MARK TWAIN AND THE NOVEL

Mark Twain was an author both drawn to and suspicious of authority, and his novels reflect this tension. Marked by disruptions, repetitions, and contradictions, they exemplify the ideological standoff
between the American ideal of individual freedom and the reality
of social control. This book provides a fresh look at Twain's major
novels, such as *Life on the Mississippi, Huckleberry Finn, A Connecticut
Yankee in King Arthur's Court,* and *Pudd'nhead Wilson.* The difficulties
in these works are shown to be neither flaws nor failures, but rather
intrinsic to both the structure of the American novel and the texture
of American culture.

MARK TWAIN
AND THE NOVEL

THE DOUBLE-CROSS OF AUTHORITY

LAWRENCE HOWE

CAMBRIDGE
UNIVERSITY PRESS

PUBLISHED BY THE PRESS SYNDICATE OF THE UNIVERSITY OF CAMBRIDGE
The Pitt Building, Trumpington Street, Cambridge, CB2 1RP, United Kingdom

CAMBRIDGE UNIVERSITY PRESS
The Edinburgh Building, Cambridge CB2 2RU, UK   http://www.cup.cam.ac.uk
40 West 20th Street, New York, NY 10011-4211, USA   http://www.cup.org
10 Stamford Road, Oakleigh, Melbourne 3166, Australia

© Lawrence Howe 1998

First published 1998

Printed in the United States of America

Typeset in New Baskerville 10.5/13 pt, in QuarkXPress™ [RF]

*A catalog record for this book is available from
the British Library.*

Library of Congress Cataloging-in-Publication Data
Howe, Lawrence, 1952–
Mark Twain and the novel : the double-cross of authority /
Lawrence Howe.
p.   cm. – (Cambridge studies in American literature and
culture)
Includes bibliographical references and index.
ISBN 0-521-56168-x (hardback)
1. Twain, Mark, 1835–1910 – Criticism and interpretation.
2. National characteristics, American, in literature.   3. Authority
in literature.   4. Polarity in literature.   5. Narration (Rhetoric)
6. Fictional – Technique.   I. Title.   II. Series.
PS1342.F53H69   1998
818'.409–DC21
97-41131
CIP

ISBN 0 521 56168 X   hardback

For Judy, Emil, and Helen

CONTENTS

ix

ACKNOWLEDGMENTS

Although some of this work was produced in relative isolation, much of it benefited from the generous support of several institutions and of some very kind and smart people. In this space, I acknowledge debts that I will never be able to repay adequately.

I thank the Regents of the University of California for permission to reprint part of Chapter 4, which appeared as "Race, Genealogy, and Genre in Mark Twain's *Pudd'nhead Wilson*," *Nineteenth-Century Literature*, 46 (1992); Duke University Press for permission to reprint part of Chapter 1, which appeared as "Transcending the Limits of Experience: Mark Twain's *Life on the Mississippi*," *American Literature*, 63 (1991); and Oxford University Press for permission to include in Chapter 1 material that appeared in a different form as the afterword to *Life on the Mississippi* in the Oxford Mark Twain (1996). I would like to thank the Mark Twain Papers for permission to quote unpublished letters and the History Game, and the Mark Twain Circle for the opportunity to present some of several chapters at one of their panels at the 1993 annual meeting of the MLA.

For fellowship and scholarship support during the research phase, I thank the Chancellor's Office and the Department of English at the University of California, Berkeley, and the Northern California Chapter of Phi Beta Kappa. Further development of the manuscript was made possible by support from the Division of Humanities and Social Sciences at the California Institute of Technology and from the Mellon Foundation.

I am also grateful to the staff of Cambridge University Press, and especially Eric Sundquist, general editor of the Cambridge Studies in American Literature and Culture series. Like all Twain scholars, I have benefited from the dedication, generosity, and cheerful expertise of Robert H. Hirst and the staff of the Mark Twain Papers at the University of California's Bancroft Library for their dedication to an invaluable project and their cheerful expertise. In addition, I owe thanks to Fred Crews for his healthy skepticism about parts of my argument, to James Cox for his endorsement of this project, to fellow Twain scholars Gregg Camfield, Vic Doyno, and Shelley Fisher Fishkin for their support, and to my shrewd students at Berkeley, Caltech, the University of San Francisco, and Roosevelt University, whose inquisitiveness has helped me to refine what follows.

I extend my warm thanks to Kevin Gilmartin and Pete Richardson for uplifting friendship and collegiality, to Mark Winokur for introducing me to *Life on the Mississippi*, to Don McQuade for steady support and for insight into the unstated protocols of the profession, and to Tom Schaub for his common sense and his uncommon kindness over the last twelve years. I am profoundly grateful to Cindy Weinstein for her counsel, conversation, and comradeship, and to Jennifer Clarvoe and Cammy Thomas, whose friendship included instructive comments on successive drafts of early versions of the manuscript – their patience with some rather tortured prose and their guidance in relieving the torture were crucial and, regrettably, unrequitable. I owe my deepest intellectual debt to my friend and scholarly mentor, Mitch Breitwieser. He has helped me confront conceptual and rhetorical obstacles that I either couldn't see or couldn't see beyond. His influence on the way that I think and teach is much more than the word "guidance" can convey.

I have also enjoyed the faithful encouragement of my family. Lucille Howe has provided the sustained love that only a mother can. My brother Greg, a picaresque traveler and an avid observer of American politics and humor, has been especially influential. Tom Frei, my father-in-law, has been not only unflaggingly supportive but also inspirational. As a Missouri native, he helped plant the idea of working on Twain at a time when I was preoccupied elsewhere. Last and foremost, I deeply thank Judy Frei and our children Emil and Helen Frei-Howe, not for what they have lent to this project but for reminding me, first, that people are more important than books and, second, that the ways in which our lives are intertwined are much more important than what I have to say about books. Because they have cared about things other than this work, and cared about me despite it, I dedicate it to them.

ABBREVIATIONS

The following abbreviations are used in citations within the text:

AC *The American Claimant.* New York: Oxford University Press, 1996. Originally published 1892.

AMT *The Autobiography of Mark Twain.* Ed. Charles Neider. New York: Harper & Row, 1959.

CTSS & E *Collected Tales, Sketches, Speeches & Essays.* 2 vols. vol. 1, *1852–1890*; vol. 2, *1891–1910*. Ed. Louis J. Budd. New York: Library of America, 1992.

CY *A Connecticut Yankee in King Arthur's Court.* Mark Twain Library Edition. Berkeley and Los Angeles: University of California Press, 1979. Originally published 1889.

FE *Following the Equator: A Journey around the World.* 2 vols. Hartford: American Publishing, 1901.

HF *Adventures of Huckleberry Finn.* Berkeley and Los Angeles: University of California Press, 1985. Originally published 1885.

HF & TSAI *Huck Finn and Tom Sawyer among the Indians and Other Unfinished Stories.* Berkeley and Los Angeles: University of California Press, 1989.

IA *The Innocents Abroad or The New Pilgrims' Progress.* 2 vols. 1869; rpt. New York: Harper & Brothers, 1911.

LOM	*Life on the Mississippi.* New York: Penguin, 1984. Originally published 1883.
LLMT	*The Love Letters of Mark Twain.* Ed. Dixon Wecter. New York: Harper & Brothers, 1949.
MTA	*Mark Twain's Autobiography.* 2 vols. Ed. Albert Bigelow Paine. New York: Harper & Brothers, 1924.
MTE	*Mark Twain in Eruption.* Ed. Bernard DeVoto. New York: Harper & Brothers, 1949.
MTHL	*Mark Twain – Howells Letters: The Correspondence of Samuel L. Clemens and William Dean Howells, 1872–1910.* 2 vols. Ed. Henry Nash Smith and William D. Gibson. Cambridge, MA: Belknap/Harvard University Press, 1960.
MTL	*Mark Twain's Letters.* 2 vols. Ed. Albert Bigelow Paine. New York: Harper & Brothers, 1917.
MTP-L	*Mark Twain's Letters.* 3 vols. *The Mark Twain Papers*, ed. Edgar Marquess Branch et al. Berkeley and Los Angeles: University of California Press, 1988.
MTNJ	*Mark Twain's Notebooks and Journals. The Mark Twain Papers*, vols. 1–2, ed. Frederick Anderson et al.; vol. 3, ed. Robert Pack Browning et al. Berkeley and Los Angeles: University of California Press, 1975, 1977, and 1979.
P&P	*The Prince and the Pauper.* Mark Twain Library Edition. Berkeley and Los Angeles: University of California Press, 1979. Originally published 1881.
PW	*Pudd'nhead Wilson and Those Extraordinary Twins.* Ed. Sidney E. Berger. New York: Norton, 1980. Originally published 1894.
TS	*The Adventures of Tom Sawyer.* Berkeley and Los Angeles: University of California Press, 1980. Originally published 1876.

INTRODUCTION: BEARING THE DOUBLE-CROSS

The novel is a prose narrative of some length that has something wrong with it.

> – Randall Jarrell, "An Unread Book"

The novel and the romance, . . . these clumsy separations appear to me to have been made by critics and readers for their
own convenience, and to help them out of some of their
occasional queer predicaments, but to have little reality or
interest for the producer, from whose point of view it is of
course that we are attempting to consider the art of fiction.

> – Henry James, *The Art of Fiction*

America is a trap: its promises and dreams . . . are too much
to live up to and too much to escape.

> – Greil Marcus, *Mystery Train*

Under the shadow of epigraphs declaring that the novel, literary
criticism, and America are all plagued by "something wrong," what
I am about to undertake might seem doomed from the start. For if
these claims are true, then to attempt literary criticism on the novels
of the writer most identified with America is to have my work cut
out for me. Nonetheless, in my view, the something wrong in Mark
Twain's novels is something worth investigating.

In part, the something wrong in Twain's work stems from the
characteristic doubleness operating at every level of his literary conception, which in turn inspired and thwarted every project he un-
dertook. The crucial term in the Twainishness that informs his texts
and persona is authority.[1] Twain was both drawn to and suspicious

1

of authority. Similarly, he was attracted to the novel, I argue, as a genre that is inherently critical of authority but that also affords a writer the opportunity to assert one's own authority. And yet writing narratives that challenge the notion of control made exercising authorial control a tortured and virtually paradoxical proposition for Twain. Although his literary performances are typically noted for repudiating figures, institutions, and traditions of control, they also invoke conservative reverence for authority almost as often as they clamor for subversion. The uneven and antithetical narratives that he produced within this conflicted process are complex expressions of a desire for power. Marked by disruptions, repetitions, and contradictions, these texts exemplify the ideological standoff between the American ideal of individual freedom and the reality of social control.[2]

Twain scholarship has often played down narrative problems, highlighting instead his ear for spoken language. Critics of this camp minimize his difficulties in controlling extended narratives as mere shortcomings, minor flaws in an otherwise artfully rendered view of American vernacular life. Among those who pay attention to structure, disagreement reigns. Some criticize the problems epitomized in the last third of *Adventures of Huckleberry Finn* as signs of Twain's profound esthetic and moral failure, whereas others find a salutary unity in the narrative structure that qualifies Twain's success. My approach is *other*-wise: I acknowledge the disruptions and discontinuities in narrative structure; however, I read these formal glitches not as signs of Twain's failed artistry but as faultlines caused by collisions of forces – literary, social, economic, historical, and psychological – that gave rise to the text. Conflating a problem of artistic control with problems of social control in nineteenth-century America, Twain's work thus articulates his equivocal stance toward literary and social authority in American society. In other words, I assume that the "something wrong" in Twain's work is meaningful. A reader who keeps an eye and an ear open to the suggestiveness of textual stresses will coax meanings from a given narrative that may complicate – sometimes even contradict or undermine – the text's explicit intentions but also signal the ideological tension in Twain's conception of American life through these patterns of semantic interference. Such an approach affords the leverage necessary to reckon with the notorious otherness of Mark Twain on its own terms, to account for both his place as a representative American writer and the complex Americanness that his divided persona represents.

This approach invites methodological flexibility – and the complex narrative texture of Twain's work requires it. Twain's major texts, in my reading, are sites where narratological theories – those of Lukács, Bakhtin, Said, Girard, Jameson, White, and D. A. Miller – cultural theories – those of Marx, Freud, Adorno, Lefort, and Foucault – and American historical interpretations – those of Perry Miller, Fliegelman, Forgie, and Woodward – collide. Within their disciplinary frames of reference, all of these scholars focus attention on the concept of authority as the agency of cultural production, and together they help to foreground the inherent problems of the subversive impulses in Twain's narratives. What I aim to show in this pluralistic approach is the heterogeneous complexity of Twain's narratives and their function as highly imaginative artistic performances that both represent and challenge cultural assumptions and anxieties.

The results of this crosscut reading emerge most clearly in my redefinition of Twain's career as a dialectic. I examine Twain's texts in pairs because Twain repeatedly divided his attention on a particular form of authority into two texts. This was due in part to the fact that his vexed sense of authority made generating and sustaining narratives a formidable task. No sooner would he launch into a topic than he would grow frustrated and shelve the unfinished manuscript, in the hope that some other project would yield a more readily marketable piece. The legendary seven-year hiatus in the composition of *Huckleberry Finn* is just such a case of writer's block, and for Twain this experience was more the rule than the exception. The texts that I examine in my first two chapters exhibit the striking effects of this pattern of compositional faltering. The interlocking compositions of "Old Times on the Mississippi," *The Adventures of Tom Sawyer, Life on the Mississippi,* and *Adventures of Huckleberry Finn* grew haphazardly from a series of experiences in which enthusiasm soon gave way to doubt and disappointment. But these texts also show that Twain's search for a new topic to rescue him from the compositional doldrums more often than not led him to a new version of the same issue – hence pairs of narratives.

Moreover, the pairs of texts do not simply duplicate or even refine

3

his efforts. Rather, I show that the pairs of texts, despite sharing an initial critical response to a given form of authority, finally stand in ideological opposition. In the first of each pair, Twain retreats from the critical project, and in the wake of the first text's insufficiency he tries again. In the second narrative, he sustains the critical edge, only to discover that another form of authority emerges to compromise the novel's critical force. The newly emergent form of authority becomes the target in the next stage of the dialectic. He tries again in the next pair of narratives, and again in the next. Ultimately, though, he discovers that the failure lies in the authority of the novel, the form in which he had invested his desire for power and control.

The consequences of this account of literary affairs are of two orders. First, Twain's discovery of the limits of novelistic authority helps to explain the shape of his career. Through his continued experimentation in the critical project of the novel, Twain came to realize the limits of the genre, its inability to do anything about the authority against which it rails. *Huckleberry Finn, A Connecticut Yankee in King Arthur's Court,* and *Pudd'nhead Wilson* end in the troubling ways they do not because Twain failed but because he could end them honestly by no other means. Despite the Twain apostles who view these narratives as esthetically and morally sound, we must acknowledge that they reflect deeply embedded problems. I differ as well with the fault-finding critics who are unsettled by these problems, disappointed by Twain's failure to resolve the narratives optimistically. Instead, I attempt to show that had Twain neatly resolved the problems in these narratives, he would have produced textual replicates of their counterparts: *Tom Sawyer, The Prince and the Pauper,* and *The American Claimant.* So rather than subscribe to the prevailing view that Twain ebbed into failure, that his artistic energy petered out when he was faced with the personal tragedies of bankruptcy and the deaths of his wife and two daughters, I argue that Twain, in fact, succeeded by confronting the limits of the novel's own authority. In other words, the "something wrong" in Twain's career was not a creative lapse that emerged late in life but a constitutive flaw present all along in the literary form he practiced.

Recognizing the differences in the pairs of texts in each dialectical stage of Twain's career leads to the second consequence: a revised definition of the American novel. This prospect is, in my view, long overdue – for no other genre has been so vaguely defined. The prevailing definition – something like the following: "a book-length, narrative, prose fiction, either set in America or written by an American" – does not help us to understand how the genre functions within American culture. Granted, some may question the need for revising the definition of such a body of recognizable literature accrued over the last two centuries. Emory Elliott, offering a virtually identical definition to the one I've just sketched, suggests that its breadth serves "to include most texts called 'novels' at the moment."[3] To be sure, it might be argued that, given the democratic diversity of American society, the most social of its literary genres should be defined as openly as possible, if it is to represent American pluralism reliably. No doubt Henry James's American background is implicit in *The Art of Fiction* when he critiques the narrowness of Walter Besant's definition of the modern English novel. But although I agree that a definition should be flexible, this principle of openness should not be so exaggerated that the definition offers no critical purchase. On the contrary, the definition should account for the motivations and effects that warrant us to call a particular category of narratives by the name "novel"; such a definition will enable us to comprehend that genre as a literary performance where esthetics and ideology intersect.

Twain's narrative pairs lend considerable insight into this problem. Both members of a given pair assume a critical stance toward authority, coinciding with the widely held view that the novel is a subversive gesture. Indeed, it's difficult to think of an American narrative that does not in some way represent either a subversive disruption of control or an alternative form of taking control. The utopian ambition motivating the culture in which these texts emerged constitutes both the literary and social projects as inspired declarations of the desire for autonomy consistent with the ethos of individualism. The preponderance of American narratives that embody a subversive theme or "escape motif" suggests that America itself must be constantly remade in order to renew its mythic ideal of individual authority.[4] But we need not assume that, despite this shared impulse, all narratives are created equal.

For example, Twain's paired texts resolve the common motivation in such strikingly opposite ways that we cannot categorize both expressions together with any degree of reliability. The first effort in each pair is so deeply invested in an idealization of authority that it either replicates or accommodates the oppressive control that it sets out to subvert. Because these texts believe in the myth of their own power, they are better understood as romances than as novels. Characterized by an unselfconscious and uncritical view of its own authority, romance is easily co-opted by the ideological hegemony, which, as contextual studies have exposed, operates throughout the culture.[5]

To be sure, "romance" is a contested term, with a long history in American culture. My use of it is not related to those of Brockden Brown, Hawthorne, or James. Indeed, the distinction between actual and invented events that Brockden Brown cites by distinguishing history from romance, or the more conventional distinction suggested in the concrete realism of the novel and the imaginative liberation of the romance has obscured much of what all fiction shares and revealed little of what differentiates a text like *The Power of Sympathy* from *The Coquette*, or *The Last of the Mohicans* from *Typee*.[6] Rather, I would emphasize that any fictional narrative assumes an authority that is romantically inspired; that is, it elevates the creative consciousness of the individual over social institutions by the power of representation. The difference that I draw between romance and novel is that romance either falls back on the authority it seeks to challenge or buys into the fiction of its own power, whereas the novel signals its critical skepticism about the authority of the literary enterprise itself.

In a letter to J. H. Burroughs, Twain projected precisely this sort of skepticism about his own romantic naiveté as a young writer by describing himself as "[a] callow fool, a self-sufficient ass, a mere human tumble-bug, stern in air, heaving at his bit of dung & imagining he is remodeling the world & is entirely capable of doing it right" (*MTP-L*, 1:289). Ever susceptible and yet suspicious of the romantic impulse, Twain often wavered. In *Innocents Abroad*, he indulges romanticism momentarily when he describes standing at the plain of Esdraelon in Palestine and wishing for the "magic of the moonlight" to create the pageantry of the epic battles that "Joshua, and Benhadad, and Saul, and Gideon; Tamerlane, Tancred, Coeur de Lion, and Saladin; the warrior Kings of Persia, Egypt's heroes, and Napoleon" had fought on that land (2:258). But in the next breath, he catches himself and dispenses with the dimly glowing

6

atmosphere that Hawthorne, in "The Customs House" preface to *The Scarlet Letter*, had hoped would inspire him. Instead Twain offers a mock biblical warning: "But the magic of the moonlight is a vanity and a fraud; and whoso putteth his trust in it shall suffer sorrow and disappointment" (2:259). Here and throughout his career, Twain was lured and repulsed by the phantoms of the imagination to concoct an image of reality that could hoodwink the unsuspecting.

The novel's problematic constitution of authority – specifically, its self-consciousness of its own limitations – is central to what I'm calling the *double-cross of novelistic discourse*. By terming this ideological and aesthetic feature of the genre a "double-cross," I mean to call up both the sense of a swindle, a literary bait and switch or "catch-22," and the notion that the novel's form and theme together bear a multiplied burden.[7] The novel holds out a tantalizing promise of authority that it finally cannot deliver.

Randall Jarrell's axiomatic definition about "something wrong" in the novel, which I've chosen as one of the epigraphs to this introduction, is a thumbnail analysis of the genre's failure of form. The novel as a form generated a contradiction from the start. For the novel is not simply a new kind of writing that appeared in the eighteenth century but a genre that constantly renews itself. A novelist, then, is faced with the dilemma of following a set of conventions that determine a text's inclusion in the genre, on the one hand, and of breaking those conventions as stipulated by the demand for newness emphasized in the genre's name, on the other hand. In short, although the genre offers the promise of freedom from conventional restraints, it compromises that freedom by enforcing convention busting as a new convention.

Edward Said gave this idea fuller articulation when he theorized the genre as a Western cultural phenomenon in which "a central purpose . . . is to enable the writer to represent characters and societies more or less freely in development." And it was Said who first called my attention to the novel's double-cross. According to his account of the novel, the authority that attracts a writer to this form is the power to begin again, to remake the world in "aesthetic objects that fill the gaps in an incomplete world." Going beyond the concept of the novel's subversive newness, Said hypothesizes that the desire for a new beginning is motivated by a cultural ambivalence toward authority. The novel's power of invention is dynamically opposed by restraint or "molestation," by which he means "the bother and responsibility of all these powers and efforts" that the novelist assumes and undertakes. Molestation consists of two difficulties: that of sustaining and completing a persuasive illusion of reality, and that of encountering continual reminders that "authority, regardless of how complete, . . . is a sham. Molestation, then, is a consciousness of one's duplicity, one's confinement to a fictive, scriptive realm, whether one is a character or a novelist. And molestation occurs when novelists and critics traditionally remind themselves of how the novelist is always subject to a comparison with reality and thereby found to be an illusion."[8] Thus the novel's promise of freedom to the writer who will control the fictive world goes unfulfilled, if not because of the sheer difficulty of the task then because this social genre runs head-on into its own impotence: institutions, ideologies, and historical realities do not respond to and are not threatened by challenges made in fiction.

Said's view is strikingly compatible with a number of theories of the novel. The currency of what D. A. Miller calls the "subversion hypothesis" within literary studies at large is most pronounced in narratology because of the novel's place as the premier narrative genre.[9] To varying degrees, the theorists of the novel to whom I refer consider the genre to be a subversive gesture that attempts both to represent a character's quest for personal authority in a fictional though realistically presented world and to achieve for the novelist a masterful authority over the representation in the text, over the text itself, and finally over the text's readers.

But Said's formulation of molestation as a limiting condition on the authority of the novel ignores the fact that molestation spurs the novel's production; that is, the desire to overcome molestation is what prompts one to indulge the novel's imaginative freedom in the first place. For the incompleteness of the world for which the novel serves to compensate is a projection of the lack of authority that the individual experiences. The world, especially the social world constituted by hierarchical institutions of power, exercises priority over the individual. Thus a writer's attraction to the novel lies in its perceived ability to compensate for the restraint that the world into which one is born imposes on one's freedom. In the epilogue to *Narrative and Its Discontents*, Miller reads Freud's grandson's game of "Fort! Da!" as a proto-narrative that illustrates a desire for control, achieved by creating an illusion of closure, but an illusion which neither eliminates or solves the motivating conflict of the narrative, just as in the manipulated plots of classic English novels. The value of this primal narrative scene for Freud's grandson is in its fictional power to control the insecurity the child feels during his mother's absence. His control over the disappearance and reappearance of the spool with which he symbolizes his mother imaginatively substitutes for his lack of actual control over her absence.

In his groundbreaking analysis of Twain's humor, James M. Cox drew on Freud to extend the discussion of vernacular in Twain criticism. And while I am interested in the way that psychoanalytic theory hypothesizes resistance and resignation to authority as an essential process of social identity, I am concerned with Freud in this study not simply as an explanatory model but because his work and Twain's resonate both thematically – say, in the way that they view the individual and the cultural as analogous – and stylistically as well. The digressive structure of *Life on the Mississippi*, for example, which formally emulates the river's meandering course, compares to the "empty stretches of road and troublesome *detours*" in *Civilization and Its Discontents* for which Freud offers a dubious apology.[10] In both texts, the metaphor of wandering serves a conceptual purpose: for Twain, it promotes an alternative authority that indulges the text's capaciousness in order to challenge the steamboat pilot's oppressively efficient control; for Freud, digression is central to the psychoanalytic process in which the seemingly irrelevant and the marginal are discovered as the truly significant and central. Aside from developing his own theory of dreams, Twain would also go on to practice a revolutionary method of autobiography, predicated on the idea that the real meaning of one's life would emerge in a random recording of events and reflections much like the psychoanalytic process. The value of these correspondences between the American fiction writer and the Austrian psychoanalytic theorist is in their revelation of the tension between freedom and control acting on the construction of identity in the thought of two very different nineteenth-century critical minds.

The cultural tensions that I emphasize are not limited to Twain's era. For example, Jay Fliegelman interprets the cultural history of the republican era in terms of a parallel conflict between patriarchal control and filial desire for autonomy and sees the literary texts at the transition from colonies to republic as a means of working out the social and psychological tensions that this conflict generates. The same is true in the American novel. For if restraint on freedom is a precondition motivating the leap into a novelistic "new beginning," then the American novel's appearance, not to mention its preeminence as the literary form of the culture, would seem to contradict the assumption that individual freedom is an automatic and paramount condition of American life.

Moreover, by focusing my readings of Twain's texts and career through the lenses of several compatible theories, I negotiate the universalizing tendencies of theory against the culturally specific concerns of Twain's place and the novel's in American studies, thus testing the ability of the theoretical conceptions to do their job. In this regard, it seems noteworthy that almost every theorist I've mentioned implies the importance of American culture to the development of the novel. Nearly every novel that Edward Said cites has some kind of New World influence, either in its setting or in some subversive intrusion within the plot. Georg Lukács, M. M. Bakhtin, and René Girard, for example, posit the novel as a form arising when the monological authority of classical or theological models of the world's unity began to disintegrate, precisely the occasion for the emergence of American culture out of the Old World. As the laboratory of the Enlightenment, America was the locus of individualism, the site where the social experiment of the modern era was tested, and it was in American soil that the very idea of the novel as the opportunity for an individual to represent reality took root. Resonating the ideal of the *vox populi*, American democracy offered a new model of literary voice, that which Bakhtin calls *heteroglossia*, within the revolutionary literary form born to this new era.

With little effort, we should recognize the novel's attempt to forge a "new beginning," its heterogeneous linguistic performance, its articulation of an epistemological shift, as fundamentally the same impulses that led to the founding of the American colonies and to the formalizing of the Declaration of Independence. Leslie Fiedler hinted as much when he recognized that "the novel and America did not come into existence at the same time by accident." And his opening remarks in *Love and Death in the American Novel* suggestively attribute to the novel the same re-inceptive inspiration that Said's theory implies: "Between the novel and America there are peculiar and intimate connections. A new literary form and a new society, their beginnings coincide with the beginnings of the modern era and, indeed, help define it."[11]

More recently, Nancy Armstrong and Leonard Tennenhouse have directly asserted the novel's American roots by challenging the consensus view of the novel as a form transmitted from England to America. They argue that since "the English novel constituted itself as an exception to the European tradition of letters," it replicates the construction of American exceptionalism. They go farther, though, in suggesting that *Narrative of the Captivity and Restauration of Mrs. Mary Rowlandson* (1682), "without question one of the most popular captivity narratives on both sides of the Atlantic," was the source for the English novel, whether one chooses to nominate Defoe's *Robinson Crusoe* or Richardson's *Pamela* as the first novel. Armstrong and Tennenhouse argue that Rowlandson anticipates Defoe's marooned hero by "representing the English in the New World as an abducted body" and Richardson's heroine by embodying "Englishness . . . in a nonaristocratic female" who is "a virtually inexhaustible source of English prose." In a study not oriented toward the novel per se, Mitchell Breitwieser shows how Rowlandson's narrative represents her grief over her child's death during their captivity as a veiled subversion of Puritan codes of mourning, despite its interpretation by Puritan ecclesiasts as an exemplum of saintly piety. Breitwieser's shrewd analysis of Rowlandson's subversiveness thus implies the importance of this captivity tale to the development of the novel. From this perspective, Rowlandson exemplifies the dilemma of authority at the earliest stage of American culture.[12]

Whether construed as the New Jerusalem where a new covenant with God would be struck, or as a *tabula rasa* where a society founded on Enlightenment ideals could be constituted, America is a constructed place where the promise of freedom was repeatedly compromised, renegotiated, or – in the worst case – revoked in favor of a restraining authority. Twain was hardly the only one to register this problem. As Richard Poirier has shown, much of American literature represents the utopian desire for "a world elsewhere."[13] But a significant portion of the texts that do so also acknowledge the limits of that desire, since, in the unfolding diegesis of many of them, the plan to escape social restraint is inevitably deferred, thwarted, or abandoned. The ideological conundrum at the core of American fiction warrants us to extend Jarrell's notion of the genre's failure of form to include the corresponding thematics of failure. What should distinguish specific texts as novels is a conscious textualizing of this reduplication of the cultural double bind in the failure of form and the thematics of failure that constitutes the double-cross of novelistic discourse.

So, in much the same way as Girard distinguishes between *romantic* narratives and *romanesque* narratives, I point to the differences between the narrative performances in Twain's various dialectical stages. The continuing debate about the closure of *Huckleberry Finn* is one index of how Twain's highly acclaimed "masterpiece" concentrates the failure of form and the thematics of failure. Others before me have pointed to the problems in *Huckleberry Finn* as a sign of a more pervasive cultural phenomenon. Louise K. Barnett draws on the insights of speech-act theory to credit Twain's most famous narrative with introducing a skepticism about the authority of speech that, in her view, marks the transition into a modern sensibility in American literature. Although I share her concern with the authority of speech, I argue that the problem she identifies as a speech-act inefficacy is the symptom of a more specific loss of confidence in the authority of a fictive linguistic performance. In *Equivocal Endings in Classic American Novels,* Joyce A. Rowe comes even closer to the problem I'm investigating. But I disagree with her rejection of genre criticism and her dismissal of categories like "romance" and "novel" as inadequate "to explain the anomalies of American fiction." I don't dispute the usefulness of her focus on the ambivalent "narrative logic" of American narratives. But her analysis is itself a kind of genre criticism without the categories. In contrast, I suggest that rather than avoiding persistent though insufficiently distinct categories, we can make greater critical headway by defining those categories more sharply according to the ideological concerns radiated in the aesthetic forms.[14]

To this end, Twain's career as a narrative artist is instructive, riddled as it is with all of what Jarrell's "something wrong" seems to imply and more. Twain's inventive, and often disruptive, combinations of genre constitute a challenge to prescriptive and proscriptive codes that conventionally authorize the shape of a narrative, codes that he alternately relied on and rebelled against. By examining how Twain's novels juxtapose and even confuse different classes of narrative – epic and bildungsroman, picaresque and heteroglot travel narrative, historical romance and dystopian novel, and slave romance and detective novel, to name a few – I will show how his texts subvert conceptions of order. For these distinct narrative classes are ideologically loaded with assumptions about the organization of social power. Consequently, his exemplary career says as much about the conflicts within American culture at large as about analogous conflicts in the American novel.

1

MARK TWAIN'S BIG TWO-HEARTED RIVER TEXT

"OLD TIMES ON THE MISSISSIPPI" AND LIFE ON THE MISSISSIPPI

> One chooses dialectic only when one has no other means. One knows that one arouses mistrust with it. Nothing is easier to erase than a dialectical effect . . . It can only be *self-defense* for those who no longer have other weapons.
>
> – Friedrich Nietzsche, *Twilight of the Idols*

Despite the ring of truth in Ernest Hemingway's often-cited praise of *Adventures of Huckleberry Finn,* he was wrong to insist that "There was nothing before" it.[1] For Mark Twain, there was *Life on the Mississippi* before there was *Huckleberry Finn.* What's more, *Life on the Mississippi* is not simply the antecedent of Twain's most recognized book; it is also some of his most personal writing, an ambitious experiment in which he worked out his complex attitude about the authority he assumed as a writer. The Mississippi book is thus an indispensable landmark for mapping Twain's distrust of and desire for authority.

Corresponding to his divided attitude toward authority, *Life on the Mississippi* is a divided text. In part 1, Twain recycled "Old Times on the Mississippi" – the sketches of his life as a cub pilot originally published seven installments in the *Atlantic Monthly* in 1875 – dividing the seven into fourteen chapters and framing them with six new chapters equally apportioned before and after the "Old Times" material. To this he joined the travel narrative of his 1882 riverboat journey down and up the Mississippi, after he had become a writer, which forms part 2 of the book. In this chapter, I reread this divided structure, not to smooth over the disparity that has prompted critical praise for the cub-pilot reminiscence and disapproval of the travel narrative but to investigate the two opposite kinds of authority Twain deploys in the book and to interpret the meanings that emerge from the conflict between them.

"Old Times" suggests that Sam Clemens was violating a paternal proscription by going on the river; having thrown off that restraint, he aspires to assume an altered form of paternal authority in the profession of steamboat pilot. Not only does "Old Times" glorify and mythologize the pilot's masterly control, but its narrative authority also emulates the directed purpose that distinguished the pilot as a uniquely American hero. Yet in part 2, where he returns to the river as a writer, Twain assumes a less practical and less rigid verbal form of authority, one that his self-description as "a scribbler of books" anxiously suggests is relatively impotent when compared to the pilot's authority (*LOM*, 166). His reaction was to devote a large portion of the Mississippi book to discrediting the pilot's authority as oppressive and restraining. Twain had professional reasons for undermining the pilot's celebrated authority. The pilot's teleological motivation of delivering his cargo in the shortest possible time is distinctly unsuited to the goals of the subscription-book writer Twain had become, for that method of marketing books required a writer to stretch his narrative to a length of at least 1,500 manuscript pages. Consequently, in the travel narrative of part 2, Twain discards the rigid control of the pilot and installs an expansive and associational form of authority, allowing the narrative to drift instead of dominating it. The Mississippi book, then, is divided because Twain's career is divided. But Twain's goal in this text goes beyond the personal; rather, it fuses the personal with the national. His career is divided, he implies, because the experience of nineteenth-century America was divided by the Civil War. The "Old Times" sketches nostalgically recall an antebellum romanticism that evokes a unity of the self, in contrast to the realism that characterizes the fragmentation of the postwar narrative. Thus, the diffuseness of the latter, for which it is often judged a failure relative to the organic unity of "Old Times," is not a measure of authorial incompetence but a sign of its formal appropriateness in representing the bustling, competitive, heterogeneous national culture.

Twain's attempt to represent his personal experience as a figure for national experience projects his desire for representativity.[2] Twain had expressed this desire as early as the preface to *The Inno-*

cents Abroad, in which he describes his intention to show "the reader how *he* would be likely to see Europe and the East if he looked at them with his own eyes" (unnumbered page), thus postulating that he observes and speaks for America. An illustration of Twain in the first edition of his book debut supports this intention by depicting him dressed in a combination of Native American and Western clothing, holding in his right hand a tomahawk with the American flag painted on the blade and in his left a satchel with the initials "M. T." over "U.S." In his autobiography, he expands his domain beyond national identity by confidently asserting, "I am the whole human race without a detail lacking" (*MTE*, xxix). In *Life on the Mississippi*, Twain's desire for representativity emerges subtly in chapter *21*, the break between the narrative's two parts, where he briefly describes his *twenty-one-year* absence from the Mississippi. The concurrence between the chapter number and the number of years since his river days calls attention to the fact that this three-paragraph chapter divides the text between his cub-pilot reminiscences and the 1882 travel narrative. And he makes clear, though with characteristic understatement, how the narrative pivots at this chapter on historical circumstance: "But by and by the war came" (*LOM*, 166). Part 2 pays considerable attention to how the Civil War changed the course of the nation as a whole, but this passage depicts the war as the catalyst for altering the direction of Twain's career in particular, transforming him from a reader of the river to "a scribbler of books." By foregrounding the war's effect on his career, he implies a correspondence between his transition from pilot to writer and the national transition from antebellum innocence to post–Civil War maturity.

Although he consciously tried to be and has been generally considered a representative American, the Mississippi book's emphasis on the Civil War as a culturally defining moment ironically underscores his difficulty in making his river life stand for national experience.[3] For Samuel Clemens was a Civil War deserter. After a two-week stint in a band of Confederate irregulars, his hasty retreat from the battlefield to the Nevada silver fields removed him from the one event that representativity would seem to have required. The dilemma he faced as a result lies in the conflict between his belief that experience was the "capital" (*LLMT*, 28) upon which successful writing relied and the fact that he lacked the central experience of the war. Twain attempts to solve this dilemma through his authority as a writer. For as a writer he can fictionalize in order to transcend the limits of his experience, transforming his actual past on the river into a series of staged conflicts with authority. Each of these agons figurally addresses the crucial experience that Twain lacks. And in each succeeding stage Twain attempts to overcome the limits of the preceding one, successively expanding the figural quality of his representativity. By redistributing value from actual to textual experience – in other words, by blurring the line between truth and fiction in the text's autobiographical sections – *Life on the Mississippi* is both a critique of oppressive control and a prototype of the novel as a genre that attempts to assert its own authority against restraining conventions. Twain invests the form with cultural meaning and exhibits the interdependence of personal and national histories and of esthetics and politics as a function of the problems of authority in a democratic society.

From Inspiration to Exasperation

The long foreground that led up to *Life on the Mississippi* provides the first suggestion of Twain's wavering resolve to write such a book. Twain hinted at his intention to write a Mississippi book as early as 1866 in a letter to his mother (*MTP-L*, 1:329). Again, in an 1871 letter to his wife, he wrote confidently about the "standard work" (*LLMT*, 165–6) he would make about the Mississippi River, but another twelve years would pass before his confident intentions yielded a book-length work. In 1874, Twain took the first step toward the book when he started in on the cub-pilot sketches, "Old Times on the Mississippi." But even that writing was marked by alternating confidence and doubt. In September 1874, William Dean Howells asked Twain to submit a story to the *Atlantic Monthly* to follow up his first submission, "A True Story," which would be appearing in the November issue. Howells judged that story to be an exceptionally strong vernacular piece and hoped that Twain had more in this line. But after trying without success to work up a subject, Twain responded regretfully, over a month later, that he had nothing to contribute. On the very afternoon of his letter to Howells, however, a conversation with his friend the Reverend Joseph Twichell produced an oral reminiscence of his years on Mississippi steamboats, which Twichell pointed out would make "a virgin subject to hurl into a magazine!" (*MTHL*, 1:34). Twain promptly wrote again to Howells with the good news and expressed his enthusiasm for a series of sketches about his steamboat experiences. Yet even before he began the writing, his proposal that the series "run through three months or six or nine – or about four months, say?" shows his expanding confidence checked by doubt about sustaining the effort.

The same pattern developed in producing the series. At first the writing went along easily. He wrote the first three installments in only five weeks. The first six appeared consecutively in the issues of the *Atlantic Monthly* for January through June in 1875, and then a seventh installment in the August issue ended the series. The two-month lapse between the appearances of the last two installments suggests the difficulty he had in continuing the series. Moreover, the consecutive appearance of the first six conceals the difficulty he experienced even before the belated final installment. Howells had to press him for completion of the sixth and the seventh installments. And Twain's complaint of "spring laziness" (*MTHL*, 1:82) indicates his ebbing interest in the Mississippi sketches. His expression of disappointment with the last sketch confirms more directly the difficulty of maintaining the effort:

> I either seem to have stopped in the middle of my subject at the editor's request, or else regularly "petered out." But No. 6 closes the series first-rate with the death of piloting, & needs no postscript. Therefore I would suggest that you leave out this No. 7 entirely & let the articles end with the June No. On the whole I think that should be the neatest thing to do. I retire with dignity, then, instead of awkwardly. (*MTHL*, 1:85)

Twain's willingness to cut himself off is striking, especially since *Life on the Mississippi* demonstrates that he clearly had more to say on the subject. But his doubt about his ability to perform and the fear of self-humiliation made an early or at least temporary retirement attractive.

The Mississippi book, which Twain had conceived as early as 1866, approached the threshold of realization in 1882. "Old Times" had enjoyed a successful reception, providing an impetus to extend the Mississippi writing. The book was now to take up from where the *Atlantic* series had left off. But the idea to build on that foundation did not alter the plan to base the book on the return trip to the river, which he seems to have considered integral to his plan all along. Since 1875 he had tried repeatedly to persuade Howells to accompany him on such a trip, but to no avail. He finally settled on his publisher, James Osgood, and a secretary, Roswell Phelps, as his traveling companions. On April 10, 1882, shortly before embarking on the voyage, Twain signed a contract with Osgood in which he optimistically promised to deliver a completed manuscript for a subscription book on October 1, 1882. Notebooks of the journey and letters home indicate his corresponding enthusiasm and confidence that the trip was yielding "volumes of literary stuff" (*LLMT*, 208).

But the project failed to progress according to his optimistic timetable. As the narrative stalled, his confidence and enthusiasm waned. The writing and revising extended well beyond the contract date and into early 1883. He wrote to Howells of the "spur and burden of the contract" as an "irritation" that he could "endure . . . no longer." In the same correspondence, he tells of composing large sections "mainly stolen from books, tho' credit given" and vows that the remaining ten-days' work will be completed in half the time by pure diligence and the desire to be rid of the project. Only five days later he admits, "I never had such a fight over a book in my life before" and takes a new vow: "I will finish the book at no particular date; . . . I will not hurry it; . . . I will not hurry myself; . . . I will take things easy and comfortably, write when I choose to write, leave it alone when I so prefer . . . [T]o follow any other policy would be to make the book worse than it already is" (*MTHL*, 1:417–18). Parallel to his experience in producing "Old Times," the confidence with which he embarked on the "standard work" also gave way to doubt. And since this effort was for a book of a specified length rather than a series of an undetermined number of installments, the doubt made the work an exasperating chore.

Twain's struggle to meet the required length for the subscription book has often been cited to support the conclusion that he carelessly padded his manuscript when his inspirational "tank had run dry" (*MTE*, 197), producing a diffuse and rambling book.[4] In this view, he failed by succumbing to extra-artistic pressure, resorting to careless execution and "spoiling" his autobiographical rite of passage, "the nearest thing to a poem Mark Twain was ever to write."[5]

Certainly, the subscription-book length requirement had an impact on the composition of *Life on the Mississippi*, just as it had influenced the production of *Innocents Abroad* and *Roughing It*. But in lamenting *Life on the Mississippi* as a failure, critics appear to assume that Twain had intended merely to continue the personal sketches they admire in "Old Times." Twain is in part responsible for this view. In chapter 51 of the Mississippi book, he claims that "the main purpose of my visit [was] but lamely accomplished. I had hoped to hunt up and talk with a hundred steamboatmen, but got so pleasantly involved in the social life of the town that I got nothing more than mere five-minute talks with a couple dozen of the craft" (354). The passing of the steamboat's flush times also had something to do with his frustrated hopes. But that he should have had those hopes at all seems rather dubious, since he already knew firsthand about the waning importance of river travel. During his 1871–2 lecture tour, he pondered the ending of the steamboat's heyday in a letter to his wife, Livy, from Steubenville, Ohio:

> These windows overlook the Ohio – once alive with steamboats & crowded with all manner of traffic; but now a deserted stream, victim of the railroads. Where lie the pilots? They were starchy boys, in my time, & greatly envied by the youth of the West. The same with the Mississippi pilots – though the Mobile & Ohio Railroad had already walked suddenly off with passenger business in my day, & so it was the beginning of the end. (*LLMT*, 172)

Even in "Old Times," he remarks how the advance of railroads and tug-boat barges had turned "the noble science of piloting" into a thing "of the dead and pathetic past!" (137). So the intention to which he alludes in chapter 51 was predictably frustrated and is thus an unlikely basis for the book. Although it may have contributed to his difficulty in completing the manuscript, critical accounts that rely on this assumption of Twain's intention – and that means virtually all of the readings of *Life on the Mississippi* as a failure – don't tell the whole story.

Ample evidence indicates that, on the contrary, Twain had intended from the outset to rely on a wide variety of sources – newspapers, diaries, histories, travel narratives, statistics, folklore, hearsay, and even tales written for but not included in *A Tramp Abroad*.[6] Moreover, the deliberate choice to compose a digressive text and the decision to pad the manuscript as a response to publishing pressures are not antithetical. The need to fill out the book to a specific length may have determined the quantity of material, but not the material itself. Whatever Twain threw into the book became its content because he chose to throw in that material as opposed to other material. He may not have been fully conscious of why he chose what he did or of all the effects that those choices created, but the material that found its way into the text represents his intention nonetheless, even if it may seem to violate organicist criteria. In fact, the entire charge of padding seems questionable in light of the fact that despite adding 11,000 words from other sources, he excised more than 15,000 words of original composition from the finished book. Thus, Twain appears to have been operating under different assumptions from those who champion formal unity. The difference between the formal unity of "Old Times" and the digressiveness of *Life on the Mississippi* stems not from Twain's failure to sustain what he had accomplished in the *Atlantic* sketches but rather from the different intentions governing the two texts. In "Old Times" he remembers the science of piloting as it was, and in *Life on the Mississippi* he describes American life as it appears on and around the river running through "The Body of the Nation" (30). The structure of each narrative is influenced by the authority exercised by the represented persona: the pilot or the writer.

When Twain began writing "Old Times," he had already established himself as a writer. But in returning to a period of his life that preceded his debut in that profession, he produced a narrative not from the perspective of the writer he had become but from that of the cub pilot he had been. By filtering the narrative authority through the perspective of his cub persona, Twain imbues the text with the innocence for which it is acclaimed. But this point of view orients the narrative teleologically, as a mimetic progression toward the pilot's authority to which the cub aspires. Telos determines the piloting enterprise: the pilot's goal is to deliver his cargo expediently, without incident, to attain the highest possible profit. He focuses narrowly on discerning a safe channel by which to achieve that goal. Accordingly, we should not be surprised that scholars with a New Critical bias for the economy of organic wholeness have preferred the teleologically motivated unity of "Old Times" over the diffuseness of *Life on the Mississippi*.

And yet, despite the praise of its unity, the form of "Old Times" is itself characteristically split, as is the book into which Twain would later absorb it. On the one hand, the critically acclaimed rite of passage of the cub pilot is a kind of bildungsroman, and, on the other hand, the panegyric of piloting is a kind of epic of the Mississippi hero.[7] He emphasizes piloting as his central focus in his request to change the title of the magazine series from the general "Old Times on the Mississippi" to the more specific "Piloting on the Mississippi" in a letter to Howells, written shortly before the series was to begin and just after he had completed the third installment: "I have spoken of nothing but of Piloting as a science so far; and I doubt if I ever get beyond that portion of my subject. And I don't care to . . . If I were to write fifty articles they would all be about pilots and piloting – therefore let's get the word Piloting into the heading" (*MTHL*, 1:47). And although the elements of bildungsroman in the sketches have garnered more critical attention, Twain seems to have offered the account of the cub's growth mostly as a credential underwriting his authority as a spokesman on the subject of piloting: "I feel justified in enlarging upon this great science for the reason that I feel sure no one has ever yet written a paragraph about it who had piloted a steamboat himself, and so had a practical knowledge of the subject" (97). His correspondence with Howells reveals markedly less restraint in his expression of self-confidence when he boasts, "I am the only man alive that can scribble about the piloting of the day" (*MTHL*, 1:47).

However, the confusion between his assertion of self-exalted uniqueness and the deprecating description of his ability to "scribble" the account of the Mississippi pilot's mastery hints at Mark Twain's uneasiness with a hierarchy of authority that places the writer beneath and in service to the pilot. The text of "Old Times" documents his comparative appraisal of the writer's and pilot's status: "[W]riters are manacled servants of the public. We write frankly and fearlessly, but then we 'modify' before we print," whereas

> a pilot, in those days, was the only unfettered and entirely independent human being that lived in the earth . . . His movements were entirely free; and he consulted no one, he received commands from nobody, he promptly resented even the merest suggestions . . . So here was the novelty of a king without a keeper, an

absolute monarch who was absolute in sober truth and not by a fiction of words ... He was treated with marked courtesy by the captain and with marked deference by all the officers and servants; and this deferential spirit was quickly communicated to the passengers too. (122–3)

Yet in contrast, he condescendingly praises a former pilot of his acquaintance who wrote Howells to propose an article on the oriental trade: "Good for Fawcett! The idea of a Mississippi pilot writing profound essays upon so imposing a subject as Ancient Oriental Trade! I think I'll ring that into a chapter, for the honor of the craft. All the boys had brains, & plenty of them – but they mostly lacked education & the literary faculty" (*MTHL*, 1:78). By entering the writing profession, Twain implies, Fawcett has elevated himself above the common horde of pilots. The excess of exclamation points, however, suggests a patronizing tone, and his intention to highlight a pilot turned writer is more a self-congratulatory gesture than a distinction of pilots in general. His language, moreover, suggests a rivalry with Fawcett; he proposes to "ring" (or the more violent "wring"?) the idea of a pilot who writes *essays* into one of his *chapters*, thereby diminishing Fawcett's output by circumscribing it within his own more voluminous production. This corresponds to the lofty inflation of his authority when he assessed his achievement in early May of 1875: "There is something charming about the lonely sublimity of being the prophet of a hitherto unsung race. There are so many prophets for the other guilds & races & religions that no one of them can become singularly conspicuous, but I haven't any rivals; my people have got to take me or go prophetless" (*MTHL*, 1:81). There is palpable irony in his haughty self-identification as "prophet," given his great concern for the *profit* he derived from his conspicuousness in the profession of "scribbler." Indeed, in "Old Times" he claims to have pursued the authoritative profession of piloting precisely because it promised the same reward of notoriety. But in spite of the irony, or perhaps because of it, he betrays a sense of rivalry with pilots. By writing, he exerts his control over the pilot's authority, which failed either to deliver on its promise or to sustain it. By writing, he not only *scribbles* but also attempts to *circumscribe* the pilot.

But only two weeks after his self-declared distinction, he suggested that the disappointing seventh installment remain unpublished so

that he could "retire with dignity." The unrivaled prophet was finding it difficult to master his material: "There is a world of river stuff
to write about, but I find it won't cut up into chapters, worth a cent.
It needs to run right along, with no breaks but imaginary ones"
(*MTHL*, 1:85). The book he would write about the Mississippi would
answer this need, freeing his subject from the narrow control that
the pilot's authority imposed and allowing the narrative "to run
right along."

The book achieves this freedom by a shift in point of view that
corresponds to the career change in Twain's self-representation.
When he returned to the Mississippi in order to convert "Old
Times" into *Life on the Mississippi*, he came as a professional "scribbler of books" and not as a former pilot. *Life on the Mississippi*, then,
is an extension of his authorial performance in the *Atlantic* series
but a departure from the teleology of piloting that dominates the
earlier text. Although the traveling scribbler follows the sequence of
his journey, his goal is not to avoid incident but to seek it out. And
with no restraints of economy (indeed, the subscription book called
for just the opposite), the scribbler delights in snags and reefs for
the picturesque variety they lend to the process. Thus the "world of
river stuff" could run freely through a text that is not governed by
the closure of telos but instead indulges a desire for openness.

By relinquishing the comparatively tighter control that he employed in "Old Times," Twain allowed an associative logic to per-
meate the Mississippi book. Toward the end of his career, Twain
would rediscover and exaggerate this method as

> the right way to do an Autobiography: Start it at no particular
> time of your life; wander at your free will all over your life; talk
> only about the thing which interests you for the moment; drop it
> the moment its interest threatens to pale, and turn your talk upon
> the new and more interesting thing that has intruded itself into
> your mind meantime. (*MTA*, 1:193)

But lest we suspect that such free play merely yields chaos, he explains further that this "apparently systemless system – only apparently systemless, for it is not that . . . is a system which is a complete
and purposed jumble – a course which begins nowhere, follows no
specified route, and can never reach an end" (*MTA*, 2:246).
Whether he knew it when he wrote *Life on the Mississippi* or not, this

system was formally appropriate to a book about the great, ever-flowing, and ever-shifting river of the North American continent.

Even before Twain articulated the value of this associative method of composition for his autobiography, Howells had celebrated this quality of his friend's prose in the 1901 essay, "Mark Twain: An Inquiry":

> So far as I know, Mr. Clemens is the first writer to use in extended writing the fashion we all use in thinking, and to set down the thing that comes into his mind without fear or favor of the thing that went before or the thing that may be about to follow. I, for instance, in putting this paper together, am anxious to observe some sort of logical order, to discipline such impressions and notions as I have of the subject into a coherent body which shall march columnwise to a conclusion obvious if not inevitable from the start. But Mr. Clemens, if he were writing it, would not be anxious to do any such thing. He would take whatever offered itself to his hand out of that mystical chaos, that divine ragbag, which we call the mind, and leave the reader to look after relevancies and sequences for himself. These there might be, but not of that hard-and-fast sort which I am eager to lay hold of, and the result would at least be satisfactory to the author, who would have shifted the whole responsibility to the reader, with whom it belongs, at least as much as with the author.[8]

By crediting Twain with having discovered a version of what Roland Barthes calls the "writerly text," a text that is repeatedly produced by readers who can never reduce it from its plurality, Howells reminds us that we gain nothing by writing off *Life on the Mississippi* as a disjointed failure.[9] Rather, we should "look after relevancies and sequences" and speculate on the meaning that may inhere in its expansive structure.

Twain's stipulation that his unorthodox compositional method is one in which "the past and the present are constantly brought face to face, resulting in the contrasts which newly fire up the interest all along like contact of flint and steel" (*MIA*, 1:193) indicates its representative value for part 2 of *Life on the Mississippi*. For this book highlights the changes that have occurred during his twenty-one-year absence from the river. Moreover, this combustible contact of past and present doesn't derive simply from the compositional method that he specifies in the *Autobiography*; rather, it inheres in the overall structure of *Life on the Mississippi*. By incorporating "Old Times" into *Life on the Mississippi*, Twain strikes the nostalgic flint of his apprenticeship reminiscence against the contemporary steel of his 1882 observations. The difference between the two narratives signifies Twain's perception of the changes in American culture: the unity of "Old Times" approximates the romantic individualism of the antebellum era, and the shift to the diffuse form of *Life on the Mississippi* parallels the realism of post–Civil War America.

But the fact that Twain absorbed the text of the magazine series into the text of the book complicates any attempt to treat "Old Times" and *Life on the Mississippi* separately and to infer that the two narrative authorities represent two discrete representational goals. The scribbler's appropriation of the cub-pilot's text effectively subordinates the pilot's authority to that of the writer. And thus the book more fully expresses the writer–pilot rivalry that his letter to Howells suggests is a latent tension in his epic praise of pilots in "Old Times." In order to sound the complex meanings at the lower depths of this rivalry, we will further examine (1) how Twain represents his conflicted relationships with authority figures, (2) how he translates that conflict with authority into the ambivalence between control and drift in the structure of *Life on the Mississippi*, (3) how he figures the conflict between democratic individualism and the authority of institutions in an historical and social context, and (4) how that conflict influences not only this text but the development of his career.

Oedipus on the Mississippi; or, Patricide and the Pilothouse Divided

When Samuel Clemens went on the river, he contracted as an apprentice under the master pilot Horace Bixby. Mark Twain recalls that in the presence of such an imposing figure of piloting prowess he was by turns either inspired to attain the grand authority of the pilot or discouraged from even trying to acquire the knowledge and expertise that Bixby demonstrated. Within Twain's epic praise of pilots, his mixed response to Bixby casts the portrait of his mentor in an ambiguous shadow. To be sure, Twain depicts Bixby as the personification of the qualities required of the craft: memory, courage, and judgment. But Twain doesn't merely offer up Bixby alone;

he reinforces Bixby's exemplary status by a comparison to Mr. Brown, another pilot under whom Bixby had temporarily placed the cub. And this comparison reflects on Twain's complex relation to Bixby.

For example, while extolling Bixby's expert ability to commit the salient details of a river to memory in short order, Twain pauses to reflect on Brown's astounding memory. The two couldn't be more dissimilar: where Bixby applies his memory to useful navigation at high wages, Brown's prodigious memory problematically exceeds the requirement. His memory is of such a peculiar stock – the mere mention of a name being enough to set Mr. Brown off on a seemingly interminable and progressively irrelevant narrative line – that Twain concludes, "His was not simply a pilot's memory; its grasp was universal," and that it "was born in him . . . not built." Such a faculty is an affliction, because in Mr. Brown's memory "[t]he most trivial details remained as distinct and luminous in his head, after they had lain there for years, as the most memorable events . . . To it, all occurrences are of the same size. Its possessor cannot distinguish an interesting circumstance from a [sic] uninteresting one. As a talker, he is bound to clog his narrative with tiresome details and make himself an insufferable bore" (117–18). But what does Brown's ability to tell a story have to do with piloting a steamboat?

At this moment in "Old Times," Twain's contemporary professional identity as a writer eclipses his former identity as a pilot and intrudes on his judgment of Brown's memory. Although his explanation of the importance of memory pertains ostensibly to piloting, Twain's own professional concern with narrative authority intrudes on his account of memory as one of three necessary requirements of a pilot. Within "Old Times," the two activities are analogous. Storytelling, like piloting, requires discretion. But because Twain's writerly interest in the authority of narration distracts his attention from the subject of a pilot's authority of navigation, he paradoxically undermines his own narrative control – in effect imitating Brown. Since Twain has adhered to the general topic of memory here, this lapse is mild enough to have escaped wide notice. However, the very installment in which Twain portrays Mr. Brown's meandering memory begins with the admission, "But I am wandering from what I was intending to do, that is, make plainer than perhaps appears in the previous chapters, some of the peculiar requirements of the science of piloting" (117–18). So, even before Twain makes Mr. Brown an example of the defects of digression, he underscores the fact that he is digressing himself at this moment. Thus, despite all of his esteem for the pilot's vigilant control, Twain shuns analogous control over this ostensibly unified text.

The illustration of Brown's narrative incompetence, in effect, humorously foreshadows the loose structure of "relevancies and sequences" in part 2 of *Life on the Mississippi*:

> Mr. Brown would start out with the honest intention of telling you a vastly funny anecdote about a dog. He would be so "full of laugh" that he could hardly begin; then his memory would start with the dog's breed and personal appearance; drift into a history of his owner's family, with descriptions of weddings and burials that had occurred in it, together with the recitals of congratulatory verses and obituary poetry provoked by the same; then this memory would recollect that one of these events occurred during the celebrated "hard winter" of such and such a year, and a minute description of that winter would follow along with the names of people who were frozen to death, and statistics showing the high figures which pork and hay went up to. Pork and hay would suggest corn and fodder; corn and fodder would suggest cows and horses; cows and horses would suggest the circus and certain celebrated bare-back riders; the transition from the circus to the menagerie was easy and natural; from the elephant to equatorial Africa was but a step; then of course the heathen savages would suggest religion; and at the end of three or four hours' tedious jaw, the watch would change, and Brown would go out of the pilot-house muttering extracts from sermons he had heard years before about the efficacy of prayer as a means of grace. And the original first mention would be all you had learned about that dog, after all this waiting and hungering. (118)

Although Twain's lengthy lampoon of Brown's shaggy-dog story is intended to show the unfortunate inclusiveness of its teller's memory, it also anticipates Twain's expansion of "Old Times" into *Life on the Mississippi*. Similar to his description of Mr. Brown's narrative, where the clauses are spliced together with semicolons and the conjunctions "then" and "and," part 2 of *Life on the Mississippi* combines materials without seeming to select them according to any discernible criteria. The narrative authority simply succumbs to the meandering current and tolerates drift, rather than exerting a control analogous to the pilot's navigational authority.

The humorous account of Mr. Brown's affliction in "Old Times" raises questions about the relation between the lack of narrative control and the exercise of authority in Twain's own practice. Could Twain have been so lacking in self-consciousness as to have unwittingly imitated in his execution of *Life on the Mississippi* the butt of one of his own jokes in the earlier narrative? If not – if he has consciously done so – does that mean that we are to see *Life on the Mississippi* itself as not much more than an extended shaggy-dog story? We can concede the obvious: Mark Twain, a professional humorist, was of course interested in jokes, and *Life on the Mississippi* is full of them. However, this doesn't warrant us to summarize the entire work as a mere joke or a tedious vehicle for a handful of mere jokes. Twain's conception of humor indicates that his intentions ran deeper than that:

> Humor must not professedly teach, and it must not professedly preach, but it must do both if it would live forever . . . I have always preached . . . If the humor came of its own accord and uninvited, I have allowed it a place in my sermon, but I was not writing the sermon for the sake of the humor. I should have written the sermon just the same, whether the humor applied for admission or not. (*MTE,* 202–3)

Moreover, he viewed the humorist label as a limiting condition. In an interview with John Henton Carter at the end of his 1882 Mississippi voyage, Twain "discussed an ancient grievance – the handicap a man suffers starting as a humorist." His resentment of being "expected ever to appear in his cap and bells and do the risible" suggests that Twain wanted appreciation as "something more" than a humorist.[10] Since this sentiment was on his mind just before he was about to begin the composition of *Life on the Mississippi,* we might speculate that the Mississippi book was part of an ambition to reach beyond the confines of what he had described to his brother as his " 'call' to literature, of a low order – i.e., humorous" to write a book that would be recognized as more than a joke, and thus qualify its author as more than a humorist.[11]

Whether Twain could have so lacked self-consciousness as to have stumbled into becoming the butt of his own joke seems disproved by the kind of humor he typically deployed. To be sure, Twain often depicted himself as the butt of a joke; however, it was a joke elaborately framed around the inadequacy of a storyteller like Brown. The framing of this kind of narrative was a clear assertion of Twain's authority. Early in his career, Twain developed narrators, "usually veterans of long service in their occupations," who were "utterly lacking in self-consciousness, perhaps because they were authority figures."[12] The lack of self-consciousness translated into a form of storytelling deficiency that took its toll on the listener. James M. Cox argues that Twain's first success as a humorist came from achieving just such an effect in "Jim Smiley and His Jumping Frog." There, Twain makes use of Simon Wheeler's deadpan oral delivery to waylay the frame tale's eastern literary narrator. But in the process, "the unwitting collaboration between the two narrators" blurs the distinction between the inept rambling of the oral and the finely executed authority of the written, transcends the East-versus-West regionalism that motivates the tale.[13] Similarly, in *Roughing It*, Twain is made the butt of a joke when lured by fellow miners to submit to Jim Blaine's inebriated narrative incompetence. Like Brown's endless and pointless narrative about a dog, Blaine's story of his grandfather's ram achieves its humor through Twain's frustrated desire for closure.[14] By turning the central narrator's affliction into a joke imposed upon the listener/frame narrator, Twain demonstrates his deft control of stratified narrative to achieve a humorous effect that asserts his authority over his audience. Twain exploits the lack of authority in these unselfconscious characters as an ironic inversion of the relationship in which self-consciousness and authority existed for him.

Indeed, authority was a topic that Twain self-consciously explored and a goal that he self-consciously sought. He entertained ambitions to be a preacher, a pilot, and a writer, because each offered an authoritative identity.[15] After recognizing that he was unfit for the first, he sought the other two with varying degrees of dedication. In the Mississippi book, Twain exploits a confusion of and difference between the authorities residing in the pilot and the writer. On the one hand, those two career paths seem nearly interchangeable to him, as the shift from navigational to narrational criteria in his judgment of Brown's memory shows. And on the other hand, the pressure to produce books of significant length encouraged just the opposite kind of authority from the pilot's discriminating control.

Unlike the pilot, the subscription-book author tolerates drift in his narrative because the market demands length, not the expediency of the shortest and fastest course. Thus, although Brown's distracting memory is decidedly an affliction for a pilot, it may be an asset for an author of subscription books. But finally, the metonymic drift of Brown's unselective memory and Twain's method in *Life on the Mississippi* differ: in Brown's case, contiguity yields pointlessness, but in Twain's, such associations produce meaning, as in the contrast implied by the juxtaposed descriptions of Bixby's able memory and Brown's disabling one. For Twain, metonymic contact often sparks a metaphoric flash, usually by a paradox of difference in apparent identity or identity in apparent difference.

When Twain recontextualized the piloting sketches in *Life on the Mississippi*, Brown assumed even greater significance, because he is, in effect, two characters. He is, first, the object of mild burlesque, as the innocently inept storyteller whose memory oppresses himself as much as it does his audience. And second, in the episodes of the cub's apprenticeship to Brown aboard the *Pennsylvania*, which Twain added to the "Old Times" material to complete part 1 of the book, Brown is the object of the cub's hatred, as the maliciously oppressive authority, ever finding fault with the cub. Brown's "dead-earnest nagging" provokes the cub to imagine killing his tyrannical master as a way of venting his resentment. Indulging in only imagined retaliation allows him to avoid actually breaking the "United States law making it a penitentiary offense to strike or threaten a pilot who was on duty" (155). If Brown and Bixby are linked in the first instance by virtue of their dissimilar memories, they are linked even more directly by contract, for Bixby loans the cub to Brown in the *Pennsylvania* episodes. This second association, moreover, would seem to amplify the contrast beyond the difference in their piloting faculties, casting noble Bixby and nefarious Brown in the distinctly polarized roles of mentor and tormentor. This opposition has been widely observed in the criticism of *Life on the Mississippi*. Edgar Burde even argues that it fundamentally informs the difference in the attitude toward authority between parts 1 and 2 in the Mississippi book. "Old Times," he contends, represents Twain's identification with the able Bixby; however, Twain's self-doubt about his competency as a pilot undermined his ability to sustain the identification with his heroic mentor, and Brown's inept drift supplants the control that marked the earlier narrative.[16] But a closer look at the cub's experiences under the two raises doubts about the good-pilot–bad-pilot distinction.

Closing the chapter in which he introduces the second characterization of Brown, Twain recalls how Brown "invent[ed] a trap" for him, ordering the cub to perform a maneuver of the vessel that he had never before allowed him to attempt. Under Brown's scrutiny, the cub is destined to fail. But as "uncomfortable" as enduring Brown's "stream of vituperation" is for him, the cub's greater distress lies in the public humiliation he suffered, "for there was a big audience on the hurricane deck." The humorous tag that Twain deploys to close off the episode ("When I went to bed that night, I killed Brown in seventeen different ways – all of them new" [156]) attenuates the impact of this public humiliation. But the similarity between this humiliation under Brown and an earlier humiliation during the climactic moment of the cub's education under Bixby betrays Twain's attempt to insulate the episode by such a rhetorical gesture. Describing the Bixby incident (which immediately follows the contrast between the mnemonic faculties of the two pilots), Twain acknowledges the humiliation he endured when Bixby played "a friendly swindle" on him for the purpose of teaching the cub to have the courage to follow his own judgment (119–21). Having instructed the leadsmen to call out an erroneous series of dangerously shallow depths, and having invited the officers of the boat as an audience, Bixby hides in the pilothouse in order to spy on the insecure cub and witness his crisis of self-doubt when challenged by information that contradicts his own knowledge. As "the leadsman's sepulchral cry" progresses dangerously to "*Mark* twain!" the cub's panic gradually increases to the breaking point. And with the emphasis of that eponymic signal, Twain avows, "I was helpless." After the cub exhibits his cowardice and lack of authority by begging the engineer to reverse engines, Bixby emerges from his hiding place and reveals the game. Subjected to "a thundergust of humiliating laughter" – not to mention months of derision, and "for years afterward" blushing "even in my sleep when I thought of it" – the cub admits, "It was a fine trick to play on an orphan, *was n't* it?" Although Bixby's clandestine scrutiny and the victim's public acquiescence in the master's lesson distinguish this experience from the cub's humiliating experience under Brown, the similarity of the two episodes and the cub's continuing rancor in the privacy of his bed undercut the division of mastery into two personae and, instead, establish an identity between his two masters.

Certainly, the cub greatly admires Bixby's navigational prowess. But the leadsman's cry in the embarrassing lesson of the cub's failed courage suggests deep tensions in that admiration by recalling an earlier reference to the cry "Mark twain!" during Bixby's risky after-dark maneuver at Hat Island. Bixby's "daring deed" at that notoriously dangerous spot on the river demonstrated his exceptional piloting ability and canonized him in the young cub's appreciative eyes. But the arrogance of attempting the ill-advised maneuver in order to impress his audience of distinguished pilots underscores the difference between the legendary pilot's public notoriety and the cub's public ignominy in the wake of Bixby's instructive "swindle." As an imposing role model, Bixby is less of an inspiration than a burden for the cub, raising self-doubt about the cub's own ability ever to measure up to his master. When the call "*Mark* twain!" sounds later, erroneously, in the cub's humiliating lesson, the disparity between pilot and cub couldn't be clearer. Richard Bridgman confidently infers that "[t]here is no doubting the intentionality of either the emphasis or the conjunction of danger and his name. The announcement of '*Mark* twain!' paralyzes him." And "as the leadsman announces the progressive fragmentation of 'twain' – 'quarter-less-twain!' " Bridgman observes, the cub's failure "to have confidence in the certain knowledge that he possessed . . . had shattered his identity."[17] This is sound reading, on one level. But we should observe a crucial distinction: the conjunction is not between his name and danger but between his pseudonym and pseudodanger. And the pseudonym is not the signifier of the cub pilot but of the author he would become. Thus it is not only the cub's identity that is shattered but also the esteem for the pilot's authority in which he has invested his identity.

Conversely, the announcement of the pseudonym suggests that he deliberately conceptualizes his authorial identity in terms of a traumatic lack of mastery. But because Bixby's stature as a pilot places him beyond the cub's reproach, the dramatization of that shattered esteem is deferred. The cub, and Twain as well, represses his resentment toward Bixby in the "*Mark* twain!" episode until he can release his wrath on an available surrogate. Enter Mr. Brown.

This compensation mechanism yields the exaggerated disproportion between the cub's deference to Bixby and his homicidal indignation toward Brown, in effect holding Brown responsible not only for the abuse he heaped on the cub but also for that which Bixby inflicted.

Still, the cub's reaction to Bixby isn't all steadfast adoration. Bixby's somewhat cruelly imparted lesson on the difference between a deadly bluff reef and a benign wind reef – an episode strikingly similar to the humiliating test of the cub's courage – provokes the cub's hostility. Although Twain resolves the episode with his famous celebration of a pilot's ability to read the surface of the water as a "wonderful book," he chafes at Bixby's seeming absence (the old hidden surveillance trick) at his moment of crisis: "[W]hy didn't that villain come!" The ambiguity created by the verb tense and the fact that the remark is embedded in the narrator's discourse without quotation marks lead us to wonder if the vilifying epithet is the thought of the annoyed cub at the moment of his panic or the expression of Twain's abiding animosity toward Bixby some fifteen years after the actual incident. When Bixby returns and embarrasses the cub with a sarcastic catechism, the cub reasserts his anger, amplifying it to the higher degree of desiring vengeance. Once he has the assurance that the responsibility is solely the pilot's, the cub eagerly follows Bixby's order and steers the boat over what he thinks is a deadly bluff reef: "I was just as anxious to kill the boat, now, as I had been to save her before. I impressed my orders upon my memory, to be used at the inquest, and made a straight break for the reef" (93–4). The cub's only hope for retaliation lies with the hope that Bixby's abusive authority might be punished by a higher authority. He assists justice in what little ways he can, by following orders and employing his memory (the very faculty that Bixby has helped him develop) to secure the testimony that will lead to Bixby's conviction. Having not yet endured Brown, the cub doesn't have anyone to whom he can transfer his resentment of Bixby's abuse. But vexed by his inability to assert himself against his superior, he takes refuge in an accommodating fantasy of revenge in which the legal system will assume his rage for him.

By claiming that Twain's esteem for Bixby, and for piloting in general, had dissipated or, at best, had been compromised by his equivocal attitude toward authority, I am calling into question

Twain's putative intention in "Old Times." But I don't mean to doubt the expression of that intention *in* "Old Times" so much as to show how Twain himself challenges it in *Life on the Mississippi.* "Old Times" makes plain that his desire to be a pilot was a desire to wield the pilot's authority. But after suffering under the yoke of that authority, he had misgivings about its charm. And when our reading of "Old Times" is refracted through the lens of *Life on the Mississippi*, Twain's doubts about the pilot's authority come into focus. The cub's humiliation under Brown sheds light on the comparable relation between the cub and Bixby, illuminating the conflict in Twain's stance toward the authority of piloting. "Old Times" portrays Brown only in his first characterization, the benignly doddering pilot with the marvelous memory. Not until Twain returned from his 1882 river trip and prepared to extend "Old Times" into *Life on the Mississippi* did he consider including the characterization of Brown as an oppressive, "bullyragging" tyrant. Notebook entries from the period indicate that, before turning his attention to the travel narrative of part 2, Twain thought of rounding out the "Old Times" sketches with either several more about his days as a licensed pilot or the chapters of his apprenticeship under Brown, including their catastrophic confrontation and the consequent death of Twain's brother Henry (*MTNJ*, 2:457). Either course would reflect his desire for closure to the elements of bildungsroman in "Old Times." To have achieved that closure with the proposed sketches of his tenure as a licensed pilot would have insured a greater degree of consistency with his explicit intention in "Old Times." Instead, he chose the Brown episodes, and in this choice Twain stages the pilot's authority in an unflattering pose. Bixby's and Brown's similar abuses of the cub go beyond the association implied by their syntactic contact within the narrative and forge an identity between them (despite the ostensible opposition that they represent). The identity suggests that in Brown Twain found a ready object upon whom to heap his resentment for all of the molestation that the authority of piloting had inflicted upon him. Contrary to Burde's speculation, Brown is not a revised model of authority (one destined to fail) to suit a digressive text; his mnemonically generated narrative excursions lack the associational coherence that *Life on the Mississippi* explores. Instead, Twain introduces Brown as a villain in order to slay, symbolically, an old model of authority before he embarks on a narrative whose intention requires the purposeful freedom of a more expansive vision.

As a result, When Twain converted the "Old Times" sketches into part 1 of *Life on the Mississippi*, he realigned their rhetorical status by virtue of the new context. All of Twain's rhetoric in "Old Times" about the pilot as "the novelty of a king without a keeper, an absolute monarch who was absolute in sober truth and not by a fiction of words" unravels in the presence of the *Pennsylvania* episodes, which deconstruct the pilot's authority. Indeed, on closer inspection we might notice that "the pilot's boundless authority" never stood on its own even in "Old Times." Rather, the pilot's authority stands by the higher authority of the law. In fact, his authority was not only *enforced* by law but also *forced* by it: "the law of the United States forbade him to listen to commands or suggestions" (123). Moreover, Twain reports that a good pilot was of such a value to a captain that the latter "took pains to *keep* him . . . I have known a captain *to keep* such a pilot in idleness, under full pay, three months at a time, while the river was frozen up" (123; emphasis added). These explicit contradictions undercut the authority that in the same breath he claims for pilots. The idea of a pilot being kept, not free to ply his trade after having been bought and paid for, implies a contract of indenture, a paradoxical kind of slavery that prohibits work. When measured in context of the contiguous references, of the respect accorded to a "stalwart darkey" because he was a fireman on the *Aleck Scott* and to a "spruce young negro" because he was the barber of the *Grand Turk* (124), the slavery implication inches a little closer to the foreground of the text, further eroding Twain's claim for the pilot's authority.

The emergence of these fissures in the unity of "Old Times" should not cause us to reassess Twain's carelessness or failure in the *Atlantic* series. For these stresses do not directly interfere with the expression of his esteem for the pilot's authority in "Old Times." However, they are latent signs of Twain's uneasiness about authority. When he adapted the "Old Times" material for part 1 of *Life on the Mississippi* and concluded with the Brown episodes, he provided a different angle of vision from which we are urged to reread the river reminiscence against the grain. This perspective exposes the disparate components in the representation of authority and challenges us to reassemble them into a new configuration. Thus, the dismantling of his esteem for the pilot's authority maintained in his cub persona becomes the opportunity to construct a new authority in the persona of a new identity: the writer Mark Twain. In this way, he supplants the authority of the pilot, which lived in "sober truth and not by fiction of words," by an authority that manifests itself precisely in the fiction of words repudiated in "Old Times."

But words were what mattered to him all along. In the course of enumerating the qualities contributing to the "Rank and Dignity of Piloting," Twain emphasizes the pilot's authoritative speech in a two-sentence paragraph: "By long habit, pilots came to put all their wishes in the form of commands. It 'gravels' me, to this day, to put my will in the weak shape of a request, instead of launching it in the crisp language of an order" (123). His esteem for the pilot's verbal authority is the ultimate extension of his admiration for rivermen's speech. This emerges in his childhood envy of the first boy to leave Hannibal for a life on the river. That unnamed adventurous boy's easy manner of inflecting his talk with "steamboat technicalities" (66) conspicuously affirmed his worldliness. Later, on board the *Paul Jones*, the aspiring cub's attempt to insinuate himself into the company of the crew is met with an awesome display of the mate's "sublime" profanity, provoking the admission (emphasized by the one-sentence paragraph): "I wished I could talk like that" (70). Even after the harsh rebuke of this demi-hero, his attraction to the talk of rivermen persists unabated, because the admirable style of the rebuke itself demonstrates the authority of conspicuous speech, thus reinforcing the promise of the authoritative identity that the youth desires to achieve.

But the cub's first recognition of the pilot's authority has nothing to do with his speech and arises merely from his desire for revenge: "I had comforting day-dreams of a future when I should be a great and honored pilot, with plenty of money, and could kill some of these mates and clerks and pay for them" (67). His acknowledgment of the power in the pilot's speech only emerges secondarily. Merely to emulate the mate's speech would relieve the abuse of subordination, but it would also yield the strife of rivalry. However, achieving the ultimate colloquial power of the pilot, a power that harnesses its colorful vitality to the force of law and the power of money, would give him a superior authority that is above molestation.

Taken together, the cub's concern with the authority of language and his patricidal desire in his stormy relationship with Brown announce an oedipal element in Twain's reconfiguration of the pilot–cub relationship.[18] In "Old Times," Twain had already employed the family discourse characteristic of Lockean philosophy to describe his position among the ship's company during his first days as a traveler aboard the *Paul Jones*: "I was now beginning to feel a strong sense of being part of the boat's family, a sort of infant son to the captain and younger brother to the officers" (69). Although he ascribes the nominal paternal position to the captain here, his later assertion that the supreme authority is legally accorded the pilot in effect displaces the former by the latter. He reinforces the Lockean resonance by alluding to the concept of the *tabula rasa* when describing his infant state as a cub. First, he admits to knowing "nothing" (75) under Bixby's examination of his knowledge of river landmarks and discredits his memory as "never loaded with anything but blank cartridges" (76). Second, he portrays himself as "a cipher in [the] August company" (80) of distinguished pilots whose talk of the river both inspires his awe of them and deflates his expectations of ever learning the river.[19] But despite the Lockean paradigm of education implied in the cub's contract to train under Bixby, the cub's desire for education is motivated by a desire for revenge against others and not by respect for the father. The contract, therefore, lacks the component of filiopiety.

On the other hand, the contract is more than the cub bargained for, because Bixby's instructional methods lack the benevolent guidance characteristic of the paternal role in the Lockean formula. The cub's reactions to Bixby's abusive tests ambiguously indicate his confusion about Bixby's paternal authority. First, his remark to Bixby upon the occasion of his public humiliation – "It was a fine trick to play on an *orphan*" (121) – applies figuratively to Bixby's abandonment of him in the pilothouse. But in declaring himself an orphan, Twain also suggests that Bixby's treatment has voided their patrifilial contract. Second, his reference to orphanhood can refer literally, since John Clemens had died when his son Samuel was eleven years old. By alluding to his biological father, the cub implies that the contract never afforded Bixby paternal status – asserting, in effect, that blood is thicker than ink. This allusion to his father, moreover, recalls the reference to John Clemens in the first installment of "Old Times": "My father was a justice of the peace, and I supposed he possessed the power of life and death over all men and could hang anybody that offended him. This was distinction enough for me as a general thing; but the desire to be a steamboatman kept intruding, nevertheless" (65–6). This reference adds another strand to the knot of confusion in Twain's ambivalence toward authority, because even though he has flouted his father's authority by his greater admiration of steamboatmen and disobeyed a paternal proscription by becoming one of them, his fantasy of becoming a pilot in order to kill the mate who had humiliated him reveals that he has transposed his father's official authority to the pilot.[20] After suffering even greater humiliation under Bixby than he had in his run-in with the abusive mate, he fantasizes similarly, only this time he separates the judge's and the pilot's authority in order to subordinate Bixby to an authority who will mete out the punishment that will avenge the cub's suffering. His fantasy emphasizes language, first by linking the authoritative word to the priority of his biological father and then by projecting his desire for that authoritative word in order to punish Bixby for his authoritarian abuse.

The cub's climactic battle with Brown adds the crowning touch that emphasizes the importance of language in the formation of credible authority. Framing this stage of the cub's apprenticeship mostly as an ordeal of verbal abuse, Twain glosses the entire experience in terms of the literary benefits he gained from it. In the opening paragraph to chapter 18, "I Take a Few Extra Lessons" (the first of the three that deal with his intensifying conflict with Brown), Twain assesses the benefits of his education under Brown:

> I am to this day profiting somewhat by that experience; for in that brief, sharp schooling, I got personally and familiarly acquainted with about all the different types of human nature that are to be found in fiction, biography, or history . . . When I say I am still profiting by this thing, I do not mean that it has constituted me a judge of men – no, it has not done that; for judges of men are born, not made. My profit is various in kind and degree; but the feature of it which I value most is the zest which that early experience has given to my later reading. When I find a well-drawn

character in fiction or biography, I generally take a warm personal
interest in him, for the reason that I have known him before –
met him on the river. (152)

Within this assurance of the literary benefit of his education under
Brown, Twain's aside that one is born a judge of men and not educated to the position, in addition to recalling his description of
Brown's memory as "born in him . . . not built," introduces its own
ambiguity. On the one hand, it implies that he will modestly refrain
from judging others, since this, or any, education cannot qualify one
for such authority. But on the other hand, if judges of men are born
and not made, the authority to judge men is a function of nature,
not nurture, and is his genetic legacy as the son of a judge. Thus,
Twain introduces his education under Brown with an *a priori* rationale justifying his consequent defiance of Brown's authority. Without
explicitly challenging the hierarchy, Twain suggests that the cub is
no longer simply subordinate to Brown; rather, they parallel each
other in relation to prior authorities. Brown artificially acquires his
authority over the cub from Bixby, and the cub naturally inherits his
authority to judge Brown from John Clemens. The restructured hierarchy provides the opportunity to move beyond either the mere
wish that the sentence of a higher authority will punish his abuser,
as he had hoped in Bixby's case, or the patricidal fantasies he entertained in retaliation for Brown's oppressive authority.

The linguistic component of this oedipal ordeal is underscored
by the fact that Brown's symbolic castration of the cub is performed
in language, by his insistent harangue on the cub's incompetence.
Finally, the threat of physical abuse provokes the cub into acting out
his oedipal wish physically (but still symbolically). Yet the most powerful effect of the cub's triumph in this final confrontation comes
not in the literal blows he deals Brown but in his subsequent verbal
denial of Brown's authority:

> Brown gathered up the big spy-glass, war-club fashion, and or-
> dered me out of the pilot-house with more than Comanche blus-
> ter. But I was not afraid of him now; so, instead of going, I tarried,
> and criticised his grammar; I reformed his ferocious speeches for
> him, and put them into good English, calling his attention to the
> advantage of pure English over the bastard dialect of the Pennsyl-
> vanian collieries whence he was extracted. He could have done
> his part to admiration in a cross-fire of mere vituperation, of

course; but he was not equipped for this species of controversy; so he presently laid aside his glass and took the wheel, muttering and shaking his head; and I retired to the bench. (158–9)

Not satisfied with soundly thrashing his adversary, the cub turns to metacommentary on the pilot's abuse to establish his linguistic superiority. On first glance, it may seem out of character for Twain, whose success rested on his use of the vernacular idiom, to represent himself extolling "the advantage of pure English over . . . bastard dialect." But the episode, nonetheless, exploits the tension between center and margin that motivates vernacular literature, because the authority accorded the pilot and his speech makes Brown a subversive target regardless of his grammatical deficiencies.

The literary conditions of this episode in language mastery point ahead to part 2 of *Life on the Mississippi*, in which the narrative authority shifts its emphasis from actual experience to textual experience. In that half of the book, Twain recalls the victims of the Civil War siege at Vicksburg. And in doing so, he installs what may seem an odd tension in the text, if not in his artistic identity. For the writer who steadfastly claimed that personal experience was the true basis of good writing reverses himself here and warns that too much actual experience can be a bad thing. Excess experience, he claims, like that of the siege victims, saps a storyteller's ability. Twain recalls how "a couple of Vicksburg non-combatants" told him their story

without fire, almost without interest.

A week of their wonderful life there would have made their tongues eloquent forever perhaps; but they had six weeks of it, and that wore all the novelty out; they got used to being bombshelled out of home and into the ground; the matter became commonplace. After that, the possibility of their ever being startlingly interesting in their talks about it was gone. (259)

A better representation of the experience at Vicksburg, Twain contends, would be rendered by one merely acquainted with the facts of history – that is, one empowered by textual experience rather than hindered by oppressive actual experience. What appears to be a virtual contradiction, though, is in fact a crucial justification, given Twain's limited Civil War service. In order to represent the nation, both personally and in writing, a shift to textual experience is a necessary compensation for the actual experience he lacks.

Perhaps nothing in part 2 better exemplifies this shift from actual to textual authority than chapter 26, "Under Fire." Composed of a pilot's own story of cowardice during his "maiden battle" of his Civil War riverboat service, this account suggestively recalls the cub's humiliations under Bixby and Brown, since, just as in the pilot's tale, both were "at his elbow to shame him [for] showing the white feather when matters grew hot and perilous around him" (192). Indeed, his ultimate confrontation with Brown is a kind of "maiden battle" in which he has been "a target," if not for "Tom, Dick and Harry," then for a man with an equally common surname. And although the cub is not guilty of cowardice in his assault on Brown, like the pilot in "Under Fire," he achieves recognition as a hero from a high-ranking officer for his illegal action. Upon a second look, this story seems designed to offset Twain's own desertion. Twain admits that this kind of story fascinated him, because, he says, "I often had a curiosity to know how a green hand might feel, in his maiden battle, perched all solitary and alone on high in a pilot-house, . . . ; so, to me [the pilot's] story was valuable – it filled a gap for me which all histories had left till that time empty." Of course, what created the gap in his experience of the historic period was the fact that he had "disenlisted" after a mere two weeks as a Confederate irregular. But the pilot's story doesn't fill that gap as neatly as he suggests. So Twain attempts to fill it himself with the episodes recounting his service under Brown on the *Pennsylvania*, which the *Gold Dust* pilot's experience resembles. In so doing, Twain recasts his personal experience as an allegorical prefiguration of the Civil War, reshaping the actual to compensate for his failure to participate in the great watershed in American history.[21]

By certifying that he values his education under Brown mostly for "the zest which that early experience has given to [his] later reading," Twain clearly implies that actual experience is subordinate to textual experience, effecting a transition between the text's two forms of authority at this pivotal moment. For though they belong with part 1 by virtue of topic and setting, the authority conflict that they play out aligns them with part 2. These transitional episodes dynamically shift the autobiographical into the metaphoric; that is, they transform the actual into the literary. For the cub's confrontation with Brown reveals Twain's anxiety about the relative value of textual and actual experience generally, and about his absence from the Civil War specifically. A close appraisal of the confrontation on the *Pennsylvania* and the ensuing catastrophe of Henry Clemens's death reveals that this episode of Twain's apprenticeship is a figure for the Civil War; in both, symbolic patricide results in the tragedy of fratricide.[22]

Initially, Twain depicts his service under Brown as slavery. The cub is, in effect, the property of his pilot-mentor Bixby. When Bixby loans him out to the abusive pilot Brown, the cub's experience parallels the trajectory recorded in Frederick Douglass's model of the slave narrative.[23] Twain recalls enduring Brown's abuse by day and dreaming of killing him by night. His antipathy reaches its climax when Brown's abuse of mud clerk Henry Clemens provokes Twain to intercede violently on his younger brother's behalf. Like Douglass's physical defiance of Mr. Covey, Twain's throttling of Brown fortifies his evolving personal strength. His report of the subsequent relief he enjoyed in the captain's lenient judgment of his criminal assault on a pilot explicitly reinforces the slavery figure: "I knew how an emancipated slave feels; for I was an emancipated slave myself" (160). Indeed, the captain's lenience circumscribes Brown's authority and metaphorically abolishes slavery. Brown's ultimatum to the captain, that either he puts the cub off the boat or Brown himself would go ashore, metaphorically threatens secession.

To insure safe navigation of the ship, the captain has no choice but to keep Brown on and to arrange the cub's passage on a boat that will follow the *Pennsylvania* to St. Louis. There the captain intends to hire a replacement pilot for Brown and to rehire the cub. However, like the futility of Lincoln's attempts to preserve the Union, the captain's solution fails to preserve the integrity of the ship once the dispute about the pilot's authority has divided the pilothouse. And like the division of Union and Confederacy, the division in the pilothouse causes the fatal separation of the two brothers. The plan to restore order is scuttled by catastrophic violence: an explosion destroys the *Pennsylvania* and sends Henry Clemens to his death. Twain reports that Henry was not an immediate casualty of the explosion; in fact, he reached shore safely but returned to the wreck to assist victims, only to become a victim himself. And for this act of fatal heroism, Twain assumes the guilt. His younger brother's return to the boat, he is convinced, was influenced by their last conversation, in which they decided that a steamboat crewman's responsibility was to "stick with the boat" in the event of a disaster (161).[24] Twain's guilt completes the allegory, transposing his patricidal assault on Brown into the fratricidal consequence of Henry's death, and thereby representing the Civil War's ultimate horror. By revising his personal experience, Twain attempts to patch up the gap in his résumé, thereby qualifying his candidacy as a representative man.

Since playing double is Twain's forte, we should hardly be surprised to find this typology of sectionalism fraught with ambiguity. Such indeterminacy prevents us from assigning a single allegorical value to any of the *figurae* in it. But ironically, instead of undermining the typology, the ambiguity affords Twain the kind of expansiveness that a representative persona requires. For example, the equation between the pilot–cub relation and the master–slave relation, though justifiably inferred from the pilots' treatment of the cub as property, is contradicted by other details in the account. Brown is not just a pilot on a steamboat called the *Pennsylvania* but also a Pennsylvania native, and during the war Bixby was the head pilot of the Union fleet, facts that locate them on the opposite side of the Mason-Dixon line from where their depiction as slaveholders situates them. In addition, Brown's interrogation of the cub in their first meeting yields the knowledge that his temporary charge was the son of a slaveholder, a biographical fact that appears to fuel the hostility in Brown's first tirade against the cub's failure to take initiative: "You've had no *orders*! My, what a fine bird we are! We must have *orders*! Our father was a *gentleman* – owned slaves – and *we've* been to *school*. Yes, we are a gentleman, *too*, and got to have *orders*!" (154). Set off by dashes, the fact that the cub's family "owned slaves" has a foregrounded importance. Thus, we can also see Brown as a northern abolitionist who is out to punish the inheritor of southern feudal authority. Viewing the cub as an heir to the slaveholder's legacy also helps explain Twain's assumption of guilt for Henry's death: the cub's refusal to accept the pilot's legally constituted authority (analogous to the South's refusal to accept the inevitability of abolition) separates him from Henry. As *figura*, then, Twain is divided between the emancipated slave and the personification of the offending South.

By allegorizing Henry's death, Twain not only compensates for his lack of experience but also bridges the two halves of *Life on the*

Mississippi, drawing other autobiographical references into the allegory. For example, upon approaching Memphis, in part 2, Twain recollects that this was the scene of "the most famous of the river battles of the Civil War." Although he represses any mention of the more traumatic personal association to Henry's death, the battle of Memphis provides Twain with another secondhand connection to the war, because two of the distinguished opponents in the battle were men under whom he had previously served: "Mr. Bixby, head pilot of the Union fleet, and Montgomery, Commodore of the Confederate fleet" (216). In effect, by having taken orders from two high-ranking counterparts in the Civil War, Twain portrays himself as both a Yankee and a Rebel, paralleling his ambiguous self-figuration as both victim and violator on the *Pennsylvania.* So whereas he had assumed a nonpartisan's role by his retreat from the Civil War, he reinsures his bipartisan's role in the allegory by portraying himself in this supplemental account as the figurative son to commanders on both sides of the battle line. The two different modes suggest a kind of synthesis of the two poles of the American representative self: the Franklinian model of the negational self, on the one hand, and the Whitmanian all-affirming self, on the other.[25]

Still, despite Twain's confidence about writing from limited experience, his doubt about the success of his allegory emerges in part 2 when he considers the profound influence that the war had on the Southerners who actually experienced it. Their habit of dating all events in relation to the war, Twain observes, "shows how intimately every individual was visited, in his own person, by that tremendous episode. It gives the inexperienced stranger a better idea of what a vast and comprehensive calamity invasion is than he can ever get by reading books at the fireside." Thus the textual experience that Twain privileges in part 2 and the war allegory he has textualized from his own experience to qualify his representativity pale in comparison to actual Civil War experience. Indeed, the idea of crediting his riverboat service with having exposed him to "all the different types of human nature that are to be found in fiction, biography, or history" appears to have come to him from a southern gentleman's explanation of the preeminence of the war in the southern consciousness: "In the war each of us, in his own person, seems to have sampled all the different varieties of human experience." The impact of this education makes the war an inevitable association, regardless of the topic. "You may try all you want to, to keep other subjects before the house," the gentleman remarks,

> and we may all join in and help, but there can be but one result: the most random topic would load every man up with war reminiscences, and *shut* him up, too; and talk would be likely to stop presently, because you can't talk pale inconsequentialities when you've got a crimson fact or fancy in your head that you are burning to fetch out. (319–20)

Twain anticipates the way in which this revaluation of actual experience compromises his representativity. Thus, when he declares his native affiliation with the South to explain his delight in the musical speech of Southerners, he appropriates a collective identity to disguise the fact that his experience doesn't measure up to that of Southerners who weren't "de-southernized," as Howells insisted Twain was.[26] And yet, as a Southerner, even a desouthernized absentee from the Civil War's defining experience, Twain's textual return to the South, a confrontation with the effects of the war, seems a compulsive return to the empty space in his identity. The war has affected this inexperienced Southerner no less than the experienced ones. The difference for Twain is that since he lacks his own war reminiscences, he can't be "shut up," as the gentleman says that other Southerners are. To the contrary, it's as if that lack drives Twain to convert what the gentleman might term the "pale inconsequentialities" of river talk into the "crimson" metaphor of consequence.

Twain's allegory of his confrontation with Brown cannot by itself substitute for actual experience of the Civil War. But this is his first, not his only, attempt to reinscribe himself into the nation's history. In order to become the "grandfather" of twentieth-century American writers, as Faulkner called him, he would have to make the leap into writing.[27] In *Life on the Mississippi*, Twain recalls making this leap by performing another patricidal gesture in his satire of "that real and only genuine Son of Antiquity," Captain Isaiah Sellers (351). In this oedipal scenario, as Twain constructs it, pilot Sam Clemens initiates his evolution from pilot to writer Mark Twain.

Steamboat and Taboo

Twain paints a fairly respectful, if formal, portrait of Sellers in his contrite explanation of his relation to the "patriarch of the craft" (349). Initially he allows that the advanced age of the "ancient mariner" gave him such priority that "his brethren held him in the sort of awe in which illustrious survivors of a bygone age are always held by their associates." Adding more detail, however, he alters the contours of the picture. Within two pages his characterization drifts into a critique of the chilling effect that Sellers's presence had on the lively brags and lies of other pilots. As a result, the pilots' awe of Sellers was, in fact, ambivalence rather than simple admiration. They resented his ability "to drop casual and indifferent remarks of a reminiscent nature" (351) that would supersede their authority, and that they could not question. Thus, whenever the venerable riverman arrived on the scene, he would spread "disaster and humiliation around him." This kind of oppressively authoritative figure shows up elsewhere in Twain: the Oracle in *Innocents Abroad* and the old Admiral in *Roughing It* are two such examples.[28] Similarly, in a deleted section of *Life on the Mississippi*, Twain comments on the prevalence of proud bluster in America's past. But he adds that this kind of irrational and defensive swaggering "has since passed away, leaving scarcely a vestige. We mourn, of course, as filial duty requires – yet it was good rotten material for burial" (293). Apparently, though, it is suitable material for exhumation in his portraits of Brown and Sellers. Much like the cub's earlier pilot masters, Sellers wields his authority to generate "disaster and humiliation." But here the pilot's tyranny is constituted not by hard lessons of navigational control or by emotional or physical oppression. Rather, by dint of his monological priority, Sellers squelches dialogue and forces an uncomfortable silence on the other pilots.

The most important distinction between the illustrious captain and the cub's pilot-masters is that Sellers was not only a pilot but a writer as well. And it was as writers that Twain and Sellers crossed paths.[29] According to Twain's account, Sellers exercised his oppressive authority in writing by publishing items about the river in the *New Orleans Picayune*. Allegedly using the pen name "Mark Twain," Sellers laced his barely literate prose with the characteristic claim to priority by which he cast his authoritarian shadow over all other pilots. In response, Sam Clemens burlesqued one of Sellers's items under the pseudonym "Sergeant Fathom." But denying any responsibility for its publication, Twain insists that other pilots, disgruntled by Sellers's authority, seized the opportunity to ridicule their victimizer and printed the lampoon in the *New Orleans True Delta*. Sellers, Twain confesses, was so humiliated by the piece that he never published again. And the author of that humiliation expresses his sorrow for his fledgling performance, because "it sent a pang deep into a good man's heart." As an act of penance and homage, Twain admits, he "confiscated" Sellers's pseudonym upon learning of his death and claims, "I . . . have done my best to make it remain what it was in his hands – a sign and symbol and warrant that whatever is found in its company may be gambled on as being the petrified truth" (352).[30]

However, a considerable amount of evidence, both internal and external, shows this account to be specious, and Twain disingenuous. First, his often reiterated explanation of the origin of his pseudonym has been cast in doubt, since extensive research has failed to discover any writing to which Sellers signed the pseudonym that Samuel Clemens was later to adopt.[31] Second, Twain's memory of the fact seems less than reliable. Sellers did write items of river memoranda, and Clemens's Sergeant Fathom piece satirizes one of those items. But Twain's account of where these appeared is suspiciously erroneous. The Sellers item that Clemens lampooned appeared in the *New Orleans True Delta*, not in the *Picayune*, and the Sergeant Fathom burlesque was published in the *New Orleans Daily Crescent*, not the *True Delta* as Twain reports.[32] The slip of Twain's memory may seem innocent and inconsequential, but the titles of the newspapers which he claims published Sellers's writing and his own spoof suggest a trivializing of Sellers's authority as "picayune" and an authentication of his own as "true delta," the real substance of the river. In light of this error, whether purposeful or accidental, Twain's certification that one might "gamble" that anything written under the name "Mark Twain" is "petrified truth" guarantees nothing. Moreover, at the outset of part 2 he indicates that he intends to collect picturesque lies, not petrified truth. In *Life on the Mississippi*, the boasts and myths that give river talk its vitality stand in diametric opposition to the dead facts. The gamble that Twain offers is, then, a sucker's bet.

In this context, the story of his remorse also begins to sound like fiction. The correspondence between his account of turning humiliation against a "patriarch" of piloting and the earlier episodes of his own humiliation at the hands of Bixby and Brown urges us to see a deeper motivation than Twain attributes to the parody of Sellers and a deeper responsibility than he is willing to accept. In his claim that Sellers never wrote again and by assuming the pen name he later attributed to Sellers, Twain constructs a classic oedipal scenario, as Richard Bridgman suggests. This later account emphasizes how he parodied what Bakhtin calls the "authoritative word" of the father in order to certify his own authority, the authority of the vernacular rebel. The Sergeant Fathom burlesque is a kind of primal scene in which Twain's ironic "internally persuasive discourse" calls into question the exclusivity and rigidity of Sellers's authoritative discourse.[33]

Bakhtin's view that the language of the novel is comprised of socially stratified discourses and that the novelist hybridizes and parodies these multiple discourses within his or her own narrational style offers insight into Twain's craft. Although the prevalence of a "mixed style" has been noted as a distinctive feature of American literature, Bakhtin's theoretical explanation helps to amplify the social underpinnings that promote this phenomenon, especially in an American context. But the double-voicedness of the Bakhtinian novel especially complements the notion that Twain was ambivalent about expressing his authority. His representation of his discourse emerging into the social arena as a challenge to Sellers's authority anticipates Bakhtin's notion that "an individual's becoming, an ideological process, is characterized precisely by a sharp gap between" authoritative and internally persuasive discourses. And it is by challenging the monolithic structure of the authoritative word, which "is indissolubly fused with its authority – with political power, an institution, a person" – and which "stands and falls together with that authority," that Twain's "individual ideological consciousness" is born.[34] The monologic authority that Sellers personifies stands opposed to what Twain most valued in the river, its ability to inspire volubility. If we take Twain's essential achievement in the transition from "Old Times" to *Life on the Mississippi* to be the production of a heterologic text that represents both the fragmented national consciousness after the Civil War and the discourses of a pluralistic society as they flood the openness of the West, then we can appreciate the importance of his subverting Sellers's stifling presence.

Like the cub's ridicule of Brown's "bastard dialect," Twain's Sergeant Fathom parody makes fun of a barely literate figure who would seem a model vernacular hero. However, Twain's parody exemplifies vernacular subversion, because it undermines Sellers's monologic hegemony. By choosing Brown and Sellers as targets for vernacular subversion, Twain underscores the fact that oppressive authorities need not be from the eastern establishment. The inclusive authority of *Life on the Mississippi* amplifies this vernacular ideal positively by accommodating the colloquial truth in a plurality of voices. Thus the pen name "Mark Twain" is, as he intended it, a verification of the truth. But instead of the "petrified truth," it verifies the vital truth of picturesque lies – those that tell the story of a self-authored identity, ambivalently subscribing to the slain father's authority, and those that make up the heteroglot chorus of the United States.

Stylistic heterogeneity also parallels a structural change in Twain's investment in and critique of the pilot's authority. Early on, the attraction to Bixby as a role model grows out of the cub's desire for superiority. The oppressive superiority that Bixby and his grotesque surrogate Brown impose on the cub gives rise to his fantasies of asserting his own superiority over them, culminating in his patricidal defiance of Brown. Sellers's dominance, however, provokes not the simple wish to enjoy superiority over him, but rather the desire to neutralize the pressure of his preemptive authority. Certainly, Twain's reverent tone in this episode is the residue of his respect for Sellers's conspicuous priority, suggesting that superiority is still a coveted asset. But his countervailing resentment of Sellers's stifling presence fosters the desire to silence the oppressive patriarch in order to liberate the voices of all those whom Sellers has silenced. By moving beyond the rivalry that compels a desire for exclusive superiority to the resentment of a single authority in pursuit of mutual autonomy of the many, Twain represents his tolerance of social diversity as a vernacularized independence from Sellers.

Twain's series of staged breaks from patriarchy gives rise not only to his self-fashioned identity but also to the metonymic emphasis in the structure of the narrative. Patriarchy must assume the intrinsic relationship between father and child on a faith allied with metaphor, unsubstantiated by the indisputable metonymic connection between mother and child. Twain's repeated rejection of the symbolic and hierarchical identity between pilot-father and cub-son translates into a privileging of metonymy over metaphor in the structure of *Life on the Mississippi*. And just as the text's associative links between Bixby and Brown establish Brown's worth as a vilifiable surrogate for Bixby, Sellers is also associated with Bixby through metonymic contiguity in the narrative. For during Twain's 1882 trip he meets up with Bixby, who invites him to join a group for a tugboat tour of the delta, and it is during that tour that Sellers's name first arises during gossiping reminiscences. The link forged in the narrative between Bixby and a river authority whom Twain symbolically slays suggests that Twain cannot introduce Bixby into his text without some translated version of his repressed conflict with his mentor also arising.

Though Twain doesn't extrapolate the consequences of his conflict with Bixby until writing part 2 of *Life on the Mississippi*, the metonymic connection between Bixby and Sellers was there even in "Old Times," just as it was in the innocuous comparison of Bixby's and Brown's differently oriented memories. Sellers appears in the sixth installment of "Old Times," though so obliquely as hardly to attract our notice. In that installment, Twain shifts his focus from episodes of his own education as a cub and writes both generally of the "Rank and Dignity of Piloting" and specifically about the labor strategy that the pilots devised to rescue their economic independence, on which much of their prestige was based, from the fluctuations of supply-and-demand market forces. The system imposed by the Pilots' Association, paradoxically, violated the autonomy that Twain celebrates in his earlier praise of the pilot's authority. Indeed, as Edgar Burde astutely observes, the association's collective system not only diminished the power of the individual but also victimized those individuals who refused to join. One such nonmember pilot, "one of the very best and oldest pilots on the river" (131), identified by the initials "I. S.," becomes the first victim when his captain must fire him to meet the demands of a member pilot. Burde astutely conjectures that the victim must have been the notorious Isaiah Sellers, whose firing represents the replacement of "individual talent . . . by economic institutions as the chief source of authority in piloting."[35] And yet the hostility of the other pilots toward Sellers that Twain reports in the Sergeant Fathom episode suggests that the issue is not simply economic. But whether economically or linguistically motivated, the collective hostility against Sellers in both scenes is an emblem of American filioanxiety.

The latent relation between Bixby and Sellers in this "Old Times" episode is even more obscure than the reference to Sellers in the 1882 tugboat conversation. Their connection in "Old Times" hinges strictly on the metonymic juxtaposition of an anecdote of Bixby's furious cursing of a captain who dared give him an order while he piloted the *Aleck Scott* and the account of the Pilots' Association that features the firing of a pilot we now know to be Sellers. In "Old Times" this juxtaposition rather easily escapes our notice, because it's embedded within a series of accounts that detail the power of pilots and their unwillingness to stand for any infringement of their authority by captains or owners. The story of Bixby's outburst is the second of two examples of a pilot's ability to get the better of a captain who violates protocol – the first being the story of Stephen W.'s ploy to scuttle a captain's attempt to undervalue his wages. Immediately after these two personal examples comes the account of the Pilots' Association as a collective tool used to gain leverage on the owners who economically violate the pilots' stature. Nowhere in the magazine installment are there any breaks in the continuity from one to the next. But when Twain divided the seven *Atlantic* installments into fourteen chapters to prepare the expanded manuscript for publication as a book, he divided the sixth installment between the stories that illustrate how both Stephen W. and Bixby keep their captains in line. So the anecdote about Bixby on the *Aleck Scott* opens chapter 15, "The Pilot's Monopoly," even though it is more thematically appropriate to the previous chapter, "Rank and Dignity of Piloting." In fact, the paragraph immediately following the story of Bixby's furious outburst displays all the rhetorical signs of a fitting introductory transition to the new chapter: "Having now set forth in detail the nature of the science of piloting and likewise described the rank which the pilot held among the fraternity of steamboatmen, this seems a fitting place to say a few words about an organization which the pilots once formed for the protection of their guild" (128). Can we assume that Twain didn't recognize the more appropriate division of his material when it came to apportioning the *Atlantic* installments into chapters? Either consciously or unconsciously, he chose this shape to the chapters for a reason: it was more important to Twain to bracket Bixby with Sellers than with Stephen, because Bixby and Sellers exerted a figurative paternal pressure that resulted in the professional transformation of Samuel Clemens, pilot, into Mark Twain, writer.

Although Twain's succession of conflicts with paternalized authorities tips the balance of the narrative structure toward metonymy, the associations generated by syntactic combination do not eradicate the metaphoric functions of selection and condensation. In part 2, Twain constructs his relationship with Sellers entirely in metaphoric terms. He had no direct personal relationship with the aged pilot, as he had in his apprenticeships under Bixby and Brown. Rather, Sellers was a patriarchal figure for the general community of pilots. And by adopting Sellers as his own oppressive father, Twain creates a metaphoric role for himself as well, a collective identity that subsumes the general experience of all pilots within the representation of his particular experience. This figural leap converts personal oedipality into a culturally representative complex, in much the same way that Freud would later extrapolate his theories of individual psychology into cultural analysis. Indeed, taken together, the publication of the Sergeant Fathom piece and Sellers's firing because of Pilots' Association pressure dramatize an Americanized version of the myth of civilization that Freud propounds in *Totem and Taboo*. From Darwin, Freud theorizes that civilization evolved into "*associations of men* consisting of members with equal rights" after the Oedipus complex was initially played out within the primal horde.[36] Twain depicts the collective action in the Pilots' Association and Sergeant Fathom episodes as two different though essentially identical versions of Sellers's ritual slaying: in both, the fraternal pilots symbolically kill the obstacle to the satisfaction of their desire for equal power. Although Freud's speculation is anthropologically invalid, his creative analysis of social organizations predicated on "equal rights" echoes Twain's representation of patriarchal tyranny and filial resentment, and both exhibit the effect of the vicissitudes of democracy in the nineteenth century on their thought.

Twain's confession of remorse for having humiliated Sellers further reveals the opposed emotions between which the Oedipus complex oscillates. According to Freud, the sons' fear and hatred of the father are counterpoised by their admiration and envy of him. Once

53

the resentful sons satisfy their hatred by patricide, guilt generates a resurgence of the kind of admiration Twain professes in his regret for his parody of Sellers. Further still, the envy of Sellers's authority indicates not only admiration but also a repressed identification that reemerges in Clemens's exculpatory appropriation of the patro-pseudonym, the *"nom de guerre* . . . Mark Twain" (352), as the signa-ture of his own authority.

The Pilots' Association episode anticipates yet another feature of Freud's primal story. The period between the association's first suc-cess, the firing of Sellers, and its eventual dominance is marked by division and conflict between the pilot-brothers. This approximates the trajectory of Freud's myth. He supposes that after the sons suc-ceed in removing the oppressive father and the primal horde dis-solves, the absence of a single unifying authority results in outbreaks of recurrent fratricidal strife, which frustrate progress toward a new social organization. The Sellers conflicts reach their fullest meta-phoric significance by establishing this pattern of crisis as a figure for America's evolving identity. Beginning with the symbolic patri-cide in the Declaration of Independence, in which King George III is portrayed as a tyrannical parent against whom the filial colonies have no choice but to act; continuing through the fraternal friction that marked the Constitutional Convention; and reaching a climax in the subsequent fratricide of the Civil War over conflicting inter-pretations of the framers' attitudes toward slavery and states' rights, American history resembles the pattern of paternal and fraternal conflict that Twain depicts in the history of piloting.[37]

But the ability of Twain's history of commercial navigation to stand for the course of the nation remains purely potential in "Old Times." Not until the Sergeant Fathom episode in part 2 of *Life on the Mississippi* establishes the collective force of Twain's identity as a writer can we begin to appreciate the allegorical meaning of the Pilots' Association struggle and the degree to which Twain's repre-sentative stature depends upon it. We should also bear in mind that this skirmish over literary authority is only the first leaning toward a more ambitious lunge at representativity. His clash with the nearly illiterate Sellers initiates Twain into a hunt for much bigger game: the literary lion Sir Walter Scott.

Twain is notorious for complaining about the South's failure to progress into the age of realism – as witnessed in its effeminate courtly indulgences, its chivalric titles, and its romantic literary style. He blames Scott and his romantic literature's pernicious influence for these stale affectations of sham medievalisms. Still, literature is not the limit of the problem. Twain even goes so far as to accuse Scott of having caused the Civil War. And, though he measures the charge as a "wild proposition" (328) himself, his invective amounts to a seriocomic attempt to bridge the national rift by rewriting history. In much the same way that the colonists depicted King George III as a tyrant, Twain makes Scott a scapegoat on whom to lay the blame for the divided Union.[38] And if the Declaration of Independence signaled the onset of the American Revolution, Twain's rallying cry for freedom from Scott's oppressive influence is a call to complete the unfinished business of the Civil War. In effect, *Life on the Mississippi* both declares a second Civil War – one in which Twain can participate with a pen instead of a rifle – and maps out his program for a literary Reconstruction.

Twain's unequivocal vituperation indicates that Scott does not threaten him with the remorse that plagued his attempt to slay Sellers. Rather, by scapegoating Scott he attempts to dispose rhetorically of the fetishized literary corpse personifying cultural stagnation. Twain's treatment of Scott appears, then, to depart from his anticipation of Freud's myth. In passing off the secessional blame, Twain doesn't patriarchalize his enemy to reify him as a totemic figure. He harbors no remorse for his desire to rid American culture of all traces of Scott.

Still, Twain's account of the South's indulgence of "girly-girly romance," while not oedipally remorseful, nonetheless anticipates Freud's theory of civilization. According to Freud, filial remorse for patricide prompts the brotherly clan later to resubmit to the father's law, to reinscribe the taboos against murder and incest. In recuperating the law of the dead father, the sons convert their desire for the mother into worship, and the culture as a whole enshrines the feminine. Correspondingly, Twain dates the contamination of the South by the "Sir Walter disease" (327) to the period between the Revolution and the Civil War, that is, after the slaying of the father and before the explosion of fratricidal conflict. And his account of Scott's influence on American cultural history during that interim depicts this romantic temper as "the fashion in both sections of the country" (328). Read against Freud's myth, this view of history implies that the youthful nation, having disposed of the English father, developed a guilty affinity for British gentility, prompting it, in Twain's view, to embrace effeminacies of the rejected paternal culture.

The parallels between Freud's and Twain's analyses are striking: both reflect their nineteenth-century perspectives.[39] The significant difference between them, however, is that Twain's critique is an explicitly historical claim for American culture. The cultural problem, as Twain sees it, lies in the disrupted equilibrium between the nation's two regions, which has resulted from the South's inability to shed its obsessional guilt. In Twain's theory of cultural kinship, fraternal strife is a healthy state of balanced diversity on which the nation thrives. The dominance of any one region, however, reasserts the narrow concerns characterizing the tyrant father's rule in the primal horde. The Sir Walter disease, Twain contends, not only emasculates and betrays what is authentically American but also violates the equality of competition that guarantees the pluralism of the cultural marketplace. The South's allegiance to what Twain condemns as British effeminacy has allowed the growing difference between itself and the North to exceed the productive friction of diversity and to reach the destructive proportions resulting in the Civil War.

Similarly, Twain's distinctly American perspective defines the difference between his cultural-esthetic theories and Bakhtin's. In Twain's account, it is not slavery per se but a more abstract esthetic-political conflict over the resurrected ideals of the dead father that has driven the sectional brothers to violence.[40] Specifically, it is the uneven response to the chivalric and romantic world view of Scott that provoked the conflict. "For the North has thrown out that old inflated style, whereas the Southern writer still clings to it" (328). Bakhtin, on the other hand, despite acknowledging the "caste consciousness" of the chivalric romance, argues that "[i]n terms of the cultural language available for its expression, this consciousness was profoundly decentralized and, to a significant degree, international." In his theory, the prevalence of the chivalric romance among different cultures indicates "a rupture between material and language" that defines "authentic novelistic style."[41]

For Twain, however, the South's attraction to Scott does not invoke internationalism but rather denies the heteroglossia of American discourse itself. The "caste consciousness" of Scott's chivalric romances has even infected the South's political ideology. In a chapter edited out of the published book, Twain reports taking four pages from the New Orleans city directory at random to indicate the "variegated nationalities" (336) that make up the population. He then argues wryly that the fact that this otherwise diverse populace could vote with staunch allegiance to only one party countermands the proverb "Many men, many minds" – a "miracle which makes all other miracles cheap in comparison." Musing on this odd feature of the South's political behavior, he notes, "How odd it is to see the mixed nationalities of New York voting all sorts of tickets, and the very same mixed nationalities of New Orleans voting all one way – and letting on that that is just the thing they wish to do, and are entirely unhampered in the matter and wouldn't vote otherwise, oh, not for anything." Although Twain doesn't directly attribute this political monism to Scott's influence in this manuscript fragment, it is clear that he has little patience with the herd mentality of *en bloc* voting and the similar lack of independent thinking symptomatic of the Sir Walter disease. By critiquing the South's homogeneity, Twain implies that he values America for its diversity. And this idea of the nation is what distinguishes Twain from Bakhtin. Bakhtin identifies nationalism with epic and with a false, unitary literary language to which the novel's heteroglossia is a realistic countermeasure. Twain, on the other hand, equates the concept of America with the kind of heterogeneity that the Russian literary theorist demanded in a novel. And Twain organized *Life on the Mississippi* in order to represent this idea of America.

The multivoiced structure of the Mississippi book is what constitutes realism for Twain. And he proffers realism as the cure for the Sir Walter disease and the national rift it produced. But despite its realism, *Life on the Mississippi* also reflects Twain's romanticized relation to the war he never actually experienced. This lack spurred all the more his desire to achieve representative status by affecting history as a writer of its text, if not as an actor in its critical events. Henry James, another writer conspicuously absent from the Civil War, noted in his life of Hawthorne in 1879 that "the national consciousness" was touched by the "great convulsion" of the Civil War. Clearly Twain's text, far more than any by Hawthorne or James, represents the changes in the nation and its consciousness destined by that cataclysmic moment in American history.[42] Fratricidal blood permanently stained the nation's idyllic self-image and mandated that history must be understood through the wide angle of realism rather than through romanticism's wrong end of the telescope. Thus *Life on the Mississippi* represents not only the division in the life of its author and his country but also a turning point in Twain's career.

Although Twain disparaged the idea of isolating separate events as independently responsible for change, *Life on the Mississippi* stands as a watershed text showing the way for the landmark novels that define the extent of his authority. In his attempt to authenticate himself as an exemplary American rebel, Twain slants the autobiography within *Life on the Mississippi* to present himself not as the self-made man that Franklin's autobiography constituted as the representative American type but rather as a self reinvented through the act of writing, conceived as a democratic enterprise. By fictionalizing his autobiography, he figuratively provides historical continuity that will authorize his identity. In the Mississippi book's pivotal chapter Twain tells us, "[B]y and by the war came." And the text shows that it hardly came and went. Rather, by and by it exercised such influence on him that it appears again and again and again in *Life on the Mississippi*. His recurrence to the Civil War indicates how much his desire to come to terms with his absence from the crucial event inspired his various autobiographical stances. As a series of creative attempts to remember his actual past as a figure for collective experience, to make his own life on the Mississippi stand for the life of America, Twain announces in *Life on the Mississippi* the immediate concerns that will steer his direction in *Adventures of Huckleberry Finn* and "The Private History of a Campaign That Failed." If *Life on the Mississippi* had succeeded, if Twain had written himself beyond the dilemma of his Civil War absence, then presumably he would not have needed to write the adventures of a southern boy who takes on the perilous responsibility of freeing a slave before the Civil War and *then* lights out for the West. And had *Huckleberry Finn* succeeded in compensating for Clemens's lighting out *during* the Civil War by his literary gesture of freeing a slave twenty-three years after Emancipation in the production of the text, then presumably he would not have had to stage another authority conflict with General Grant in "The Private History." The pattern assumes the contours of a repetition compulsion and indicates the psychological toll of negotiating the price of representativity.[43]

On the Threshold of Novelistic Discourse

In the expansion of "Old Times" into a book, Mark Twain clearly abandoned the epic intentions that guided the *Atlantic* sketches. But just what kind of a text is *Life on the Mississippi*? To call it a travel narrative is inadequate, because that classification applies only to part 2 of the divided text. By grafting the travel narrative onto the "Old Times" sketches, Twain created a hybrid text that challenges such a simple generic label. To unravel the tangled genre of the Mississippi writings, we should look again at the Brown episodes, because the deconstruction of the pilot's authority – and, by analogy, of the epic – at the pivot of the text provides a clue to the relation between the overlapping Mississippi texts. In the course of discrediting the corrupt authority that Brown represents, Twain not only invalidates the epic but also provides a denouement for the bildungsroman latent in "Old Times," thus foregrounding the novelistic impulse embedded in the praise of piloting. This generic shift that resulted from Twain's adaptation of the *Atlantic* sketches to fit the book signals the text's evolution into novelistic discourse and Twain's own emergence as a novelist.

Part 2 is obviously not a bildungsroman, but as a travel narrative it shares a kinship with the picaresque tradition of the novel. Like the picaresque novel, part 2 follows the sequence of a journey, amplifying the temporality that was muted in the "Old Times" sketches, and Twain's traveling "scribbler" persona is a modern specimen of the roguish picaro who wanders the landscape pricking the sensitive areas of cultural convention. Immediately after the Brown episodes, in chapter 21, Twain describes himself as a picaresque wanderer, successively drifting through a series of occupations during his twenty-one-year absence from the river. The syntactically stressed prose of this transitional chapter between parts 1 and 2 performatively imitates the metonymic drift of the picaresque figure he has become. Although the two parts of *Roughing It* portray his metamorphosis from miner to writer similarly, the career transformation in *Life on the Mississippi* concentrates the issue of authority. By splicing the two Mississippi texts together, Twain forges a necessary link between the two versions of authority they represent: the cub pilot's conflict with authority informs the writer's exercise of authority and gives rise to the often-cited dualism of Mark Twain's identity.[44]

Doubtless, the discriminating judgment he learned while training as a cub pilot has given way to the experience of the "roving reporter" or the "scribbler" of subscription books, whose need to fill columns or pile up pages has encouraged an inclusive temperament. However, the residual influence of Twain's river apprenticeship can be seen in the traveling writer's ploy to arouse the rivermen's desire to assert their superiority and then circumscribe that response by his own exercise in authority. Having "remembered that it was the custom of the steamboatmen in the old times to load up the confiding stranger with the most picturesque and admirable lies" (167), Twain intended to prey on the pilots' own predatory instincts, thus tricking the unsuspecting rivermen into helping him fill his "standard work" with errant content – with lies, fictions, and ambiguous statistics that he would weave into a colorful tapestry. To the picaresque author, pilots are a bunch of inveterate liars whom he can roguishly play for all they're worth.

Just as Twain portrays himself as an ambivalent heir to the authority of father figures, the incorporation of the epic "Old Times" into the context of the novelistic *Life on the Mississippi* also signifies the novel's ambivalence toward the legacy it inherits from the epic. The cub's rivalrous triumph over Brown, which stems from the desire to assume a position of sole superiority over the father, effects the transformation from epic to bildungsroman in the adaptation of "Old Times" into part 1. And Twain's subsequent conflict with Sellers, which was generated not by the simple desire to replace the father as a monological voice of authority but by the desire for colloquial heterogeneity, stimulates the metamorphosis from the bildungsroman that closes part 1 to the picaresque that opens part 2. The novel's loose form enables the traveling "scribbler" of the picaresque to suspend the various discourses that organize the diversity of American experience in the fluid medium of American prose. Thus *Life on the Mississippi* embodies the Bakhtinian heteroglossia that defines the novel as an expansive social genre.[45] Twain didn't fail to extend "Old Times," as some critics have complained; rather, by beginning to enunciate in *Life on the Mississippi* the novelistic tendencies that lay dormant in the *Atlantic* sketches, he succeeded in creating a heteroglot text that represents the democratic pluralism of the nation.

Although the transformation of the Mississippi writings from the stable unity of the epic/bildungsroman's monological discourse to the subversive heterogeneity of the picaresque's double-voiced discourse is clearest at the transition between parts 1 and 2, the three introductory chapters of *Life on the Mississippi* announce the intention to revise "Old Times" by reframing it in the new context of the book.

In the first of the three introductory chapters, Twain explicitly states the value of context when contemplating the history of the Mississippi:

> To say that De Soto, the first white man who ever saw the Mississippi River, saw it in 1542, is a remark which states a fact without interpreting it: it is something like giving the dimensions of a sunset by astronomical measurements, and cataloging the colors by their scientific names; – as a result, you get the bald fact of the sunset, but you don't see the sunset. It would have been better to paint a picture of it.
>
> The date 1542, standing by itself, means little or nothing to us; but when one groups a few neighboring historical dates and facts around it, he adds perspective and color, and then realizes that this is one of the American dates which is quite respectable for age. (41)

The same critique could be leveled at "Old Times." When Twain says that he had been a cub pilot in an unspecified time period, he states a nearly similar fact without any "neighboring historical dates and facts," and complicated further by his disingenuous self-portrait as a callow youth. The Mississippi book, though, has more of the context he calls for in the passage just quoted. When he contextualizes the account of his apprenticeship, by grafting on the prefatory chapters before and the travel narrative after, he not only adds "perspective and color" but also *re*interprets it.

In the second of the introductory chapters, "The River and Its Explorers," Twain quotes extensively from the historical writing of Francis Parkman, whose picturesque, narrative style might initially appear to be a model for Twain's own book. Indeed, Parkman's writing would seem to exemplify the kind of narrative that Twain

says, in part 2, would adequately depict the experience of the Vicksburg siege: one made by someone who had access to "the materials
furnished by history" (258) rather than actual experience, and that
comes "nearer to reproducing [the event] to the imagination" of
the reader than could one made by an actual participant in the
event. But Twain interpolates the quotations from Parkman's authoritative discourse with his own colloquial commentary. The juxtaposition defamiliarizes the official history and alerts us to the prej-
udicial hues in which the historian's lush literary style colors his
account of the events. Parkman dubs La Salle's laying claim to the
Mississippi Valley "the stupendous accession" for "the Sultan of
Versailles" (49); Twain labels it a "robbery" "consecrated with a
hymn" for "Louis the Putrid" (48). Where the historian marshals
the conventions of the "picturesque" and the "sublime" in nineteenth-century American landscape painting to convey the paradox
of "a feeble human voice" exerting control over the magnificence
of the American landscape, Twain eschews both pictorial and rhetorical conventions in order to emphasize his critique of colonial-
ism.[46] In his double-voiced discourse, the vernacular writer calls attention to the interpretive acts that constitute the record of any
historiographer, whether the annals of the "quaint chroniclers"
(45) of the seventeenth century or the accounts of the distinguished
historian of nineteenth-century America. Despite his own stylistic
emphasis on picturesque narrative, Twain looks critically beneath
the surface of Parkman's picturesque conventions to challenge the
historian's elitist, ideological assumptions about American destiny.

Still, Twain does share an affinity with a relevant trait of the nineteenth-century American landscape painter, who, by venturing out
into the wilderness, as Barbara Novak describes, substituted himself
for the epic hero of European convention: "The artist became the
hero of his own journey – which replaced the heroic themes of
mythology – by vanquishing physical obstacles en route to a destina-
tion."[47] Twain's 1882 trip on the Mississippi was just such an "artist's
Quest" in preparation for his novelistic undertaking. And if *Life on
the Mississippi* has a hero, it is the writer, as both represented traveler
in the world and representing consciousness *of* the world. For the
representative figure in the novel is no longer the great man of
action, like Aeneas or Brutus, the eponymous heroes of texts and
nations. Nor, for that matter, will Columbus, De Soto, Joliet and

Marquette, or La Salle serve the identity function. That kind of hero may have suited the epic intention of "Old Times," but in *Life on the Mississippi* the writing "I" fills the vacancy left by the symbolic death of the pilot as epic hero. But Twain's self-representation mixes the conventional arrogance of the heroic artist with vernacular humility. As one who can identify with the lower strata of society, he serves as a conduit through which the motley national character can be represented without reinscribing the fraudulent high-culture monism. Thus, in Twain's hands, the novel exposes the cultural hegemony underlying the epic aspirations of American art and challenges the ability of such a discriminatory attitude to represent America accurately.

In fact, by appropriating Parkman's discourse to reinterpret "Old Times," Twain questions the canonical assumption that America's great destiny is to extend Western culture by textual instruments of European colonial appropriation and religious dogma. Twain's critique implicitly challenges both the Calvinist notion that America was a New Eden over which Christian idealists would hold dominion and the Americanized versions of the medieval concepts of *translatio regnii* and *translatio studii*. In Europe, these latter two notions were used to validate one's own culture as the descendant of a former great civilization, whose legacy was to translate the political and intellectual greatness of the cultural heritage around the globe. Eighteenth- and nineteenth-century American orators often adopted this model to project similarly, thus imagining for themselves an epic role in this great destiny.[48] Twain's reinterpretation of "Old Times," then, is also a critical interpretation of the self-privileging heritage Parkman represents. Even before he assumes the role of the picaro in part 2 and destabilizes the epic unity of "Old Times" with the novel's heteroglossia, Twain breaks the ancestral line of the epic tradition by challenging the hegemonic assumptions behind it.

Twain never expressly classified *Life on the Mississippi* as a novel. That label was reserved for works of fiction wherein invented characters are embroiled in some kind of a realistic plot. But if his heteroglot text doesn't quite satisfy the structural conventions, the creative license Twain exercised in the autobiographical reminiscences indicates the text's fictional proclivity. Furthermore, Twain's commentary on Parkman's historical writing indicates his appreciation for the effect of fiction in works other than those strictly in that mode. He notes with awe the effect of Parkman's account of Joliet and Marquette's party discovering "the footprints of men in the mud in the western bank – a Robinson Crusoe experience which carries an electric shiver with it yet, when one stumbles on it in print" (46). Although the actual events are not unimportant, what appears to matter more to Twain is that they make good reading, that they can be experienced – just like Robinson Crusoe's discovery – by a reader of a text. The value, then, is found not so much in the literal accuracy of facts as in the "truth" of the tale, a truth that results not in spite of the fiction but almost because of it. This truth is metaphoric: literally false, but true in its appeal to our sense of a figurative representation of reality. Thus, "The Mississippi is well worth reading about" (39) because it offers the truth of this kind of textual experience, and *Life on the Mississippi* is the vehicle for that experience.[49]

The third chapter, which completes the introduction to the "Old Times" sketches, demonstrably inaugurates the role of fiction in *Life on the Mississippi*, since it is composed of the famous section that Twain borrowed from the manuscript of *Adventures of Huckleberry Finn*. Thus, the recontextualizing frame for the epic text formally represents the novelistic spirit in which the entire work participates. The full force of the varied performance that Huck witnesses aboard the raft can also be understood in light of the heteroglossia embodied in the raftsmen's talk. First, "the one they called Bob" and "the Child of Calamity" stage their famous tall-tale, verbal joust; then the raftsmen sing

> "Jolly, jolly raftsman's the life for me," with a rousing chorus, and then they got to talking about differences betwixt hogs, and their different kind of habits; and next about women and their different ways, and next about the best ways to put out houses that was afire; and next about what ought to be done with the Injuns; and next about what a king had to do, and how much he got; and next about how to make cats fight; and next about what to do when a man has fits; and next about differences betwixt clearwater rivers and muddy-water ones. (56)

This topic leads to a joke about the claim that there's greater nutrition in the Mississippi than in the Ohio, the proof manifest in the superior trees in a St. Louis graveyard as opposed to those in a Cincinnati graveyard: "It's all on account of the water the people drunk before they laid up. A Cincinnati corpse don't richen a soil any." The topic of graveyards steers the conversation to ghosts and finally to the tall tale of the haunted barrel from which Huck takes one of his many aliases.[50]

Like the metonymically displaced narratives generated by Brown's "universal" memory, or like the syntactical representation of Twain's drift through a succession of careers after leaving the river, the flow of the rivermen's talk is also a contiguously associative discourse. And although the prosiness here doesn't progress to a meaningful closure as it does in the career history, neither is it completely irrelevant, as the digressions in Brown's frustrating stories are. Not only does the raftsmen's talk indicate the dominance of associational drift in the material written in 1882; it also indicates the meaning generated by the association between the introductory chapters and the autobiographical reminiscences. Bridgman has observed an implied association between Huck in this episode, whom the raftsmen refer to as "nothing but a cub" (62), and Twain's cub persona in the apprenticeship sketches that immediately follow.[51] Huck's witnessing of the performances in the raftsmen's contest further reinforces the parallel between Huck and Twain on his 1882 river trip: Huck, traveling incognito on the river, gets "loaded up" with the kind of information that Twain attempts to compile when he returns incognito to the river in preparation for writing his Mississippi book. The raftsmen's passage, then, is a *mise en abyme*, an emblem in miniature of the book's shape overall. Since *Life on the Mississippi* mirrors itself in a passage from what would become Twain's most notable novel and construes Huck's identity as that novel's protagonist/narrator parallel to his own traveling "scribbler" persona, the text distinctly exhibits the temperament of fiction.

The inclusion of Huck's brief stay with the raftsmen also reasserts Twain's interest in language. At the beginning of "Old Times," it was colorful talk that initially drew Sam Clemens to the river. So, too, the language of the river draws him back after twenty-one years away, only this time he returns as a "scribbler of books," not an impressionable naïf. His dictation of data to his secretary on the 1882 trip, though similar to his note taking of the river's features in his memorandum book during his apprenticeship, is not an attempt to fix the physical signs of the river in his mind for piloting purposes but to appraise the mutability of the culture surrounding the river.

Twain's firsthand experience with the fallacy that lay behind the pilot's arrogant attempts to control the mighty river indirectly influenced the novelistic authority governing *Life on the Mississippi*. As a writer, Twain has come to see the river not as a mere current of water to be controlled solely for man's commercial purposes but as a current of stratified discourse that, in its vast capacity to represent the nation, threatens to overflow the levees of narrative design. He therefore respectfully acknowledges the tenuousness of his authority over the talk he represents. Speaking through Huck's report that the rivermen's "yelling and jeering . . . and roaring and laughing" is of such vitality that "you could hear them *a mile*" (61, emphasis added), Twain subtly disputes Parkman, who, in a quotation that sounded the conclusive note in the preceding chapter, observes the irony of La Salle's claim to such a vast territory "by virtue of a feeble human voice, *inaudible at half a mile*" (49, emphasis added). For Twain, the human voice in the Mississippi Valley is not "feeble" but vigorous; it reverberates across the landscape. Unlike the historian, who arrogantly projects his ideological desire for America's great destiny on the history of the river, Twain suggests in *Life on the Mississippi* that a true document of the river cannot be written from the unifocal bias that recognizes only the elite white power structure. Rather, it must be multifocal and, moreover, multivocal, representing the robust, if sometimes cacophonous, sound of speech in its fullest array. A text true to its object must include the apocryphal, the loud-mouthed, the off-color: in short, it must be vernacular. Language, especially vernacular, is the *life* in *Life on the Mississippi*.

To be sure, *Life on the Mississippi* isn't all vernacular, for the encyclopedic range of representation in the book encompasses more than speech alone. Much as the Mississippi erodes its banks from headwaters to delta, yielding a richly saturated suspension of varied materials, *Life on the Mississippi* collects all relevant discourses – historical documents, newspapers, narratives of European travelers, confessions, Civil War diaries, statistical reports, travel brochures, Indian legends – and suspends them in its current. These multiple discourses, written and oral, literary and extraliterary, compose a text openly illustrative of novelistic heteroglossia. This profusion of languages in *Life on the Mississippi* recalls the encyclopedic breadth of *Moby-Dick*. Like Ishmael, Twain's traveling "scribbler" persona stands in opposition to an Ahabian navigational authority, whose urge to dominate nature results in a monomaniacally restricted vision. However, unlike Ishmael, who undertakes his epistemological quest to know the whale by observing it through as many different discourses as are available to him, Twain shows that these multiple discourses aren't merely the various planes of a prism through which our knowledge is refracted; rather, together they constitute the varied texture of Mississippi life and, more broadly, American life.

In 1895, Twain indirectly indexed the novelistic properties exhibited in *Life on the Mississippi* when he refuted Paul Bourget's analysis of American character and society in his book *Outre-Mer*. Discounting Bourget's ability to know the soul of Americans because he was a foreigner, Twain insists, "There is only one expert who is qualified to examine the souls and the life of a people and make a valuable report – the native novelist." With twenty-five years of training, of "unconscious observation – absorption," to qualify the native novelist's authority,

> he lays plainly before you the ways and speech and life of a few people grouped in a certain place – his own place – and that is one book. In time he and his brethren will report to you the life and the people of the whole nation . . . And when a thousand able novels have been written, *there* you have the soul of the people, the life of the people, the speech of the people; and not anywhere else can these be had. And the shadings of character, manners, feelings, ambitions, will be infinite. (*CTSS&E*, 2:167–8)

Certainly, Twain distinguished himself as such an expert. And though he underscores the importance of the collective industry of a corps of native novelists in these late remarks, he appears to have attempted the valued accretional effort single-handedly in *Life on the Mississippi*. His emphasis on accretion in the novel's ability to represent "the soul of the people," and on the division of *Life on the Mississippi* between "old times" and "new times," formally endows his "standard work" with the authority of the Bible, perhaps the most exemplary heteroglot text. Of course, the traditional view of the Bible in the nineteenth century was as the ultimate monological authority, but here again Twain anticipates contemporary narrative theory by converting the model of what Bakhtin calls the external and monological "authoritative word" into a formal version of the dialogized "internally persuasive word."[52] Twain's formal imitation of Scripture adds one more stratum of hybridization to the architectonics of *Life on the Mississippi*. In effect, Twain creates the epitome of the novel by broadening the text's representative horizons, both propelling the form forward and formally encompassing the textual origins of Western culture.

Twain points to the example of the sacred bipartite text in an analogy to the pilot's ability to remember river details:

> To know the Old and New Testaments by heart, and be able to recite them glibly, forward or backward, or begin at random anywhere in the book and recite both ways and never trip or make a mistake, is no extravagant mass of knowledge, and no marvelous facility, compared to a pilot's massed knowledge of the Mississippi and his marvellous facility of handling it. (116)

A similar kind of memory is required of the reader who tries to navigate *Life on the Mississippi*. The associations between pilot figures, and the evolution of the authorial persona across the two halves of Twain's text correspond to the biblical typology that theologians find in the Old and New Testaments. But a deeper conceptual analogy joins Scripture and Twain's Mississippi book, which the two Greek terms for time, *chronos* and *kairos*, help to illuminate. *Chronos* refers to natural time, seasonal succession as a circular recurrence. *Kairos*, on the other hand, refers to cultural time, a linear progression distinguished by a critical event that separates all that went before from all that comes after. This meaningful crisis is what distinguishes a chronicle from a narrative by ordering events according to a pattern of interpretive emphasis. The birth of Christ functions as such a kairological event both theologically in the transition from the Old Testament to the New Testament and historically in the Western practice of dating events as either B.C. or A.D. *Life on the Mississippi* has its own kairological moment in the Civil War, the demarcation between parts 1 and 2 and the event in relation to which American history is measured.[53] And whereas the Christian conceptualization of *kairos* informs the interpretation of the New Testament as the fulfillment of Old Testament prophecy and emphasizes the future salvation of all believers of diverse ethnicity over the epic past of a single nation of people, part 2 of Twain's text fulfills the implied prophecy of oedipality in "Old Times" and emphasizes the progressive, diverse culture of postwar Realism over the fatuous unity of antebellum Romanticism.

What encourages the textual comparison is the implied hinge between them: the Civil War underwrites Twain's biblicizing of *Life on the Mississippi*. The war exaggerated the cultural habit of reading historical events as dramatic enactments of biblical lessons. Daniel Aaron notes that "In the 1860's, passages from Milton's poem and allusions to the heavenly struggle he recorded came readily to the minds of clergymen, orators, versifiers, and novelists."[54] If the Civil War was a kind of *kairos*, a critical moment that indelibly changed the course of American history, it was such a moment for Twain as well, whose life, as he represents it here, was irrevocably altered. For though he was absent from the war, his depiction of his brother Henry's death as a kind of personal analogue to the war at the pivot of *Life on the Mississippi* reinforces the kairological structure of the text. Moreover, in a letter to his sister-in-law dated June 18, 1858, Twain inflects the same event as a kind of Christic self-portrait. The two accounts taken together cast his career shift from pilot to writer as a kind of resurrection linked with the salvation of the nation from its sin of slavery.[55]

At the same time, Twain's ambivalence toward his role in this kairological progress can be detected in the attention he gives to the cycle of natural time, of *chronos*, as figured in the river's indifference to human history. The synthesis of the two concepts of time amplify the text's formal tension. For the text is neither strictly divided between past and present of human history nor cyclically representative of the river's natural course. Rather, *Life on the Mississippi* is a chiasmus – a structural device that will emerge again in *Adventures of Huckleberry Finn* – a mirror of itself, in which the linear progress of history and the repetitive process of nature are dynamic and reflexive. The transitional chapter between parts 1 and 2 is the reference point of this structural dynamic.

For example, at either end of the book, Twain indulges in boyhood reminiscences. In part 1, he leaves Hannibal for a life on the river and becomes a cub under Bixby. In part 2, upon reaching New Orleans at the end of the southern leg of his 1882 journey, he meets Bixby again and books passage with his former master back north for a return to Hannibal. Likewise, on board the *Paul Jones*, before he signs on as a cub, he is humiliated for his gullibility by a night watchman who tells him an outlandish autobiography plagiarized from an adventure narrative; in part 2, in his return to Hannibal, he recalls the carpenter who frightened him with an autobiography plagiarized from Bird's *Nick of the Woods*. His later Hannibal memories include the story of a boyhood companion who drowned when he became entangled among submerged barrel staves, suggestive of Charles William Allbright of "Haunted Barrel" fame in part 1.

The symmetry of episodes aligned on opposite sides of the narrative pivot is not, however, mere repetition. More often than not, the later episode critically reverses the rhetorical value of its antecedent. In part 2, when Twain heads north from Hannibal to the upper river, back to the source, he observes lumber rafts,

> but not floating leisurely along, in the old-fashioned way, manned with joyous and reckless crews of fiddling, song-singing, whiskey-drinking, breakdown-dancing rapscallions; no the whole thing was shoved swiftly along by a powerful stern-wheeler, modern fashion, and the small crews were quiet, orderly men, of a sedate business aspect, with not a suggestion of romance about them anywhere. (401)

Although this points to a discrepancy between the past delineated by Huck's raftsmen's passage and the commercial progress of the present, the nostalgic longing for romance complicates his thesis honoring the productivity of Realism.

Finally, Twain closes his travel narrative by reversing the tenor of the historical, prefatory chapters. Contrary to the grand heroic destiny that the quotations of Parkman's history invoked at the outset, Twain attributes the advance of civilization to the importation of whiskey. It is neither religion nor great imperial vision nor epic destiny but whiskey – the "Jug of Empire," a title that adapts Berkeley's "Westward the Course of Empire," a nineteenth-century version of the *translatio* concepts – that lubricates the movement of Western culture across the continent. This discredited return to the dawn of Western history on the Mississippi provides the opportunity to include the native legends that white culture deleted from the official history of the Mississippi.

Twain's playful critique of the "Legend of White-Bear Lake," though, doesn't offer patronizing reverence for the mystical legend. His account of the legend itself reads like an Indian translation of Cooper: two young lovers are united when the young brave kills the "white and savage beast" (a bear) that has abducted the young maiden. And Twain faults the implausible action of the plot and the questionable relevance of a prop, the young brave's blanket, in much the same way that he criticized "the American Scott" in his famously hilarious "James Fenimore Cooper's Literary Offenses":

> It is a perplexing business. First, [the Indian maiden] fell down out of the tree – she and the blanket; and the bear caught her and fondled her – her and the blanket; then she fell up into the tree again – leaving the blanket; meantime the lover goes war-whooping home and comes back "heeled," climbs the tree, jumps down on the bear, the girl jumps down after him – apparently, for she was up the tree – resumes her place in the bear's arms along with the blanket, the lover rams his knife into the bear, and saves – whom, the blanket? No – nothing of the sort. You get yourself all worked up and excited about that blanket, and then all of a sudden, just when a happy climax seems imminent, you are let down flat – nothing saved but the girl. Whereas, one is not inter-ested in the girl; she is not the prominent feature of the legend. Nevertheless, there you are left, and there you must remain; for if you live a thousand years you will never know who got the blanket. (415)

Like Brown's defective stories, this legend, Twain lightheartedly claims, fails to fulfill the expectations it raises. But although his con-centration on the blanket warrants a laugh, his complaint punningly shows where our attention should be in *Life on the Mississippi*. Just as the "Legend of White-Bear Lake" is not about the lake or the bear or the Indian lovers, so Twain's text is not about the Mississippi or pilots or himself. But whereas the Indian legend is, in Twain's inter-pretation, about a blanket, a literal textile woven from literal yarns, *Life on the Mississippi* is about the figurative tapestry woven from fig-urative yarns, constituting the fabric of Mississippi life in the speech of the people.

Life on the Mississippi represents Twain's conception of the novel as an expansive literary form that answers Whitman's call for a dem-ocratic literature. Twain achieves this representative status not in the transcendental unity of Whitmanian paradoxes but in the conflict of authority deeply embedded in vernacular humor – a mode of discourse that honors lies, honors the truth that is figured in well-told lies, and honors the wisdom that is contained in criticism of ineptly told tales. Although this sort of discourse had been a staple of his earlier writings, not until the Mississippi book did he realize that it could provide the terms of a penetrating cultural critique. Twain's conflict with authority in *Life on the Mississippi* led to his discovery of novelistic discourse. The pursuit of this literary endeavor defined the direction of his subsequent work.

2

CATCHING MARK TWAIN'S DRIFT

THE ADVENTURES OF TOM SAWYER
AND
ADVENTURES OF HUCKLEBERRY FINN

━━━━━

The prototype of all revivals is each man's
wistful sense of his own childhood.

The American temperament leans generally to a kind of mystical anarchism, in which the "natural" humanity in each
man is adored as the savior of society.

— Walter Lippmann, *Drift and Mastery*

If the textual evolution from "Old Times" to *Life on the Mississippi*
initiates the dialectic of Twain's novelistic career, the production of
The Adventures of Tom Sawyer and *Adventures of Huckleberry Finn* completes its first full cycle. The two boyhood fictions readily testify to
their complementary relationships with the ostensibly nonfiction
texts. There are significant similarities between the "Old Times"
cub and Tom Sawyer. Just as the cub learns to read the signs of the
river in order to become a respected and highly paid pilot, so Tom
learns to read and manipulate the conventions of the social code in
order to become a conspicuous American success. Even one-upping
Twain's cub pilot persona, Tom wins not only fame and fortune but
also the girl. In addition, the form of *Tom Sawyer* is, like "Old
Times," a kind of bildungsroman–epic hybrid. After Tom survives
his trial in the underworld of McDougal's cave, Judge Thatcher compares him to George Washington, the epic hero of whom *McGuffey's
Reader*s so often sang.[1] Tom thus metamorphoses from an irritating
yet amusing juvenile delinquent into something like an American
epic hero.

Huck's story, on the other hand, drifts along like part 2 of the

Mississippi book, incident following incident without the kind of teleological goal that motivates Tom's calculated quest for celebrity. And just as *Life on the Mississippi* questions the reverence expressed for the pilot's authority in "Old Times," Huck's meandering narrative also challenges the authority depicted in *Tom Sawyer*. Dismissing civilized lies like Tom's romanticism and the Sunday school moralism of the widow Douglas and Miss Watson, and fearing the all too genuine violence of Pap's primitive authoritarianism, Huck attempts to escape from both the genteel and the brutal oppressions that confine him.

But Twain's characteristic double vision prevents us from rigidly assigning attributes both of Twain's "Old Times" persona to Tom and of his *Life on the Mississippi* persona to Huck. Although Tom's desire for heroic notoriety reflects his similarity to the cub, Tom also strives to maintain and prolong the theatrical effects of his play. By exploiting every predicament in order to maintain control over the performance (indeed, in *master*minding Jim's escape he must even invent difficulties), Tom resembles the writer who needs to fill up his book with picturesque extravagances. For Huck, on the other hand, adventures are predicaments that he must negotiate his way clear of, not inflate into grand performances. Thus, his temperament resembles that of the pilot who needs to avoid the dangers of the river to deliver his cargo.

Reversing direction yet again, Twain portrays Huck as the author of a book about his river adventures, much like himself, the traveling "scribbler" who produced *Life on the Mississippi*. Tom's meager, occasional output – a love note, an oath, two short notes on sycamore bark (*TS*, 55, 80, 113), a list of "mournful inscriptions" for Jim's coat of arms, and two anonymous letters for the "evasion" (*HF*, 322, 334) – just don't stack up to Huck's forty-three-chapter volume. Furthermore, Huck is a vernacular character whose uncultivated tastes run toward the heteroglot diversity that distinguishes part 2 of *Life on the Mississippi* from "Old Times." At the outset of his narrative, Huck complains that the fare at the widow Douglas's table pales because "everything was cooked by itself. In a barrel of odds and ends it is different; things get mixed up, and the juice kind of swaps around, and the things go better" (*HF*, 2). When describing his picaresque journey, his narrative style is oriented likewise. Ostensibly free of the conventional restraints to which Tom subscribes, Huck documents his journey in a narrative whose juice "kind of swaps around," unencumbered by strict adherence to conventions of genre. So, like part 2 of *Life on the Mississippi*, *Huckleberry Finn* is not merely a sequel, an extension of what Twain intended in an earlier text in a similar mode, but rather a novelistic revision of a romanticized fiction of unity. The mercurial and often overlapping characterizations of Twain's personae and of his boy heroes suggest that generic distinctions of the texts are not reducible to clear-cut oppositional thinking. Rather, like his own duplicitous identity, Twain's texts are double-voiced, both in form and in their equivocal stances toward freedom.

As Twain drifts into Huck's story of his flight to freedom, his hero manifests an ambivalent attitude that is no doubt a reflection of his author's as well. The impulse for freedom from anterior authority that characterizes both Huck's story and Twain's literary identity is a fundamental motivation embedded in the novel as a literary form and in the structure of American society. Both the novel and America promise the freedom of starting over, but that promise is finally compromised by the durability of the conventions the novel resists or flouts and by the recalcitrant facts of the society it tries to alter in fiction. In *Huckleberry Finn*, this dilemma emerges forcefully, revealing novelistic discourse as a kind of confidence game into which Twain is himself drawn, a double-cross in which the authority that the novel promises is already compromised.

In this chapter I suggest that, by virtue of the double-cross that Twain discovered in *Huckleberry Finn*, his most significant contribution to the American novel is an explicitly deconstructive text that demythologizes its hero. *Huckleberry Finn* does not reassert the value of nature over culture and invention over convention, as widely interpreted; rather, it ironizes the ideal return to nature. Twain's text shows this romantic notion to be a myth that fails to escape its own status within a cult of primitivism and instead merely relocates cultural authority in a romantic ideal of nature's priority. As Sam Clemens discovered in his own flight to the territories, no one gets out of culture alive, because one is not simply in the culture but the other way around. And no sooner does one arrive in a world elsewhere than culture sets up its newest trading post on the frontier.[2] When Clemens turned his back on the cultural polarity of the Civil War in 1861, he didn't realize how the culture had already consumed him, had already contributed to the construction of his identity. Even reinventing himself as "Mark Twain" could not turn the trick. In *Life on the Mississippi,* his nostalgic reminiscence of the halcyon days of cub piloting gives way to an allegory of the national crisis he had tried to elude. *The Adventures of Tom Sawyer,* likewise, started out resisting cultural authority but caved in, if the pun may be pardoned, to a desire for notoriety within the social hierarchy. After Tom's accommodation to society, Twain started again with Huck's escape from and troubled critique of social injustice. Twain intended Huck's story to be a triumph of the heart over the dictates of conscience. But Huck fails both to exonerate himself from cultural complicity and to redeem Sam Clemens's absence from the actual battle. This vernacular hero squares off against the American mythology that exalted Nature, and what he unwittingly discovers is the ineluctability of culture. *Huckleberry Finn* documents Twain's discovery that cultural history is inscribed within the consciousness of all citizens, regardless of their active investment in society. As Huck's enterprise shows, the patterns of thought informed by that history both impose limits on social freedom and inspire literary freedom in the attempt to overcome restriction. And yet Twain's text finally exposes the complicity of novelistic discourse: the genre of the novel promulgates the myth of breaking free, a myth that always betrays those it inspires, because one cannot extricate the self from the culture that has constructed it.

This was the long-evolving lesson in the career that began when Clemens headed west to avoid the Civil War and the divisive issue of slavery. When he tried to compensate for his own escape by altering Huck's course in order to stand up to slavery, at least fictionally and twenty years too late, he discovered that history, either his own or that of the nation, could not be so easily altered.

Riffs on Rafts

Twain's dialectical composition of the Mississippi quartet frames the issue of anterior authority in terms of textual production. The relationships among the four texts call our attention to the fact that *Huckleberry Finn* is the culmination of a process. It exists within a genealogy of texts that shapes its meaning. Still, that genealogy is by no means a straight line of descent. Twain began the fiction manuscripts prior to their respective nonfiction counterparts, but he would not have completed either novel as we know it if he hadn't previously written the cub-pilot sketches and the Mississippi book. For the overlapping compositional histories of the four Mississippi texts indicate that Twain's examinations of authority in the nonfiction texts were catalysts for completing the fictions. Thus, the nonfiction works were not simply diversions from the difficulty Twain encountered in assuming authority for the fictional reconstructions of boyhood but provided opportunities for working out different stages of his troubled attitudes toward authority.

Moreover, in the Mississippi quartet's interdependent composition Twain not only transacts a bargain that earns him enough control to complete his texts but also complicates the notion of anteriority in their confused lineage. Twain's concern with authority becomes a structuring principle of the Mississippi quartet in which the actual anteriority of the stalled *Tom Sawyer* manuscript was virtually usurped by the appearance of the "Old Times" sketches in the *Atlantic.*[3] A similar relationship characterizes *Huckleberry Finn* with respect to *Life on the Mississippi.*

In reading the dialectic of Twain's career, then, some caution is advised in order to resist oversimplifying the effect of his uncertain control on the production of these texts. As I argued in Chapter 1, Twain's recourse to the nonfiction texts didn't relieve the anxiety of asserting authority but simply rechanneled it elsewhere. The raftsmen's passage clearly illustrates how this works. When Twain introduces it into the Mississippi book as an excerpt from the manuscript of *Huckleberry Finn*, he describes the latter as "a book which I have been working at, by fits and starts, during the past five or six years, and may possibly finish in the course of five or six more" (*LOM* 51). Twain's raid on the dry-docked *Huckleberry Finn* manuscript implies his concern with bringing *Life on the Mississippi* to subscription length. The merging of manuscripts indicates his compositional struggle with both texts. But more importantly, beyond indexing authorial frustration, the sporadic composition also yields an intertextual dialogue. *Huckleberry Finn* doesn't simply absorb and synthesize the tensions of the earlier texts but reciprocally influences the production of *Life on the Mississippi* as well. These last two Mississippi narratives coexisted in Twain's imagination, and though either one occupied his attention alternately, the presence of each is felt in the other. Shared images cross-fertilize the texts, generating a dialectical compensation by which any representation of authority seems to evoke its antithesis. The frustration of producing sufficient quantity of manuscript, then, also contributes to thematic interference, exemplified by the inclusion of the anarchistic raftsmen's life in a book that alleges to be about the grand authority of steamboating.

Huck's book contains an even more complex version of this interference, because, despite its commitment to the theme of freedom symbolized by raft travel, the text's ambiguous freight includes steamboat images from both halves of *Life on the Mississippi*. As symbols of culture, the wrecked *Walter Scott*, on the one hand, and the monstrous steamboat that wrecks the raft and separates Huck and Jim, on the other hand, respectively signify the cultural decay diagnosed as the "Sir Walter disease" in part 2 of *Life on the Mississippi* and the powerful dominance of culture over nature propounded in "Old Times." These conflicting images reflect Twain's ambivalence toward the culture–nature opposition often imputed to the steamboat and the raft.

By adding the wreck of the *Walter Scott* to *Huckleberry Finn* Twain appears to reinforce the steamboat's symbolic value of cultural decay developed in *Life on the Mississippi*. Written after the completion of the Mississippi book, in which Mark Twain documented the steamboat's fall from grace, Huck's account of the "steamboat that had killed herself on a rock" (80) similarly implies the demise of a corrupt civilization. The *Walter Scott*'s diseased cultural cargo, Bill and Packard's sham "good morals" (84), signifies the treachery justified by the society's self-contradictory codes, which prompts Huck's flight. In contrast, the egalitarian camaraderie that Huck and Jim enjoy on the raft and their shallow-drafted vessel's invulnerability to the kind of navigational suicide that has befallen the *Walter Scott* might appear to rank the raft over the steamboat and nature over culture.

On the other hand, the episode of the raft wreck inverts the hierarchy. Huck's account of the steamboat as a fearsome, devouring monster, "Big and scary, with a long row of wide-open furnace doors shining like red-hot teeth" (130), compares to an experience that Twain recollects from his days as a cub, except from the opposite perspective. In "Old Times," the navigational nuisance posed

by "small-fry craft" such as the raft is understood from the steers-
man's point of view:

> All of a sudden, on a murky night, a light would hop up, right
> under our bows almost, and an agonized voice, with the back-
> woods "whang" to it, would wail out . . . Then for an instant, as we
> whistled by, the red glare from our furnaces would reveal the scow
> and the form of the gesticulating orator as if under a lightning-
> flash, and in that instant our firemen and deckhands would send
> and receive a tempest of missiles and profanity, one of our wheels
> would walk off with the crashing fragments of a steering oar, and
> down the dead blackness would shut again. (*LOM,* 101)

In the transition from "Old Times" to *Huckleberry Finn,* the narrative
perspective shifts from the cub's station high up in the pilothouse
to Huck's low position on the raft. Neil Schmitz argues that this shift
signals Twain's change of heart: the scene announces a new relation
to the river in *Huckleberry Finn,* one unmediated by the social hierarchy and technology of civilization.[4] Yet Schmitz's insistence that
the raft symbolizes an unmediated relation to nature signifying
Twain's revision of the culture–nature hierarchy doesn't square with
the fact that the episode dramatizes the destruction of Huck's and
Jim's raft by the sublime techno-leviathan. Wrecking the raft clearly
corresponds to the "Old Times" notion of the steamboat's powerful
authority. Although the raft's drift draws an analogy to the discursive
narrative that I have valued as an asset of part 2 of the Mississippi
book, here the drifting raft is a severe liability. Due to its passive
navigation, the raft doesn't simply fail to elude civilization's awesome power; rather, it maximizes the raft-dweller's vulnerability to
the steamboat juggernaut. Despite the romantic admiration that critics have heaped upon Huck's rude Rousseauvian vessel – complete
with the shelter of the noble savage, a wigwam erected on a raised
earthen floor – the raft is no match for the force of civilization, even
during Twain's earliest work on the manuscript. Furthermore, the
river's indifference to man's social needs is hardly a blessing in this
case, because its southward current progressively imperils the runaway slave. Indeed, despite all of the critical celebration of Huck's
praise for the raft's "free and easy and comfortable" (155) life, what
Huck and Jim really need is to stow away on that northbound steam-

boat, as Roxana shrewdly does in *Pudd'nhead Wilson.* Undermining the raft as a symbol of freedom, Twain casts doubt on Huck's entire enterprise of "lighting out."

The prevailing interpretation of the raft as a symbol of nature that outstrips the discredited steamboat as a symbol of culture needs qualification, then. The wreck of the *Walter Scott* serves in this capacity because, even though Twain wrote the episode fairly late in the composition of *Huckleberry Finn,* he spliced it into the narrative before the raft is wrecked by the monstrous steamboat, so that the syntax of the unfolding narrative undoes the nature–culture hierarchy reflected in these images. Moreover, the *Walter Scott* episode itself is not as clear-cut as it seems. Huck's Tom Sawyerish desire for adventure aboard the *Walter Scott* signifies civilization's centripetal tug on his sensibilities. No sooner do the raftmates indulge Huck's fascination with the foundering steamboat and discover the real-life outlaws on board than the raft slips its moorings and drifts downstream, stranding Huck and Jim among very dangerous company. The only remaining means of escape is the plunder-filled skiff of the outlaws. True to romance-adventure form, Huck commandeers the outlaw craft, but he is no outlaw in this episode. Rather, he begins as a play outlaw, imitating Tom Sawyer's investment in the literature of romantic adventure, and he ends as a conventional "good boy." Although he uses the authority of romance texts and Tom Sawyer's notoriety to refute Jim's cautious appeal to the ultimate textual authority of "de good book" (80), when confronted with the real treachery of real outlaws, Huck responds with a respect for the law and a Christian sympathy for his victims that he proudly imagines would earn him the approval of the widow Douglas. Though Huck begins these adventures to satisfy himself, he ends up serving the widow's altruistic instruction to "never think about myself" (13), as he puts it. So even if the *Walter Scott* were to stand for social and cultural corruption, Huck's action in this scene mimics conventional cultural models no less. The notion that he represents the self as distinct from society is emphatically denied by this scene. Instead, the very concept of self appears determined by the society to which it stands opposed. And finally, the booty Huck and Jim acquire from this adventure furnishes their raft with fragments of culture, notably the literature that Huck set out to imitate. Huck, by assuming the role of authoritative explicator of their new textual property, reveals the degree of his Tom Sawyerish bent.

We might construe the raft's destruction as poetic justice, now that this symbol of nature has been defiled with culture. When Twain returned to the manuscript after the dry spell that he hit in the midst of the Grangerford–Shepherdson episode, he found that one way to get the story going again was to resurrect the raft. But if bringing the raft back into the narrative breaks the spell of narrative inertia, it doesn't do so by reinvoking the raft as a symbol of the value of nature in opposition to the steamboat of culture. After Huck's nearly fatal encounters with the monstrous steamboat and the brutal gentility of Compromise, Kentucky, he would, presumably, find it easy to repudiate civilization further and cling to the security of his floating retreat. But reunited with Jim on the repaired and reequipped raft, Huck regains temporary equanimity, waxing poetic about how "lovely" it is "to live on a raft" and in virtually the same breath admiring the steamboat as a thing of beauty: "Once or twice of a night we would see a steamboat slipping along in the dark, and now and then she would belch a whole world of sparks up out of her chimbleys, and they would rain down in the river and look awful pretty" (158). As harrowing as his experience with the monstrous steamboat has been, its picturesque appeal has endured. When the king's plan to swindle the Wilks heirs includes a ride on a steamboat, Huck admits his eagerness: "I didn't have to be ordered twice, to go and take a steamboat ride" (204). Contrary to the opposition Schmitz draws, imputing polarized meanings to Tom's deck passage on a steamboat and Huck's bivouac in the wigwam of the rough-hewn raft, the text and Huck equivocate, suspending absolute judgments that repudiate the one and elevate the other.

Schmitz's argument is valuable, nonetheless, because it clearly articulates an exemplary problem in the critical perception of Tom and Huck as an opposition: the boy of culture versus the boy of nature. On this ground, critics have staked out the prevailing interpretation of *Huckleberry Finn* as Twain's great expression in honor of individual liberty. This fundamental opposition follows the negative definition of liberty, "an absence of institutional restraint," that David Noble claims was a dominant feature of liberal thought from 1880 to 1920.[5] But to adhere strictly to this definition is to impose an ideology on which the text itself equivocates. This sort of ideological blindness has led to the unrelenting debate about the ending of *Huckleberry Finn*. Whether critics proclaim that Twain succeeds in maintaining Huck's essential desire for autonomy from all prior authorities or complain that he fails by resubjecting Huck to Tom's dogged adherence to authorities as models for behavior, both sides cling to the Tom–Huck opposition. But perceiving Tom and Huck in these terms is, I contend, a mistake. Despite Huck's ostensible investment in unqualified autonomy, he conforms to traditional forms of authority throughout. By foregrounding their functionally equal investments in controlling representations of culture, I will show that *Huckleberry Finn* is a text that merely "lets on" to free itself from institutional restraint. Understanding this ambivalence to authority in Twain's vernacular first-person narrative reveals the inadequacy of prevailing interpretations to account for the text, its relation to Twain's career, and its status as an American novel.

First, we need to be clear that to challenge the opposition between Tom and Huck is not to deny their differences. Huck is not simply a shabbily arrayed Tom Sawyer. Twain's creative logic prohibits such an identity. When he came to write the first-person sequel to *Tom Sawyer*, he disqualified Tom as a candidate for the narrator-protagonist. The first-person narrative that Twain had in mind required a more complex figure, and he judged Tom as merely another of the "one-horse men of literature" (*MTHL*, 1:91). Presumably he saw Huck as more than Tom's double or reciprocal. Were Huck, after all, either Tom's ragged copy or his opposite number, Twain would have saddled his narrative with yet another one-horse man. Instead, what qualified Huck as Twain's narrator-protagonist was his vernacular status – and yet it is a misreading of Huck's vernacular status as an affiliation with nature that has led to the culture–nature opposition construed between Tom and Huck. For the conflict between vernacular and mainstream culture is not so much a stable opposition as a dynamic between margin and center. As a speaker on the margin, Huck is precariously balanced between the centripetal pull of social restraint and the centrifugal push of individual freedom. Still, to be on the margin is to be part of the circle, a cultural participant. And although Huck's vernacular authority both criticizes the conventional authority to which Tom subscribes and reflects a desire to steer clear of the center, society's gravitational attraction keeps Huck within its orbit. In his teetering equilibrium, Huck embodies the ambivalent attitude toward authority that epitomizes Twain's enterprise, the novel as a genre, and America's democratic project.

Like the novel's essential difference from convention, Huck's vernacular status is defined as an opposition, a relation that correspondingly defines his participation in culture. Consequently, he is in his own way as much a part of the society as Tom is. The significant difference between Tom and Huck lies in the kinds of authority that their central and marginal positions represent. A comparison between them and Twain's two personae in *Life on the Mississippi* is instructive, because Tom's and Huck's different attitudes toward authority parallel the two versions of oedipality that describe Clemens's professional course from pilot to writer in the Mississippi book.

In his quest for heroic notoriety, Tom views figures of authority as rivals over whom he strives to gain superiority, just as the cub desires the pilot's unchallenged authority as a rivalrous response, first to the abusive mate aboard the *Paul Jones* and later to Bixby and Brown. The embarrassments that the cub endures for failing to read and memorize the river – a piloting ability likened to knowing "the Old Testament and New Testament by heart" – compare to two scenes of embarrassment in *Tom Sawyer*. In the first, Tom bares his ineptitude at memorizing Scripture when tested in Sunday school by Judge Thatcher. The examination's importance for Tom escalates beyond the theological matter because of who examines him. The judge is both the community's leading citizen – the civic pilot of St. Petersburg, so to speak – and Becky's father, so the authority he represents is doubly assured of provoking Tom's humble respect and his humiliating rivalry. In the second scene, Tom humiliates himself by vainly attempting to gain celebrity in his abortive attempt to recite Patrick Henry's famous classroom set-piece of nationalist scripture. Ironically, it is the content of his disastrous attempt at oratory that reveals Tom's difficulty, for he does not want liberty, after all, but glory. And not until Tom can stage the theatrical spectacle of his resurrection from the fictional death fortuitously achieved in the Jackson's Island sojourn can he dominate the community's attention and realize his goal of celebrity. In other words,

Tom can muster little commitment to Patrick Henry's hallowed American words, because Tom's motto, as attested by his resurrection, would take the verbal form, "Give me death in order to attain notoriety."

On the other hand, *Huckleberry Finn* emulates the revisionary impulse of part 2 of *Life on the Mississippi*, because Huck desires autonomy rather than superiority over a rival. James M. Cox has noted the similarity between the portrait of Mr. Brown as a tyrant in *Life on the Mississippi* and the depiction of Pap as an abusive and ignorant authority.[6] But unlike the cub, who symbolically slays Brown, Huck checks his oedipal desire, despite sighting his oppressor down the barrel of a loaded shotgun. More like the pilot Sam Clemens, who resented the stifling authority of Captain Sellers, Huck merely seeks freedom from, not dominance of, an oppressive force. This distinction underscores as well the difference between Huck and Tom. Just as Twain's "Sergeant Fathom" piece imitated Sellers's river memoranda, Huck imitates Tom to formulate a fiction of his own death. However, Huck's staged death is not for the purpose of attaining heroic status upon resurrection but merely to liberate himself from the private authority of Pap, the public authority of the community's symbolic parents, Judge Thatcher and the widow Douglas, as well as the romantically invested authority of their heroic heir, Tom Sawyer. Moreover, in contrast to Tom's failure to recite the "Give me liberty or give me death" speech, Huck's assembly of misleading clues to his fictive violent demise unwittingly stages his escape from the terms of Patrick Henry's ringing dictum: he attains liberty *through* death, or at least a persuasive dramatization of death. And consequently, Huck subverts not only Pap's abusive authority but a founding father's cultural authority as well.

Huck also differs from Tom in that Huck's subversion is double – composed of the narrated action, by which he explicitly escapes the authorities within the story, and the act of narrating, by which he implicitly escapes the authority of his textual father, Mark Twain. And it is by the appropriation of textual authority at the opening of his narrative that Huck fully mimics the second version of oedipality in *Life on the Mississippi*. Similar to Twain's account of his circumscription of Captain Sellers's authority, Huck's narrative begins with the famous assertion of his own authority in implicit defiance of "Mr. Mark Twain":

You don't know me, without you have read a book by the name
of "The Adventures of Tom Sawyer," but that ain't no matter.
That book was made by Mr. Mark Twain, and he told the truth,
mainly. There was things which he stretched, but mainly he told
the truth. That is nothing. I never seen anybody but lied, one time
or another, without it was aunt Polly, or the widow, or maybe
Mary. Aunt Polly – Tom's aunt Polly, she is – and Mary, and the
widow Douglas, is all told about in that book – which is mostly a
true book; with some stretchers, as I said before. (1)

This opening expression of Huck's assertion of authorship reveals
the same ambivalence that leads to Twain's mixed resentment of
and respect for Sellers's authority. Huck appears to make allowances
for the fact that Twain committed a few "stretchers" as a common
human trait, but the dismissive remark "That is nothing" is ambiguously misplaced; although it appears to refer to the fact that
"[t]here was things which he stretched," it follows the clause "but
mainly he told the truth." Even as Huck tries to minimize Twain's
lapses into falsehood, his language dismisses any credibility Twain
may have earned for telling "mainly . . . the truth." Closing the paragraph, he ostensibly stresses the veracity of *Tom Sawyer*, but he can't
resist reiterating his emphasis on the "stretchers." This faint praise
of Twain's authority recalls the author's own equivocal verification
that anything appearing under Sellers's pseudonym "may be gambled on as being the petrified truth" (*LOM*, 352). Just as Twain
expressed his resentment of preemptive authority by lampooning
Sellers's arrogant authority, Huck assures us that to have read *Tom
Sawyer* or not "ain't no matter," thereby asserting the autonomy of
his text by devaluing Twain's anteriority even as he tries generously
to respect "Mr. Mark Twain." In effect, Huck tells us that Twain's
work is of no consequence because this narrative is his own. He has
stepped out of the text in which Twain's questionable authority contained him and will set the record of his own adventures straight, in
his own words.

Although the rather sharply drawn authority conflicts between
Huck and Tom in the Phelps farm episodes have distressed many
readers, it seems rather ironic that more readers have not been
dismayed by the violation of authority in this first paragraph. For
this necessary expression of freedom from Twain's authority is
where Huck's critique of authority begins to run into problems.

Huck is, after all, Twain's fictional creation; his putative ability to step outside the domain of his creator's authority is the ultimate fiction, and an absurd one. But that is precisely what readers are rooting for when they lament or excuse Huck's failure in Pikesville. To believe, finally, that Huck could transcend that authority – and he must, in order to be a completely autonomous creature – is to assume a naiveté on the order of Huck's when, first, he believes that the drunkard at the circus, who steps out of the audience to mount a wild horse, is just a belligerent member of the audience, and then – more absurdly – when he believes that the drunkard, who reveals himself as a highly skilled member of the show, has acted independently, to subvert the ringmaster's authority. The enduring belief that Huck can return to the state of nature is a nostalgic fraud that Twain teases the reader into – he knows what will seduce his audience as well as the duke knows what will titillate the rubes of Bricksville. To be sure, part of the delight in reading the novel comes from believing in Huck's independence, from suspending our knowledge that Huck is fully under the control of his author. But ultimately, the fiction of Huck's autonomy cannot be sustained. Twain's exploitation of our desire for fiction should force us to acknowledge our own ambivalent investment in authority: we admire the author who can artfully draw us into the characters and plot of the novel – and we root for the character to defy the authorial control that we so admire.

The significance of Huck's collapsed autonomy is not simply his obvious inability to escape Twain's control but that even his break from cultural, community, and paternal control, a break that we vicariously desire, is impossible. Throughout his narrative, Huck recurs to the contrasting wisdom he has garnered from Pap and the widow, as exemplified in the compromise between Pap's euphemistic semantics of "borrowing" (80) versus the widow's condemnation of stealing. And though Huck's motives are at times different from Tom's, he repeatedly expresses his admiration for Tom's ability to work up an adventure.

Deceit, Desire, and the Raft

Huck as nature boy is not, however, an identity simply invented by readers who desire an idealized romantic hero of American individualism. Huck's perceived romantic stature originates in *Tom Sawyer*. The genteel narrator of the first novel introduces Huck as "the juvenile pariah of the village . . . cordially hated and dreaded by all the mothers of the town, because he was idle, and lawless, and vulgar and bad" (*TS*, 47). Even if we were to miss the oxymoron in the fact that mothers "*cordially* hated" Huck – implying that society requires scapegoats as object lessons – it's unlikely that we would fail to hear the mixed emotions when the avuncular voice of respectability goes on to portray Huck as the object of admiration, "the romantic outcast":

> Huckleberry came and went, at his own free will . . . [H]e did not have to go to school or to church, or call any being master or obey anybody; he could go fishing or swimming when and where he chose, and stay as long as it suited him; nobody forbade him to fight; he could sit up as late as he pleased; he was always the first boy that went barefoot in the spring and the last to resume leather in the fall; he never had to wash, nor put on clean clothes; he could swear wonderfully. In a word, everything that goes to make life precious, that boy had. So thought every harassed, hampered, respectable boy in St. Petersburg. (49)

The last sentence attempts to confine this impression of Huck to the unregenerate little boys who resent the oppression from which Huck is immune. But the fond description of Huck's autonomy from the dictates of genteel convention belies the narrator's shared envy of Huck's freedom. The narrator's duplicity in overtly upholding the community's genteel standards while covertly admiring Huck's indifference to those standards exemplifies a cultural ambivalence regarding the trade-off between autonomy and society. And the fact that legions of readers have accepted Huck as the "romantic outcast" indicates that this is neither the envious dream of little boys chafing against restraints on their liberty nor a particular quirk of the narrator but a general phenomenon of the compromise exacted by social conformity.[7] Every prohibition assumes a preexisting desire so powerful and prevalent as to warrant institutional interdiction. Huck's indifference to the behavioral code appeals to all the civilized readers whose desires have been inhibited by the code to which they have submitted. Just as Tom's diversionary spectacle with the pinch-bug and the poodle offers the St. Petersburg congregation a

87

half-secret relief from the boredom of the parson's discourse, so Huck's liberty offers a similar vicarious escape from the authority that checks desire. There's little doubt that Tom's subversive acts place him consciously within the scope of convention, but Huck, too, unwittingly assumes a role in the social drama: the pariah who dares to indulge desire.

Huck's posture of liberated desire clearly affects his self-image. But we can believe in his determination to escape society only if, seduced by the promise of vicarious freedom, we ignore Huck's dubious ability to evaluate himself honestly and allow his self-perceptions to sway our critical estimation of his character. This is not to pronounce Huck guilty of "stretchers"; he firmly believes that he can exist outside of society. But Twain's text is an ironic portrait of its hero. The ambivalence toward authority reflected in Huck's self-deception undercuts his declaration of individualism in *Tom Sawyer*, "I ain't everybody" (257), revealing the social underpinnings of his identity as a kind of ragged everyman. In *Huckleberry Finn*, the text's irony warrants a reading that goes beyond the critical tradition of measuring Huck's final degree of success in his escape and that, instead, accounts for the ways in which Twain urges us to question Huck's commitment to that escape and to reassess his underlying commitment to society.

Tom Sawyer shows just how unaware Huck is of his social role. He believes he is immune from all paths of conformity and fails to recognize that his desire to live outside of the social code is countered by a nearly equal desire for social interaction. The Jackson's Island episodes in *Tom Sawyer* expose the unacknowledged desire behind the pariah's mask, thus limiting his romantic-outcast stature early in Twain's first "boy book." Initially, Huck shows no interest in the society from which they have escaped and enjoys his stay on the island because of the relative ease with which his needs are met. He expresses indifference to Tom's delighted suggestion that their adventure would inspire the envy of their Hannibal playmates: "I reckon so . . . anyways *I'm* suited. I don't want nothing better'n this. I don't ever get enough to eat, gen'ally – and here they can't come and pick at a feller and bullyrag him so" (103). But within a day, the firm resolution with which he professes his outcast's creed begins to crumble. Like his fellow runaways, Huck loses interest in their self-imposed exile when the oppressive seclusion induces a longing for civilization:

> The stillness, the solemnity that brooded in the woods, and the sense of loneliness, began to tell upon the spirits of the boys. They fell to thinking. A sort of undefined longing crept upon them. This took dim shape, presently – it was budding homesickness. Even Finn the Red-Handed was dreaming of his doorsteps and empty hogsheads. But they were all ashamed of their weakness, and none was brave enough to speak his thought. (109)

The roundly shared emotions indicate how alike the pretending pirates are. Despite the difference between Huck's hand-to-mouth vagrancy and Tom and Joe's middle-class roots, Huck longs to return to his place in society, marginal as it is. His ability to experience the same embarrassment as his more respectable comrades reveals that his determined outcast swagger is an ambivalent posture of defiance hardly more resolute than Tom's and Joe's self-exhortatory insistence that "they would never return to civilization" (102).

At the end of *Tom Sawyer*, Huck's penultimate move is the reverse of his desire to return to St. Petersburg; that is, he retreats from the center of civilization back to the margin, reverting to his ragged liberty among the hogsheads after enduring too much of the widow Douglas's regimentation. Huck consistently resents being picked at and bullyragged, but his repudiation of civilization here seems oddly adamant, because he criticizes the comforts of order in terms precisely opposite to those in which he originally praised his island retreat. On Jackson's Island he enjoyed the rare satisfaction of a full stomach, but he complains that under the widow Douglas's care "grub comes too easy – I don't take no interest in vittles, that way" (257). The reversibility of his terms in the two instances suggests the ambivalence underlying his claims. Thus he no sooner steadfastly declares, "Now these clothes suits me and this bar'l suits me, and I ain't ever going to shake 'em any more" (258), than Tom easily negotiates him back to the bothers of civilization with the promise of adventure. Satisfied with the bargain, Huck "shakes" his hogshead, gainsaying his freshly uttered dedication to waywardness: "I'll stick to the widder till I rot, Tom; and if I git to be a reglar ripper of a robber, and everybody talking 'bout it, I reckon she'll be proud she snaked me in out of the wet" (259).

In light of Huck's propensity to "shake" and "stick" to antithetical propositions at the close of *Tom Sawyer*, it's no surprise to find him correspondingly disillusioned with the unfulfilled promise of life in Tom Sawyer's gang when his own narrative opens. His disappointment, however, doesn't cause him to revert automatically to his vagrant life. For the most part, he has become inured to the tight clothes and rigors of education. But after Pap abducts him, it takes but a brief taste of the carefree life, "lazy and jolly, laying off comfortable all day, smoking and fishing, and no books to study" (30), to reaffirm Huck's resistance to the widow's cramped up, "sivilized" ways. And yet Pap's authoritarian abuse, at the other extreme, proves more than a mere bother. Self-preservation inspires Huck's plan to escape, to "tramp right across the country . . . and so get so far away that the old man nor the widow shouldn't ever find me any more" (32). Huck's cycle of oscillation between autonomy and subscription to authority represents the kind of dynamic that fuels Twain's own attitude and correspondingly afflicts his creative process. The solution that Huck finally hits on appears to offer a way out of the cyclical trap for both protagonist and author, but anxiety about freedom and control so informs the structure of identity within the culture that such an escape is impossible.

Rather than stick to his plan to "tramp right across the country," Huck's chance discovery of a canoe suggests that he alter the means and direction of his escape. But the choice also alters the quality of Huck's liberation, because the river as an avenue of escape also offers access to society on either bank. Had Huck adhered to his original plan, he would have had little opportunity for social interaction; he'd have been a solitary man in nature. The river allows him to continue to indulge his ambivalence: he can immerse himself in nature, and culture is never farther away than the nearest shore.

Still, the structure of Twain's ambivalence denies a simple opposition between two poles. Rather, each one is both a remedy for oppression and an oppression to be remedied: nature relieves the irritation of society but yields dullness which social interaction in turn relieves. So, while Jackson's Island offers a peaceful retreat from society, it isn't long before the satisfaction of being the "boss" of the island wears thin, and Huck admits that "by and by it got sort of lonesome" (48), repeating the pattern established in *Tom Sawyer*. Jim's arrival helps break the boredom of solitude temporarily, but even companionship proves not enough stimulation for Huck. He complains that "it was getting slow and dull, and I wanted to get a stirring up, some way" and suggests a return to the town "to find out what was going on" (66). Huck doesn't have to work too hard to manufacture an adventure in this instance, because as a fugitive Jim has created a "stirring up" that Huck crowds himself into. Although only Jim is sought, Huck declares, "They're after us!" (75) when he returns to the island. Huck doesn't think twice about signing on to such an adventure. It promises to fill up the void of lonesomeness more easily than having to find ways on his own "to put in time" (156).

Conversely, after his experience of well-mannered violence among the uncompromising Grangerfords, Huck relishes the simple pleasure of having nothing to do but "put in time" on the raft. Chapter 19 opens with a rambling description of the uneventful respite in which clauses are strung together by a profusion of semicolons and conjunctions, indicating the continuous sequence of passing time:

> It was a monstrous big river down there – sometimes a mile and a half wide; we run nights, and laid up and hid day-times; soon as night was most gone, we stopped navigating and tied up – nearly always in the dead water under a towhead; and then cut young cotton-woods and willows and hid the raft with them. Then we set out the lines. Next we slid into the river and had a swim, so as to freshen up and cool off; then we set down on the sandy bottom where the water was about knee deep, and watched the daylight come. (156)

This catalog of Huck and Jim's routine leads to an even longer, more discursive description of dawn on the river:

> The first thing to see, looking away over the water, was a kind of dull line – that was the woods on t'other side – you couldn't make nothing else out; then a pale place in the sky; then more paleness, spreading around; then the river softened up away off, and warn't black anymore, but gray; you could see little dark spots drifting along, ever so far away – sometimes you could see a streak on the water which you know by the look of the streak that there's a snag there in a swift current which breaks on it and makes that streak look that way; and you see the mist curl up off of the water, and

the east reddens up, and you make out a log cabin in the edge of the woods, away on the bank on t'other side of the river, being a wood-yard likely, and piled by them cheats so you can throw a dog through it anywheres; then the nice breeze springs up, and comes fanning you from over there, so cool and fresh, and sweet to smell on account of the woods and the flowers; but sometimes not that way, because they've left dead fish laying around gars, and such, and they do get pretty rank; and next you've got the full day, and everything smiling in the sun, and the songbirds just going it! (156–7)

This famous passage of Huck's evocative pastoralism is the center-piece of Leo Marx's praise of Huck's appeal; Marx regards it as the most concentrated moment of lyrical intensity in American litera-ture.[8] I quote the passage at length for two reasons. First, this mo-ment of lyrical intensity may be unparalleled, but it is also the last of its kind in the text. In fact, it seems not so much an endorsement of pastoralism as a poignantly emphatic farewell to nature in this novel, because the raft is about to be invaded by the king and the duke, who contaminate the raft and the remainder of the story with the corruption of civilization. Twain underscores the ironic shift that the two confidence men incur by staging Huck's encounter with them while he is berry picking. Earlier, when Jim admitted that before he teamed up with Huck foraging provided the staple of his diet, Huck was appalled. Now, however, Huck's own recourse to this primitive means of subsistence brings him in contact with the bank, allowing the opportunity for cultural degradation to take command of their floating refuge.

Second, and more importantly, despite Marx's praise of this pas-toral ode, the passage fails to motivate or even to constitute narrative in any significant way. In effect, Huck's description is distantly akin to Mr. Brown's storytelling defect in "Old Times." Huck doesn't digress to the degree that Brown does, and his description follows the temporal progress from darkness to the light of full day, but his chronicle of the unfolding moments of daybreak, one after the other, shares a pointlessness with the metonymically connected mat-ter spewed by Brown's capacious memory. Huck's incessant se-quence gives the illusion of narrative momentum to what is virtually a static observation of nature. In *The American Claimant*, Twain will lampoon the idea of cluttering up the narrative action with descriptions of atmospheric conditions by including an appendix of quotations borrowed from "qualified and recognized experts" of this "literary specialty" (*AC*, ix). Twain encourages the reader to "turn over and help himself from time to time as he goes along," whenever a craving for weather strikes. For *Pudd'nhead Wilson*, Twain toyed with the idea of dispensing with discursive weather passages anywhere in the text, replacing them instead with a system of symbols that would alert the reader to climatic conditions throughout. As he humorously tells us in *The American Claimant*, devices such as these serve both the reader, who is often deterred from reading a tale through "because of delays on account of the weather," and the author, whose progress is often halted by "having to stop every few pages to fuss-up the weather" (2). Huck's lyrical moment, however, doesn't interfere with the narrative progress because his narrative progress has stalled on its own, a serious problem for an adventuresome boy and the maker of a book whose title boasts "Adventures." In fact, the metonymic accumulation of detail after detail is a literary version of what Huck calls "putting in time," until the king and the duke can revive the narrative momentum.

Furthermore, Huck's pastoral digression here does not elevate nature as an ideal but posits it as one pole of the dynamic that divides his attention between nature and culture. For example, the woods in this predawn moment appear as a "dull line," reminding us of the stultifying lonesomeness that Huck finds in nature. Gradually, Huck's attention alternates between natural and cultural features. Other river craft appear as "little dark spots" in the distance of the gray river, their sweeps "creaking" and their occupants' voices carrying through the dimness. As the light comes up, Huck's gaze falls on the streak of a snag on the river's surface and a mist rising off it, and then a distant cabin of a wood-yard on the opposite shore. And the aroma of the woods and sweet flowers gives way to the stench of dead fish that an unidentified "they" have left to rot on the banks. In each sensory instance, Huck's ambivalence directs his oscillating attention between observations of nature and signs of human activity, indicating his fluctuating attraction to both nature and culture.

In both the history of American settlement and the tradition of the American novel, the significance of nature is subordinate to that of culture. As raw material whose potential is activated when shaped into a cultural meaning, nature is appropriated into the novel, a fundamentally social genre. In Twain's novel, this social function is disguised by Huck's presumed inclination toward nature and by the fact that Huck's story pretends to be an autobiography – a factual account of events. But as Twain has shown in *Life on the Mississippi*, autobiography itself is an artifice no less than the novel, because it recasts selected events of one's life to project retrospectively a pattern of meaning on the otherwise random accumulation of experience. As a meaningful construct, Huck's narrative is a cultural product, just as his identity is. If Huck were the nature boy so many critics have wanted him to be, we might expect that the entire narrative would look something like his lyrical description of dawn. Like the river's continuous flow or the inseparable moments in which the day subtly emerges, "Adventures of a Nature Boy" might be one long sentence. But, in fact, such a text would not exist at all, at least not in the first person. For the very act of making a book, of assuming authority over a representation of experience, inscribes one within culture. The final product – indeed, one might argue, the *only* product – of *Adventures of Huckleberry Finn* is not Huck's escape from civilization but his narrative. And while he undertakes this project to exercise his autonomy from Twain's anterior authority, Huck works within language. Like Tom's, Huck's identity is embedded in a matrix of textual forces that define the culture and his place in it, whether he knows it or not. Moreover, in having written a book – an accomplishment of which even Tom Sawyer can neither boast nor be rotten glad to be rid – Huck is not just a product of culture but a producer of it.

Thus, for all of the ways in which his identity is a construction of culture, we might also see his name as a subtle satire of the nature worship that Thoreau embodies in *Walden* when he writes, "A huckleberry never reaches Boston; they have not been known there since they grew on her three hills. The ambrosial and essential part of the fruit is lost with the bloom which is rubbed off in the market cart, and they become mere provender. As long as Eternal Justice reigns, no one innocent huckleberry can be transported thither from the country's hills." Twain's Huckleberry naively imagines himself as the same kind of natural fruit, only to deny this sense of uncultivatedness in his every move.[9]

However, to identify both boys within the sphere of culture is not sufficient. To account for their differences, we might measure their different orientations in their project to free Jim as opposite poles of narrative impulse. Huck's goal is to free Jim, whereas Tom's is to keep the project running. In their different aims, the two boys personify the narrative impulses of closure and what D. A. Miller terms "narratability."[10] Because Jim's imprisonment has raised the stakes to a greater peril, Huck desires closure to be rid of all the bother of adventure. But enervated by the challenge and the lonesomeness of his companionless state, his dedication to closure is initially half-hearted at best. Of course, when Tom arrives to relieve Huck's loneliness and to whip up the sagging narrative momentum, Huck is reactivated and recommitted to his goal of Jim's freedom. But the two boys do not act in concert so much as in spite of each other's desires. They embody the conflicting energies that motivate the act of narration.

Huck, for example, articulates his renewed teleological purpose not when Tom gets into the act but when the master of juvenile theatrics is forced to compromise his standards of execution and use picks to dig Jim out rather than case-knives – as his literary authorities would have it. Animated by his victory, Huck enunciates his creed of pragmatism:

> *Now* you're *talking!* . . . your head gets leveler and leveler all the time, Tom Sawyer, . . . Picks is the thing, moral or no moral; and as for me, I don't care shucks for the morality of it, nohow. When I start in to steal a nigger, or a watermelon, or a Sunday school book, I ain't no ways particular how it's done, so it's done. What I want is my nigger; or what I want is my watermelon; or what I want is my Sunday school book: and if a pick's the handiest thing, that's the thing I'm agoing to dig that nigger or that watermelon or that Sunday school book out with; and I don't give a dead rat what the authorities thinks about it, nuther. (307)

This is a very different Huck from the one who earlier in the novel spoke admiringly of Tom's ability to put in the fancy touches on a project and about his own need to "put in time." This later Huck voices Twain's own frustration after laboring on and off for nearly seven years without concluding the novel. Correspondingly, Huck expresses relief at the end of his narrative, now that "there ain't nothing more to write about, and am rotten glad of it, because if I'd a knowed what a trouble it was to make a book I wouldn't a tackled it and ain't agoing to no more" (362).

Tom, on the other hand, as the agent of narratability, expresses annoyance only with the trouble of making such a simple enterprise into a suitably bothersome one. He requires adversity to motivate his narratable agency. The negligence of Jim's captors, Tom complains, "makes it so rotten difficult to get up a difficult plan . . . [I]t's the stupidest arrangement I ever see: You got to invent *all* the difficulty" (298). But Huck provides the necessary resistance against which Tom can mobilize his theatrical ambitions until he can stir up the community of adults later.

Moreover, the ambivalence that the two contending adventurers represent goes beyond narrative in general to signify a cultural ambivalence about race relations. As Tom reveals that his idea of invention is no more than "gerry-rigged" convention, a performance that is "regular" according to "all the best authorities" (299), his "romantical" (294) plan escalates into an absurd concoction of conventions that pointedly illustrates the civil rights abuses that continued after Reconstruction, all in the name of freeing the Negro. Huck recalls Tom's enthusiasm for his plan to free Jim:

> He said it was the best fun he ever had in his life, and the most intellectural; and said if he only could see his way to it we would keep it up all the rest of our lives and leave Jim to our children to get out; for he believed Jim would come to like it better and better the more he got used to it. He said that in that way it could be strung out to as much as eighty year, and would be the best time on record. (310)

Here it would appear that Jim is not the only prisoner: Tom's slavishness to the cultural code demonstrates his own incarceration within a closed system of signs. But Tom's blind adherence to the conventions of romance literature does not mean that the concept of Jim's freedom is beyond his grasp. In the end, Tom proves that he has understood that concept all along – in fact, his knowledge that Jim was already free afforded him the opportunity to indulge himself in his stylish pageant of Jim's escape. The fact of Jim's emancipation is the trump card that Tom is ready to play should he lose control of the game. Thus, Tom displays narratability as an allegory of white culture's subjugation of blacks. Twain represents that injustice not simply as an unconscious, internalized cultural assumption but as a conscious manipulation of the concept of freedom, overtly justified as moral though covertly understood as corrupt.

The narrative's conclusion problematizes the application of Miller's theory of "discontented" narrative to explain Twain's text. Miller argues that the narratable conditions that give rise to a story are never actually resolved but only appear so by means of narrative repression. Closure is, therefore, an artificial way of bringing that conflict under illusory control. But early in *Huckleberry Finn*, Twain represents the narratable conflicts of the story as merely temporary conditions. The literal motivations of Huck's adventures – Huck's vulnerability to Pap's lawful hold on him and Jim's to the law of slavery – have been neatly undone, and the fact of their undoing repressed, earlier in the plot. In the end, Tom's revelation that Jim is in fact a freedman and Jim's revelation that Huck is in fact free of Pap mean that the odyssey has been unnecessary.[11]

Still, although Twain invalidates the motivating conflict of Huck's *Adventures*, he suggests, by including Tom's "evasion," that the narratable condition of racial injustice in the story of American culture is insidiously alive, not only in the novel's antebellum setting but in the post-Reconstruction era in which Twain wrote it. Insofar as Tom finds elaborate ways of enslaving Jim, all in the name of setting him free, despite Tom's knowledge that he is already free, Tom's pageant represents the de facto slavery that persisted during and beyond the period in which Twain composed the text. Twain's 1882 Mississippi voyage into the South afforded him the initial opportunity to witness the failure of Reconstruction. Despite his confident claim in the manuscript of *Life on the Mississippi* that the "horror" of slavery "is gone, and permanently" – a claim that he edited out of the published text – Twain registers his concern in the same passage for the South's "solid" support of the Democratic Party (332). This political dominance enacted the Black Codes and Jim Crow laws shortly thereafter as a way of returning blacks to a subordinate role in southern society.[12]

This is the reason that so much importance has been assigned to Huck's crisis of conscience at the moment when he defies the culture's slavery code and defiantly damns himself to hell in order to save Jim. Indeed, compared to Tom's harrowing ordeal in Mc-Dougal's cave, Huck's verbal descent into hell confronts cultural repression much more directly. To be sure, in Tom's adventure Twain constructs a much more elaborate allegory of the cultural unconscious. But Tom's confrontation with his mirror image, the real half-breed outlaw, is a repressive rite of passage into a cultural identity, a moment of identification and complete denial of that identification with the dreaded outcast "other," from which Tom emerges into the daylight of social acceptance. Conversely, in his own trial, Huck squarely faces the cultural abuse of the racial other. Though he tries to invoke the rhetoric of theological justification, he cannot, finally, repress the truth. Instead, he is deeply impressed by the truth of Jim's humanity, and he repudiates the society that has endorsed slavery.

His ignorance of Jim's emancipation does not invalidate this humanitarian moment of civil disobedience in the name of racial equality, but, of course, nearly every other act he performs mitigates it. Ever since Huck first shamefully acknowledged Jim's humanity after playing him for a fool in their first reunion on the fog-shrouded river, he has been easily distracted from honoring Jim's dignity by the adventures in which he becomes embroiled, especially after teaming up with the king and the duke. Huck's heralded moment of self-damnation is the crucial dilemma between conscience and heart that Twain was after, the conflict between social authority and moral autonomy. But despite Huck's reiterated stake in liberty, it is not long before he submits to Tom's "regulations" (301), failing to free Jim in much the same way that Emancipation and the Union victory in the Civil War ultimately failed by giving way to the civil rights abuses of the post-Reconstruction South.

We could hardly expect the Phelps's farm episodes to turn out differently, especially because Huck has been "born again" as Tom Sawyer. After having invoked Tom's ability to manage an adventure during the course of his journey, Huck has finally found the one identity that he finds "easy and comfortable" (282). Thus, akin to the way that Huck's and Jim's perils motivating the journey are voided of necessity, the fundamental psychological condition motivating Huck's adventures – his desire for freedom outside of civilization – is comparably futile.

As far as Huck has traveled from St. Petersburg, he has never been far from the culture that Tom embodies. Although literal, concrete, utilitarian products of culture like fishhooks, frying pans, and castoff articles of clothing are Huck's most conspicuous acquired materials, his imaginative resources are also acquired materials from cultural sources, many of them acquired quite directly from Tom. All along the way – with Judith Loftus, the raftsmen, the bounty hunters – Huck succeeds in lying only after those he has failed to deceive provide him with acceptable premises. As early as his escape from Pap's cabin, he acknowledges his debt to Pap for the inspiration of the plan itself. Pap's warning that the prowlers Huck had invented intended them harm, Huck admits, "give me the very idea I wanted" (39). Although this appears to be a measure of Huck's resourcefulness, his failure to invent his own ruses and his reliance on materials presented to him indicate the extent of his bricoleur identity, and his reliance on Tom as a model defines this identity more sharply.

In Huck's elaborate staging of his death, Tom's influence is waiting in the wings. Huck reverses his earlier rejection of his stylish comrade's theatricality: "I did wish Tom Sawyer was there, I knowed he would take an interest in this kind of business, and throw in all the fancy touches. Nobody could spread himself like Tom Sawyer in such a thing as that" (41). In light of Tom's influence here and Huck's explicit attraction to Tom as an adventurous ideal in the *Walter Scott* episode, Huck's escape to Jackson's Island begins to look like a patent imitation of the idyllic retreat to the same location in *Tom Sawyer*. So even the integrity of Huck's defiant act, a blow struck for liberty, is undermined by its dependence on a model.

Huck's sojourn on the island follows the same pattern of adventurous exploration and loneliness that characterizes the *Tom Sawyer* episodes. He even echoes the approval he admitted during his last vacation here with Tom and Joe Harper when he proclaims to Jim with satisfaction, "[T]his is nice . . . I wouldn't want to be nowhere else but here" (60). His vacation on the island in the later story lasts at least three weeks before Huck's ensuing restlessness prompts his return to the village, much as Tom returned to eavesdrop on his aunt Polly's grief. Huck's return to the village suggests that he has forgotten about his original plan to escape civilization for good. We might even speculate that had Huck been assured of both his own and Jim's safety, the *Adventures* would have been over much sooner, because not until he learns of the bounty being offered for Jim does the actual journey begin. Under different circumstances, he would have simply returned to the comfort and bother of civilization, wrapped in the celebrity to which Tom Sawyer had introduced him.

Huck's affinity for emulating a model individual like Tom characterizes what René Girard calls "triangular desire." In *Deceit, Desire, and the Novel,* Girard illustrates the structure of this desire mediated by imitation of a model in *Don Quixote,* a novel that consciously reveals the presence of a mediator. And it is precisely this conscious revelation that, in Girard's view, distinguishes Cervantes' text as "romanesque" – roughly equivalent to what I am calling "novelistic" – as opposed to "romantic," an unselfconsciously imitative performance.[13] Girard's reading of this structural principle of novelistic discourse is a valuable paradigm for understanding *Huckleberry Finn.* Moreover, his use of *Don Quixote* is especially fortuitous, because that text was an important one for both Twain and Tom Sawyer.

Twain singles out Cervantes' novel for admiration in *Life on the Mississippi* for having "swept . . . the medieval chivalry-silliness out of existence" (329), in contrast to the romanticism of Scott's *Ivanhoe,* which, Twain self-contradictorily laments, undid all the benefits of *Don Quixote.* In these remarks, Twain distinguishes himself from the romantic reader of *Don Quixote,* of whom Girard writes, "The romantic reader, by a marvelous misinterpretation which fundamentally is only a superior truth, identifies himself with Don Quixote, the supreme imitator, and makes of him the model individual." Of course, Tom Sawyer does not escape this criticism. He is the apotheosis of this characterization, overtly emulating the notorious windmill tilter as a model hero. Tom's explicit appeal to the authority of *Don Quixote* early in *Huckleberry Finn* makes clear that he is an exaggerated version of Girard's romantic reader, who, by misinterpreting Cervantes' novel, unconsciously imitates the literary madman. Nowhere is this more striking than in the Phelps farm episodes: there, Tom not only imitates Don Quixote and the heroes of romantic adventure stories but exemplifies the contradictory behavior that Girard claims characterizes romantic readers: "All this untimely rescuing ends by harming what it sets out to save. It is not surprising that every generous romantic gesture has such catastrophic consequences . . . [T]he 'victim' to be rescued is never more than a pretext for asserting oneself gloriously against the whole universe." In the case of Tom's vainglorious acts, the issue is even more duplicitous, because

Jim is no longer a slave. So Tom is not really opposing the slavery code but rather reenslaving Jim in the name of freeing him.[14]

But if Twain's readers have recognized Tom's misreading, they appear, correspondingly, to have failed to recognize themselves as romantic misinterpreters of *Huckleberry Finn*, the text in which Twain transplanted the motivations of Cervantes' novel into American soil. By maintaining their belief in, or their desire for, Huck's ideal freedom they have committed themselves to the romantic fallacy that the "romanesque" text seeks to expose. For the triangulated desire that Girard identifies in *Don Quixote* and that we can readily perceive in Tom Sawyer's emulation of heroic models motivates Huck as well. Huck's ridicule of Jim's misunderstanding of King Solomon's wisdom and of the difference between French and English echoes Tom's ridicule of Huck's ignorance, which itself echoes Don Quixote's complaint about his sidekick. Indeed, Huck's emulation of Tom throughout his adventures shows that internal mediation operates within his text, as opposed to the external mediation that structures Tom's behavior; that is, Huck's model of action is internal to his story, in contact with the hero, whereas Tom's model exists in another textual realm outside of his immediate contact. For Girard, the presence of both external and internal mediation is what distinguishes a text as romanesque, a narrative that consciously reflects the presence of a mediator.

The difference between external and internal mediation is the difference between fantasy or play and action. Tom's activity is all fantasy, and Huck's is for the most part action. Even in *Tom Sawyer*, Huck was saving the widow Douglas by his valiant surveillance of Injun Joe while Tom was off cavorting with Becky in McDougal's cave and planning to spend the night with her, though not in the nightmarish union they ultimately share.

But Huck's most sincere action in his narrative occurs at that one moment when he appears to relinquish his triangulated desire and to act autonomously by damning himself to hell for Jim's freedom. The outcome of Huck's crisis of conscience is taken as the triumph of essential goodness over cultural conditioning. Yet in the novel's opening scene, Huck judges that there was "no advantage in going where [Miss Watson] was going" and resolves not to put in his bid for "the good place." Instead, Huck takes heart in Miss Watson's assurance that Tom was destined for damnation, "because," he admits, "I wanted him and me to be together" (4). His early indifference to theological definitions of fate, however, is not motivated by the kind of crisis that prompts his climactic self-damnation. And Huck's surprise that a boy of Tom's upbringing should take part in freeing a slave suggests that he sees his own act as somehow different from Tom's participation in what Huck presumes is a subversion of a cultural taboo.

Yet Huck has seen Tom violate an oath before, to save Muff Potter, because it was the "right" thing to do, even if it would place him in personal jeopardy. And when Huck is reborn as Tom Sawyer, he is relieved because he knows how to fill this role, not dismayed because the act he is about to commit will earn Tom the undeserved reputation of an abolitionist. Instead, what ought to come as a greater shock to Huck is the fact that Tom has betrayed his trust by pretending to free Jim when Jim has been free all along. Huck has staked his soul and what little reputation he has to subvert the slave code for Jim's sake, only to find out that the entire enterprise was a fiction. Those readers who have accepted the premise of America and the novel, and who have, thus, believed in Huck's quest for autonomy, have felt similarly betrayed, or at least disappointed, by the novel's ending.

Readers so oriented reiterate the misunderstanding of metaphysical desire that Girard insists epitomizes *Don Quixote*'s romantic readers. Metaphysical desire, Girard contends, consists of a "perpetual contrast between what is normal and what is exceptional . . . Don Quixote is the exception and the dumbfounded spectators are the rule." Novelistic discourse is activated by a dialectic of the exception and the rule. In Twain's novel, Huck personifies this dialectic. Like Sancho Panza, who provides what Girard calls "the indispensable rational decor," Huck represents the rule when he stands behind Tom Sawyer. And he becomes the exceptional hero himself when he opposes the conventional wisdom to which Tom subscribes. Girard argues that "[r]omantic criticism does not understand the novelistic dialectic" and "thereby destroys the very essence of novelistic genius. It re-injects the Manichean division between Self and Others which that genius has overcome only with great difficulty."[15] The romance of democracy, in which the individual is valued over the mob, gives an American slant to the romantic criticism in Twain's novel. However, I do not mean to suggest that Twain was in some way above or immune to this romance. To the contrary, Colonel Sherburn's defiant speech, widely accepted as Twain's own sentiment, converts his cold-blooded killing of Boggs into a dramatic portrayal of the stalwart individual's virtue. For Twain, though, the dialectic remains dynamic, and so, too, this quality of the novel is not resolved. Although Girard's formulation of the dialectic is finally transcended by the hero's *disengaño* in the conclusion, Twain's novel suggests that such a triumph over metaphysical desire is elusive. Certainly, Huck's narration of the novel fits with Girard's claim that the hero of a novel becomes capable of writing it. But Huck's authorship, signed off "Yours Truly," accompanied by an illustration of Huck bowing decorously to the reader, is not to be confused with the complete union of the hero and his creator that, as Girard claims, novels achieve. Certainly Huck and his creator share a number of characteristics, but the complete fusion of self and other that Girard posits indulges the romantic notion that the novel can achieve what it sets out to do. And what Twain discovered in *Huckleberry Finn* is the seduction and betrayal of the novel's fictional power.

To blame Twain for the novel's failure burdens him unfairly. Twain, too, is betrayed by the novelistic discourse in which he set out to restructure the world. Huck's enterprise was a way for Twain to make up for his own absence from the Civil War, a way to free a Negro slave and to light out for the territory before the Civil War rather than to light out during the war without having recognized the moral urgency of racial freedom for which it was waged. And in the double-cross of novelistic discourse Twain began to sense the authority of history and to doubt that fiction could stand up to the determinism of historical circumstance.

Huck's emulation of Tom Sawyer is but one instance – the most self-conscious one – of his internalization of cultural codes of behavior. Under the widow Douglas's and Miss Watson's tutelage, the village pariah has been formally introduced to literacy, for which he alternately earns the community's approval and Pap's contempt. Although Huck demonstrates a marked imprecision in his specific references to his formal education through the course of his narrative, much of his journey reinscribes Western cultural history in a way that demonstrates Huck's osmotically acquired stock of cultural literacy. His debate with Jim over the moral of the story of Solomon's wisdom is a revealing case. Jim's interpretation of Solomon's cruelty is informed by his experience under the patriarchal oppression of slavery, where a slaveholder can dispense with human lives on a whim. Although Huck has endured a kind of slavery under Pap's authority – complete with Pap's emblematic prohibition of Huck's literacy, in their first dramatic encounter – he has absorbed the accepted, culturally informed irony of Solomon's astute sensitivity to human feelings. Despite his self-image of estrangement from any sense of community, Huck's narrative dramatizes not only his drift within a specific cultural community and historical setting but also his immersion in an historically informed cultural tradition about which he is only peripherally aware.

By depicting the authority of history over his vernacular protagonist, though, Twain gives the lie to his own novelistic authority. If Huck's autonomy is a fiction in the face of history, then Twain's own claim to personal autonomy as a representative American also rests on fiction, in principle as well as in practice. Sensing this, Twain counters the linear historical progression of Huck's adventures with a chiasmic, ironic repetition of narrative incidents, as a way of inverting historical authority against itself.

Huck's Story and History

Whether lamenting Huck Finn's failure to make good on his moral maturity or endorsing the formal symmetry of the novel, critics have commonly observed that *Adventures of Huckleberry Finn* ends where it began, with Huck and Tom Sawyer playing games.[16] Yet games are featured not only at both ends of the narrative but also throughout. Nearly all of Huck's actions are a kind of trickery on the order of a game, though often a serious one. And the social relations into which he is drawn – the raftsmen's tall-tale telling, the Grangerford–Shepherdson feud, and the various confidence schemes of the king and the duke, to cite a few examples – are not much more than games. Twain himself was fascinated by games. He even invented one, not surprisingly around the same time that he was writing *Huckleberry Finn*. The "History Game" – or "Mark Twain's Memory Builder," as it was also called – was another of Twain's many brainstorms that evolved through several phases: originally an outdoor game in which the reigns of English kings were measured out on the ground; then an elaborate board game that included a chart of various empires and an accompanying history book that detailed the biographies of English royalty; and finally a simple board game with rules suggesting a variety of methods of play. Twain abandoned the History Game as he had numerous other projects, but, like all of the schemes that incited Twain's entrepreneurial enthusiasm, it caused him much excitement and optimism at the outset.[17]

Twain's nephew Samuel Webster suggested that the author's absorption in the History Game's complexities had distracted him from the completion of *Huckleberry Finn*. Jeanie Wagner expanded on Webster's assertion to infer that the failure of the novel's final chapters was due to the History Game's hold on Twain's attention. Wagner argues that the "burlesque incidents, graphic portraits of backwoods religious types, and satire on Tom Sawyer's quixotic approach to life and its problems" that comprise the final chapters "would have made easy writing for Mark Twain at this stage of his career." She concludes that rather than "sustaining the theme developed in the middle section of the novel," Twain took the easy way out and "[fell] bac[k] on" familiar devices so that he could divert more of his energy to the History Game.[18]

Webster's assertion and Wagner's speculation imply their agreement with the widely held view that the end of *Huckleberry Finn* is a failure. Given my different take on the notion of failure, I suggest that we might better understand the relation between *Huckleberry Finn* and the conception of history that the game propounds if we avoid the disappointment of those who subscribe to the possibility of Huck's autonomy and think of the game as an extension of the novel rather than a distraction from it. For Huck's narrative is saturated not only with games that reenact or exploit social conventions but also with reenactments of cultural history. And where Twain literally staked out the various reigns of the English kings spatially on the ground in the outdoor version of the History Game, in his novel he spatializes Western culture as a collective narrative in a series of allusive emblems that unfold episodically in Huck's journey downriver. Huck's tale shows that the celebrated autonomy of the most noted rebel in American literature is compromised by his culturally constructed consciousness, reflected in the novel's representation of history as a river of cultural data shaping his identity. Moreover, by depicting the authority of history over his vernacular protagonist, Twain discovers that his own novelistic authority is similarly compromised. If Huck's autonomy is a fiction in the face of history, then Twain's own claim to personal autonomy as a representative American also rests on fiction, both in practice and in principle. Finally, in his attempts to mitigate the determinism of history by elaborate architectonic manipulation of the narrative structure, Twain registers his awareness of what I am calling the "double-cross" of novelistic discourse.

It was during his Mississippi voyage of 1882 that Twain first became aware of the river as a metaphor for history. *Life on the Mississippi*, the book that resulted from that voyage, makes this clear in the way that it reframes the cub-pilot sketches Twain wrote in 1874 and 1875. In the earlier sketches the river is a kind of timeless, primordial flow to be mastered, whereas the writing generated by his 1882 voyage emphasizes, instead, the river's historicity, because during the trip Twain was struck by the changes he witnessed on the river, changes motivated by economics, technology, and not least by the Civil War. As I showed in Chapter 1, Twain displays his idiosyncratic view of history in the opening chapters of *Life on the Mississippi* and ironizes the florid historiography of Francis Parkman. Twain's concern with history also permeates *Huckleberry Finn*.

In Huck's story Twain treats history as an evolutionary process, conforming to the cultural assumption of the Whig hypothesis. But in *Huckleberry Finn*, this process is characteristically duplicitous. On the one hand, Twain turns back the clock on the Civil War and its aftermath and depicts Huck as a vernacular freethinker who opposes slavery, at least in Jim's case. And on the other hand, Huck is unconsciously implicated in the development of Western culture, even as he attempts to step outside of it. I will begin with the second of these two treatments of history, and, through an extended sketch of the narrative diegesis, I will show how Huck's journey allusively represents the cultural influence that informs his identity.

From the very start, in his escape from Pap's oppression to Jackson's Island, Huck unwittingly dramatizes the founding idea of America as a society that fulfills biblical promise. The island is an American Eden described in Miltonic echoes, and Huck's retreat there regenerates the Adamic myth from the debasement of Pap's depravity. Pap, you will recall, is a drunkard well known for "rais[ing] Cain around town" (29), and his filthy appearance after a night in the gutter leads Huck to suggest that "[a] body would a thought he was Adam" (33). But insofar as Huck's flight is an attempt to be free of this degraded cultural myth, the Adamic repetition in his escape suggests the futility of trying to shake off the genetic narrative that partly underwrites American ideology. Twain further exploits the American theme of biblical renewal by evoking the story of Noah in the torrent and flood from which Jim and Huck find shelter in a cave on the high ground of the island. Old Testament mythology and Jewish history combine in their flight to the island's Edenic haven. For the exodus that the raft-bound refugees reenact, in which Huck is a juvenile American Moses leading a slave to the freedom of the Promised Land, brings Huck, first, to the lively colloquy of rivermen in the timber-raft episode. When discovered and forced to identify himself, Huck claims to be Charles William Allbright, the phantom baby in the haunted barrel about whom he has just heard one of the raftsmen tell, an American vernacular version of Moses in the bulrushes. Shortly thereafter, Huck avoids the Jonah-like fate of being swallowed by the technological leviathan – the steamboat that devours the raft. And he washes ashore into the conflicted territory east of Eden, where the names of the Grangerford and Shepherdson families signify that their agrarian–pastoral feud is a recreation of the Cain and Abel agon. This fairly extensive biblical typology exhibits just how much of the culture Huck has unconsciously digested and come to personify, despite believing that he has escaped the Christianizing program of the widow Douglas and Miss Watson.[19]

As his story progresses, the Old Testament patterns give way to a range of other cultural analogues. In his transvested encounter with Judith Loftus, Huck imitates Achilles, who attempted to avoid the Trojan War by cross dressing. Like the Greek warrior, who could not disguise his masculine spear-throwing prowess, Huck cannot hide the incompetence with needle and thread nor the skill in throwing a lump of coal that reveal his youthful masculinity. Medieval feudalism reigns in Compromise, Kentucky, where the warring families, adhering to a code of aristocratic honor, are a vestige of a pre-democratic age. The bogus identities of the king and the duke also hearken back to feudalism, but as fallen royalty they signify a shift toward democracy. The mob that pursues Sherburn emphasizes this shift by echoing Carlyle's descriptions of the mobs in *The French Revolution*.[20]

The Grangerford–Shepherdson feud also draws on Shakespeare, the benchmark of English *literary* history, and the dramatic productions of the king and the duke explicitly show Shakespeare as a mainstay of nineteenth-century American popular culture, as Lawrence Levine has established.[21] Together these Shakespearean moments in Huck's tale reflect cultural changes stemming from the burgeoning of individualism. In the Kentucky adaptation of *Romeo and Juliet*, Huck assumes the role of Friar Laurence to the feud's forbidden lovers, promoting their self-determined union outside of the patriarchal tradition that prohibits it. Straightforward enough. The king and duke's Shakespearean sequences function less obviously because of the humorous purpose they serve. Huck's hilarious description of the rehearsals of the bard's greatest hits aboard the raft are so memorable as to overshadow the fact that the public performance was a failure, earning hardly more than a few lines in Huck's tale. What does earn our attention, though, is the plan to swindle the democratic rabble of Bricksville with the kind of entertainment that the duke predicts would "size their style" (194). Such ignoble behavior raises Jim's suspicions about the royal raftmates. Huck's attempt to explain yields a confused history of royal shenanigans as context for the king and the duke's fol-de-rol. Still, Jim's nose for the genuine tells him the truth about the king, that "dis one do *smell* like de nation" (200). Jim's keen sense of smell, implicitly questioning aristocratic privilege, should also alert us to the politico-historical evolution recorded in their journey. As aristocratic authority decomposes, democratic authority rises in its place. Thus in the first Shakespearean sequence, the patriarchal authority of the medieval feuding tradition is subverted, and in the second, royalty is a fraud whose authority is supplanted by the mass market.

From here, Huck's journey proceeds apace into the bourgeois age. Right after Jim expresses his doubts about the confidence men, the chapter closes with his pathetic and remorseful recollection of how he once struck his daughter, having mistaken behavior caused by her deafness for disobedience. This is precisely the kind of tale featured in the sentimental literature of bourgeois society, on which the king and the duke soon rely in their charade as Peter Wilks's heirs. Using what Huck terms so much "tears and flapdoodle . . . rot and slush . . . soulbutter and hogwash" (213), the bunko artists exploit the sentimental mode to prey on the emotionally vulnerable. The king and the duke, then, represent the degeneration of that mode into conventionalized insincerities. And Huck's disapproval of the king's performance introduces the critical terms of Twain's realism. Realism is not antithetical to sentiment. Huck, after all, is as swayed by Jim's sentimental tale and the plight of the Wilks family as the community is by the king's bathetic eulogy. But an important distinction lies between genuine sentimentality and hackneyed sentimentalism.[22] This development in Huck's sensibility is crucial because it prepares him to challenge Tom Sawyer's devotion to empty romanticisms and his lack of concern for the true pathos of Jim's incarceration in the final and controversial stage of the novel.

Similar readings of many of these episodes have been rendered before by one critic or another.[23] But to my knowledge, the claim that the allusive progress of the journey represents the trajectory of cultural history has not previously been made. Nor has an interpretation emerged that accounts for the influence of culture on the text's emphatically countercultural protagonist or on his escape, and about what that might mean for the novel and for Twain's career. I suggest that Huck's reenactment of cultural history dramatizes Twain's view of the formation of the American ethos in a manner that was becoming popular in the late nineteenth century. Frederick Jackson Turner's "frontier" thesis about the renewal of American culture in successive stages of westward expansion is widely known, but Turner's thesis is itself an extension of the primitivism in the cultural theory of recapitulation that, as T. J. Jackson Lears has shown, was popularized by the educational psychologist G. Stanley Hall, among others. "Drawing on the dubious biological theories spawned by German romanticism, Hall restated the common analogy between the child and the race in an influential formula: ontogeny recapitulates phylogeny."[24] The cultural stages that Huck's journey represents bring this theory into the structure of the narrative and dramatizes how the American subject is constructed within culture. In other words, since *Huckleberry Finn* is about how the story of the American self is told, the journey shows how, as Stephen Greenblatt has quipped in another context, "ontology recapitulates philology" in the American novel.[25] And here the History Game comes into play.

Twain's enthusiasm for the History Game sprang from a desire for capital gain and a personal fascination with historical influence. But he also harbored an educational concern for inculcating historical awareness in American youth, the kind of awareness that Huck lacks. In the "Remarks" he included to justify the game, Twain complained, "Many public-school children seem to know only two dates – 1492 and 4th of July; and as a rule they don't know what happened on either occasion. It is because they have not had the chance to play this game," suggesting the grand role that he envisioned for his invention.[26] Yet the game does more than facilitate rote knowledge of American history. After converting his original idea to an indoor version, Twain settled on a design for the game board that would allow players to employ their knowledge of history synchronically, as the rules suggest:

1. The board represents *any* century.
2. Also, it represents *all* centuries.
You may choose a particular century and confine your game to one nation's history for that period;
Or you may include the *contemporaneous* history of all nations.
If you choose, you can throw your game open to all history and all centuries.
When you pin your fact in its year-column, *name the century*.

Of the 100 boxes on the game's cribbage-style board, a given box, say "42," can represent 1542, the year in which De Soto first glimpsed the Mississippi River and in which Mary Queen of Scots was born; 1642, the beginning of the English Civil Wars; 1742, the end of the Great Awakening in the American colonies; and 1842, when the Webster–Ashburton Treaty established the northeastern border of the United States and when Dickens published *American Notes*. The variety of ways Twain imagines the game may be played suggests that he conceived of history not simply as a linear development but also as multiple strata that overlie each other in a synchronic representation on the game board. The game, then, is a corollary to Huck's reenactment of Western civilization in the course of his journey.

Twain assumes that, like Huck, the History Game's players have large stores of historical facts over which they have very little control; indeed, if Huck is representative of the game's players, history has control over them. Playing the game will bring these facts to the light of consciousness, where the subject can then exercise control over them. Twain remarks,

> This is a game of *suggestion*. Whenever either player pins a fact it will be pretty sure to suggest one to the adversary. The accidental mention of Waterloo will turn loose an inundation of French history. The mention of any very conspicuous event in the history of any nation will bring before the vision of the adversaries the minor features of the historical landscape that stretches away from it.

The closing visual image of an historical landscape suggests Twain's interest in travel narratives, which contributed much to his interest in history.[27] He implies that a spatialized historical perspective, which the History Game was designed to promote, will enable one to *master* history and no longer be a *slave* to it. Thus, knowledge of history is a prerequisite if an individual – the kind that Huck is often supposed to be – is to achieve emancipation from the restraint that history imposes. Indeed, Huck's inescapable problem is not Tom's domineering power over him or his lack of critical insight into social structures such as the slavery system but, rather, his failure to know the history that has produced the culture within which his own identity is constructed.

Yet despite Twain's claim that his "Memory Builder" will put the skillful and attentive player in control, the language of this passage suggests that Twain himself is in its control. For example, in the clause "Waterloo will turn loose an inundation," the name of Napoleon's last battle generates repetitions of sound – in the last syllable, "loo," and the word "loose" – and of imagery – in the first two syllables "Water" and the word "inundation" – that demonstrate the associative control that words have over Twain. Moreover, the memory built according to such lexical suggestions does not necessarily lead to mastery; rather, as in the case of Mr. Brown in "Old Times," a pilot with a memory so capacious as to have become a liability, such a memory makes one a slave to the flood of facts that gush forth at the slightest cue, not to mention the misery it inflicts on the audience of the tedious, protracted, sorriest excuse for a story that such a memory generates. Yet even if we assume that one might use the Memory Builder successfully, and thus escape Mr. Brown's susceptibility to suggestion, we still might ask, Will the player's control mean anything beyond the game itself? Judging by Twain's own "Remarks," the game seems more like a one-way system for building one's memory, with no purpose other than to succeed at playing the History Game:

> In the ordinary ways, dates are troublesome things to retain. By this game they are easy to acquire (from your adversary), and they stick fast in your head if you take the trouble to *use them a few times in playing the game.*
>
> Play all the dates you are sure of, and take sharp note of those which the adversary plays – *for use next time.*
>
> In your daily reading seize valuable dates *for use in the game at night.* (Emphasis added.)

We might ask a similar question about *Huckleberry Finn*: Is there a purpose outside of the text's own game? To which the novel's prefatory "NOTICE" suggests an answer: "Persons attempting to find a motive in this narrative will be prosecuted; persons attempting to find a moral in it will be banished; persons attempting to find a plot in it will be shot." These warnings read like the rules of a board game and underscore the fictionality of the novel, even before it begins.[28] By extension, the American ideals of self-determination and autonomy that the course of Huck's narrative seeks to recover are perhaps fictions as well, especially in light of the coercive institutions, such as the paternal authority of the family and the patriarchal authority of slavery, that motivate the narrative.

This bodes ill for Twain's own authority. Because the action of the novel is a fiction, because it takes place in an imagined – and, therefore, when compared to the actual, an ineffectual – space, the authority of novelistic discourse is at best compromised, at worst nullified. This is the double-cross of novelistic discourse: its promise of authority, of power to remake the world, is undercut by the fact that institutions, ideologies, and historical realities may not – and very likely will not – respond to challenges made in fiction. The text of *Huckleberry Finn* indicates that Twain was awakening to this double-cross. Not only was his novel inadequate compensation for his own absence from the Civil War, but he was becoming increasingly aware that an entire history of racial injustice could never be fully redressed by real actions, let alone by fictional ones. This is the reason, or, rather, one of two reasons, why Huck ends up where he begins. On the one hand, Huck's return underscores the fact that cultural determinism is inescapable, and, on the other hand, just as Huck has tried to escape and even plans a second escape to the territory, Twain tried to cross up the double-cross of novelistic discourse by also representing the movement of Huck's journey as a chiasmus, in order to ironize the linear thrust of history that diminishes the authority of the individual.[29]

Although the raft adrift in the river's current is analogous to the individual's course in history, Twain simultaneously resists the concept of historical determinism by ironically reflecting the first half of the narrative back against itself in the second, just as in *Life on the Mississippi*. In so doing, he adopts the trope that Henry Louis Gates identifies as Frederick Douglass's "major contribution to the slave narrative . . . in which a slave-object writes himself or herself into a human-subject through the act of writing." That is, in Douglass's pivotal, self-defining, declaration, "You have seen how a man was made a slave; you will see how a slave became a man," he escapes the objectifying determinism of historical oppression. Twain, too, deploys the chiasmus as a negational structure to contradict the determining force of the linear structure in the journey and to imply Huck's identification with his self-emancipated companion. But the difference between the slave narrative and the novel is significant. For if, as Thomas Mermall argues, the chiasmus is "an incipient but unconsummated form of dialectical argumentation" that "arrests progressive movement toward the resolution of the contradictions it generates," it rhetorically imitates the novel's own incipient but unconsummated form of expression. The slave narrative's deployment of the trope performatively affirms the subjectivity already achieved *in life*. The novel, on the other hand, represents the desire to begin again *in fiction*. The logical force of this trope in the novel is a purely literary resistance to the historical determinism that threatens to expose the genre's impotence.[30]

Mapping the novel's chiasmus will help us to analyze the underlying ambivalence, the double-cross, of novelistic discourse that Twain confronts in *Huckleberry Finn*. If we align the ironic reflections in the text, we'll notice that the narrative divides roughly in half at the resurrection of the raft, and similarities between episodes on either side of this division begin to emerge.[31] The king and the duke, for example, parodically personify the booty of romantic literature that Huck and Jim acquire from the wrecked steamboat *Walter Scott*. The Grangerford–Shepherdson feud's gentlemanly warfare degenerates into the chaotic cowardice of mob psychology in the Boggs–Sherburn duel. Huck's skillful manipulation of the bounty hunters' imaginations, by which they come to believe that his "father" has smallpox aboard the raft, finds its ironic echo in the duke's plan to disguise Jim as a "Sick A-rab" (203). Huck's absurd attempt to pass himself off as Charles William Allbright, about whom he has just heard a tall tale when discovered aboard the timber raft, is mirrored in the king and duke's attempt to pass themselves off as the brothers and heirs of Peter Wilks, after pumping an unsuspecting yokel for information to support their claim on the estate. And finally, perhaps the most striking example is the symmetry between Huck's initial escape and the Phelps farm sequence. Huck's wish that "Tom Sawyer was there" to "throw in the fancy touches" on his escape from Pap's cabin is ironic, first, because Huck has just recently become disillusioned with Tom's singular ability to "spread himself . . . in such a thing as that" (41). Second, and more importantly, Huck's remark typifies a larger structural irony by foreshadowing his frustration with Tom's stylish plan to free Jim from his similar prison at the story's end.

The chiasmus that these reversals construct attempts to defer the inevitability of historical determinism by maintaining possibilities and is thus related to the Christian redemption foreshadowed in the biblical typology Huck imitates at the outset of his journey. In this way, Huck and Jim's slipping past the fog-shrouded town of Cairo, Illinois, has more than geographical significance. For Cairo fortuitously marks the kairological moment in the narrative, the moment of crisis after which all that came before is ironically replayed by the chiasmic repetition.

The final effect of the chiasmus in *Huckleberry Finn* is not, however, a redemptive typology. Rather, the attempt to still the momentum of historical determinism ultimately reveals the novel's hollow center. Perhaps this emptiness is why Huck is a virtual absence in the central episodes. But even on the outer edges of the narrative, where Huck is most active, the hollowness is still audible. It echoes most loudly in Huck's meeting with Judith Loftus and his meeting with Tom at the Phelps farm. In the earlier scene, when Judith Loftus tells Huck that the community has assumed that Jim has murdered him, he begins to blurt out a defense of his companion but holds his tongue: " 'Why *he* – ' I stopped. I reckoned I better keep still. She run on, and never noticed I put in at all" (69). Later, when Huck admits he plans to steal his companion out of captivity, Tom similarly checks his near revelation that Jim has in fact been free ever since his manumission was declared in Miss Watson's will two months before.

> "What! Why Jim is – "
> He stopped, and went to studying. I says:
> "*I* know what you'll say. You'll say it's a dirty low-down business; but what if it is? I'm low-down; and I'm agoing to steal him, and I want you to keep mum and not let on. Will you?" (284)

I call attention to these self-censored speeches because their symmetry belies the apparent similarity between the speakers: Huck checks his speech so that Jim will remain free, whereas Tom cuts his revelation short to keep Jim a slave to his theatrical desire. This distinction is deeply embedded in the antithetical meanings that Twain plays out in the verb "to let on": for Huck, it means to reveal the truth, but for Tom, it means to pretend, to conceal the truth in a fiction. The effect of these antithetical meanings is a semantic chiasmus. Huck's request that Tom "keep mum and not let on," as Huck construes it, is tautologous – "to keep mum" is to "not let on" – whereas for Tom the two are anything but synonymous. Tom can "keep mum" about Huck's plan, but to do so requires that he "let on" that Jim is not already free. So although Tom will "not let on" by keeping Huck's secret, he cannot resist the impulse to "let on" that he is freeing Jim.

Until Huck absorbs Tom's meaning of "let on" while they plan the "evasion," he has consistently used the expression to mean "to reveal," except in one instance. The single exception occurs at the moment of his crisis of conscience. Repulsed by his violation of the law, Huck is on the verge of a conversion experience. But when he attempts to pray for forgiveness and the strength to reform, he comes up short. And he realizes,

> It was because my heart warn't right; it was because I warn't square; it was because I was playing double. I was letting *on* to give up sin, but away inside of me I was holding on to the biggest one of all. I was trying to make my mouth *say* I would do the right thing and the clean thing, and go and write to that nigger's owner and tell where he was; but deep down in me I knowed it was a lie – I found that out. (269)

Realizing that he could never go back on Jim, Huck affirms that he will "take up wickedness again," because he was "brung up to it" (271). Ironically, all the soul-searching and self-abasement preceding this resolve indicate exactly how he was "brung up." His self-damning is a liberation from "letting on" to give up "sin" by endorsing the values of his culture. And only after having dedicated himself to Jim's freedom can he really "let on" – admit – that he had been "letting on" – pretending – that he could have denied Jim's humanity.[32] Of course, this moment of freedom from corrupt social morality occurs when Huck is isolated. Such autonomy is an ideal that cannot endure in a social setting, because society has another agenda.

In this light, and in light of the fact that Twain's novel was published in 1885 – which is to say that it was both *preempted* by the Emancipation and the Civil War and *compromised* by the kind of reenslavement enacted during Reconstruction that Tom's charade imitates, Twain's novelistic authority appears to be doubly double-crossed, as we might have expected. After all is said and done, it is not the chiasmic structure that ironizes the historical determinism of Huck's linear journey, but history itself that ironizes the novelistic impulse to begin again. In effect, *Huckleberry Finn* "lets on" – reveals – that its mode of challenging reality amounts to nothing more than "letting on" – pretending. The failure that this represents is not a sign of Twain's artistic shortcoming but of the insight he gained in pursuing a promise that was destined to fail. I am not suggesting that Twain was irrevocably enlightened by this discovery. His reliance on the structural chiasmus suggests that at some level he sought a way out of the dilemma, even if by way of a carnival huckster's trick mirror. Furthermore, the fact that he went on to write *A Connecticut Yankee in King Arthur's Court*, which radically manipulates the authority of history, suggests that either Twain failed to recognize fully the failure of the novel or he refused to give in to that failure without a fight.

3

REINVENTING AND CIRCUMVENTING HISTORY

THE PRINCE AND THE PAUPER
AND
A CONNECTICUT YANKEE IN KING ARTHUR'S COURT

———

[I]n ... the common analogy which likens the life power of
a nation to that of an individual ... lurks the recognition of
an obvious truth – the truth that the obstacles which finally
bring progress to a halt are raised by the course of progress;
that what has destroyed all previous civilizations has been the
conditions produced by the growth of civilization.

— Henry George, *Progress and Poverty*

In his work on the History Game and *Adventures of Huckleberry Finn,*
Twain was not simply awakening to history but exploring a long-held
fascination. In an interview in December of 1885, Jane Clemens
recalled that her son "was always a great boy for *history,* and would
never get tired of that kind of reading."[1] Exactly four years before
her interview and the publication of *Huckleberry Finn, The Prince and
the Pauper* had already publicized Twain's fascination with history.
Four years after Jane Clemens's recollection, *A Connecticut Yankee in
King Arthur's Court* would carry that fascination in a radical direction.
Taken together, the two texts reflect in their divergent conceptions
of history Twain's changing outlook. *The Prince and the Pauper,* produced as a respite from the frustrations of *Huckleberry Finn,* accepts
historical tradition as the model for America's cultural destiny,
thereby exhibiting the first inklings of the historical conditioning
allegorized in Twain's most highly acclaimed text. *A Connecticut Yankee,* conversely, reacts aggressively to the ways in which history and
historiography circumscribe the freedom that propelled both the
novelistic conception of America and the genre Twain explored as
a writer.

Clarence Stedman was perhaps the first to notice the linkage between *The Prince and the Pauper* and *A Connecticut Yankee*, observing in an 1887 letter to Twain that his latest manuscript "is an extension of the text called 'The Prince and the Pauper' – and perhaps 'twould not have been written, or not written as well, but for that pioneer . . . the little book was checkers: this is chess."[2] This linkage was not news to Twain. In a canceled preface to *A Connecticut Yankee*, he iterated the line of argument that he had adopted from J. Hammond Trumbull's *True-Blue Laws of Connecticut and New Haven* as the premise of *The Prince and the Pauper*, indicating the close alliance he intended between the two texts. But how the one is "checkers," the other "chess," needs fuller explanation. Although Stedman didn't define the difference, the two texts exemplify the differential definitions of romance and novel that inform my reading of Twain's career. Like *The Adventures of Tom Sawyer* and "Old Times on the Mississippi," *The Prince and the Pauper* begins subversively but recoils to a conservatism that accommodates traditional authority. In technique, structure, and historical outlook, *A Connecticut Yankee* amounts to a radical novelization of history that has no patience with the romance compromise of *The Prince and the Pauper*. Twain deployed a radical strategy, both to overcome his own accommodation of history in the text that slipped from a critical fiction into a monumental romance and, more generally, to expose the ideological blind spots that he thought distorted historiographical practice. Consequently, the novelistic premise of *A Connecticut Yankee* becomes a test of the genre's critique of the authority of history. Yet the results of this test expose not only the weaknesses of historiography but also the limits of the novel. Thus, the opposition between the naive optimism of *The Prince and the Pauper* and the jaded pessimism of *A Connecticut Yankee* generates the terms of the next dialectical stage of Twain's novelistic career.

The antithetical positions of this stage represent Twain's shift toward a critical understanding of history, of cultural assumptions about tradition and progress. This dialectical interpretation revises the conventional view that Twain's interest in history is a steadfast reflection of his reading in Hume, Macaulay, Lecky, and Taine, who postulated that history was a continuous march of progress.[3] Doubtless, these Whig historians influenced Twain. But as reflected in the shift in his two historical narratives, as well as in "1601," "A Private

History of a Campaign That Failed," and *The Secret History of Eddypus*, his developing conceptions of history suggest a more complex understanding of historiographical problems and a more antagonistic stance toward history than the critical assertion of Twain's fidelity to acknowledged influences implies. Overall, the transition in historical perspective from *The Prince and the Pauper* to *A Connecticut Yankee* signals the erosion of Twain's confidence in Whig historiography. Although this shift in Twain's attitude occurred largely in *A Connecticut Yankee*, even *The Prince and the Pauper* equivocates on the reliability of historiography, generally.

The bifurcated critical reception of *The Prince and the Pauper* reflects Twain's divided intention, between the "democratic thesis," which invalidates the monarchical tradition of genealogical legitimacy, and the "nostalgia thesis," which looks back fondly on the legendary nobility and pageantry of an earlier historical era. The critical disagreement is noteworthy for the mutual blindness of both sides to the text's equivocation on these two rhetorical positions. Taking stock of the text's staging of this antithesis, I contextualize these opposite narrative inclinations in light of their connection to what T. J. Jackson Lears has called "the crisis of cultural authority" in late-nineteenth-century America. The antimodernism that symptomatized this crisis, in Lears's view, stemmed from a concern for the growing disparity between the prosperous and the poor. Anxiety about modern conditions propelled an esthetic fascination with medievalism in retreat from what was viewed as a modern assault on individuality.[4]

The narrative tensions in Twain's literary representation of this cultural anxiety, and the ambiguities they lend to interpretations of Twain's intention, open up to a deconstructive analysis of two awkward stances in the text. First, *The Prince and the Pauper* is a text generated by Twain's reading, but the narrative rhetorically discredits reading and invests greater value in lived experience. The conflict between textual and actual experience in *The Prince and the Pauper* introduces an important issue in Twain's evolving professional identity. Anticipating the authority he would soon associate with a writerly identity in *Life on the Mississippi*, Twain frames the conflict between reading and experience in *The Prince and the Pauper* in order to foreground his professional activity as participating directly in a textual universe whose boundaries and topographical descriptions are subject to challenge.

Second, the tale is a fiction. Culturally, and even within the text itself, this mode of storytelling ranks below historiography as a standard of truth. In the competition between these two modes, Michel de Certeau argues, historiography

> establishes a certain distance between itself and common assertion and belief; it locates itself in this difference, which gives it the accreditation of erudition because it separates itself from ordinary discourse . . . The technical discourse [historiography] capable of determining the errors characteristic of fiction has come to be authorized to speak in the name of the "real." By distinguishing between two discourses – the one scientific, the other fictive – according to its own criteria, historiography credits itself with having a special relationship to the "real" because its contrary is posited as "false."[5]

Only two years after *The Prince and the Pauper*, Twain would make a similar claim against fiction in *Life on the Mississippi*, arguing that romance spread the "Sir Walter disease" throughout the South, corrupting cultural consciousness.

But not all fiction was created equal. As *Life on the Mississippi* reveals, Twain came to regard novelistic fiction as a means of overcoming the "dead facts" of history. The difference between the romance and the novel lay in the critical attitude that inheres in the latter. In *Huckleberry Finn*, though, he confronted the inadequacy of novelistic discourse to break free from historical conditioning. This text was the catalyst for Twain's realization that the authority of history dilutes, if not entirely dissolves, the imaginative opportunities of the novelist's alternate fictional world. Twain's desire to rescue the novel's critical potential gave rise to *A Connecticut Yankee*. This highly imaginative narrative met history head on and licensed him to dispense with the plot constraints of historical fiction. *A Connecticut Yankee*'s challenge to history is specifically American and radically novelistic, attempting to eliminate history by remaking the past according to the American blueprint of republicanism and industrial capitalism. Finally, though, *A Connecticut Yankee* is consumed with power. By recycling authoritarian oppression, the tale nullifies confidence that modern advancements can ameliorate the human condition and casts a cynical shadow over the regenerative powers of novelistic discourse both in literature and in American ideology.

Twain's two historical narratives reveal that his historical consciousness was more complex, and more ideologically conditioned, than the "Trivial Pursuit" mentality he projected in his parlor-game version of memory building. Even in *The Prince and the Pauper*, Twain's historical inventiveness shows his imaginative boldness. But more importantly, the two narratives together delineate the problem that history poses for a culture that defines itself in a paradoxical relation to history. America is both a break from history, a discontinuity of social and political traditions, and the culmination of Western culture, the fulfillment of the Enlightenment's latent promise. This paradox nagged at America's cultural consciousness, raising doubts about the promise that a 250-year-old rhetorical tradition had constructed. Despite assertions about America's role in realizing the Enlightenment enterprise, American writers had long grappled with their uneasiness about their nation's shallow history even as they emphasized the value of breaking from history. The often-cited obstacle to establishing a truly American art was thought to be the newness of its culture, the very feature that validated its revolutionary status. Twain's experiments in historical fiction highlight this paradox as a cultural precondition for the double-cross of the American novel.

The Principles of Democracy and the Popularity of Antiquarianism: A Tale of Two Readings

To offer more than a passing comment on *The Prince and the Pauper* may seem somewhat unusual, for this text is perhaps the most neglected of Twain's major works. When critics have noticed it at all, they've given it short shrift. Disapproving critics have faulted it as a nostalgic indulgence lacking the immediacy and edge of Twain's American narratives. Much has been made of a critique by Joe Goodman, one of Twain's friends from Virginia City, who, suggesting that Twain had misfired, questioned why he had set his tale in sixteenth-century England "when he could have been so much more at home in the wash of today." Often this "nostalgia thesis" is linked to Twain's desire for genteel recognition. Justin Kaplan characterizes the text as "an act of culture," an attempt to "cater to the fashionable taste for monarchical England . . . [Twain] was determined that the book would exhibit him not as a humorist . . . , but as a serious practitioner of polite, colorful literature . . . He was determined to give genteel culture exactly what it wanted." Reading the text as part of Twain's calculated strategy of legitimation is warranted. The text shows the influence of his having read Charlotte Yonge's successful *The Little Duke* and *The Prince and the Page*, and Twain intimated his desire for affiliation with such genteel writers as Yonge and Frances Hodgson Burnett, as well as Whittier, Emerson, Holmes, and Longfellow, by sending them inscribed copies of his book. Though the book was not a commercial success, the kind of admiring audience it attracted, among whom were the author's wife and daughters, has been cited as justification of critical disapproval. The genteel influence that Olivia Clemens exerted on her husband is part of the legend that Twain himself helped promote. Since most critics concur that Twain's literary strength lay with his vernacular aesthetic, Olivia Clemens's approval of *The Prince and the Pauper* has been reason enough for some to dismiss it as a capitulation to genteel society's esthetic fascination with Britain.[6]

However, what has often been passed over as a sign of Twain's failure also registers an ideological dilemma that Twain shared with the genre he practiced and the culture in which both writer and genre were immersed. For example, although the tale is not literally set in "the wash of today," it nonetheless addresses contemporary concerns. Pauperism was a much-studied social condition and the topic of many sermons of the day. To be sure, reformers had spoken out against poverty, especially the plight of poor children, for some time. Hannah Foster's *The Coquette* and Susannah Rowson's *Charlotte Temple* represent poverty as one of the miseries endured by their fallen heroines in the early national period. These texts inferred an association between poverty and moral decline. When the poor were fewer in number, the cultural assumption that they were makers of their own destiny had currency. But when economic depression struck in the nineteenth century, the effects were broad enough to have made it harder to blame such large numbers of people for their condition. Joseph Tuckerman's *On the Elevation of the Poor* (1840) helped convert poverty relief to a noble cause. In the wake of the Panic of 1873, poverty emerged as the leading reform issue, taking the place of antebellum abolitionism, as indicated in a letter from Thomas K. Beecher to Twain's close friend Joseph Twichell:

> Whatever you and I have felt in days bygone as the sacred fugitives from slavery came shivering to us by night showing cracked pit scars, and in rags, until we could endure *slavery* no longer – the same I feel daily and hourly as the unending procession of my neighbors files by me – anxious, heartbroken or worse, with eyes of hate and envy. They know themselves the bleeding grist of our great financial mill.

By the late 1870s, the young field of sociology staked its scientific interest in the link between pauperism and crime in noted studies like Robert Dugdale's *The Jukes*. The *Atlantic Monthly*'s "Contributors' Club," a regular feature of unsigned short pieces, included two items during the period when Twain was writing *A Tramp Abroad* and *The Prince and the Pauper* that urged esthetic appreciation for the picturesqueness of "tramps" and indignation at the unfairness of the current vagrancy laws and the institution of workhouses. As good Republicans, Twain's Hartford neighbors were deeply committed to compassionate work for the poor.[7]

Among all of the discourse on pauperism, Henry George's treatise on political economy, *Progress and Poverty* (1880), is particularly noteworthy because his analysis of the paradoxical rise of pauperism in an era of growing prosperity shares philosophical resonances and specific historical examples with Twain's text. George's critique of American political economy is committed to the advancement of civilization, and he rejects the "noble savage" doctrine of those who urge the simplicity of rural life. But George also admits that a member of "the lowest classes in such a highly civilized country as Great Britain . . . would make infinitely the better choice in selecting the lot of the savage. For those classes who in the midst of wealth are condemned to want suffer all the privations of the savage, without his sense of personal freedom." After comparing the contemporary conditions of poverty in New York and London, George traces the problem to an historical cause, "the monopolization of land during the reign of Henry VIII," and then reinforces the linkage between the conditions in Tudor England and the contemporary American scene: "[T]hat there was a reduction in common wages, and great distress among the laboring classes, is evident from the complaints of 'sturdy vagrants' and the statutes made to suppress them. The rapid monopolization of the land, the carrying of the speculative rent line beyond the normal rent line, produced tramps and paupers, just as the like effects from like causes have lately been evident in the United States." I'm not suggesting that George's comparative analysis was a source for Twain's decision to focus his tale on the plights of Tom Canty and Edward VI; Twain's notebook shows that he had settled on the exchange between "Edward VI & a little pauper" as early as 1877. But the likenesses between George's economic analysis and Twain's narrative representation suggest the cultural influence that inhabits both texts.[8] Within ten years, concern for social conditions would lead to the groundswell of literary attention to urban squalor as represented by Crane's *Maggie*, Riis's *How the Other Half Lives* and *The Children of the Poor*, and James's *The American Scene*.

Twain's indirect mode of representing contemporary social conditions in the mirror of sixteenth-century English society surely softened the impact of the implied critique. But the historical displacement is an important feature because, as Lears has shown, the American esthetic fixation on Anglo-Saxon ancestral legends was prompted by cultural anxiety about American social instability in this period, which bred a nostalgic desire to recover some sense of heritage missing from the young culture.[9] Here again, George's work is illuminating. In one of his closing chapters, "The Current Theory of Human Progress – Its Insufficiency," he observes a cultural dilemma very similar to the crisis that Lears describes. For George, the crux of the dilemma stems from the contradiction between the cultural belief in civilization's evolutionary improvement and the "fact" that "the majority of the human race to-day have no idea of progress; the majority of the human race to-day look . . . upon the past as the time of human perfection."[10] *The Prince and the Pauper* embodies the very phenomenon that George laments, exhibiting a nostalgic acquiescence awkwardly fused to a belief in Enlightenment progressivism. So, despite failing to satisfy the frontier tastes of John Goodman, the tale does speak to its contemporary audience's anxiety about history.

Judging from the narrative development of *The Prince and the Pauper*, Twain was anxious about "cater[ing] to the fashionable taste," as Kaplan suggests. For although he was clearly attempting to break from his relatively low status as a humorist and to secure a place for himself within polite literary circles with this tale, the text also hints at his misgivings about ingratiating himself with the elite, as exhibited in his inconsistent imitation of the diction and syntax of English in the Tudor period. This narrative charade has been a source of either admiration for genteel readers (Susie Clemens admired the language of the text as "perfect") or irritation for those who prefer Twain's vernacular style. But within this antiquarian performance occur anachronistic lapses into mining and riverboat metaphors. Surprisingly, critics of either stripe have not really explained these interferences with the narrative tone. Some have spotted these momentary intrusions, but usually, like Everett Emerson, only to comment on how they "reveal the writer's background." Sloane goes a bit farther, recognizing that these breaks in consistency connote "the American milieu through anachronism . . . to generate a democratic atmosphere against which he can raise an aristocratic world in opposition." But a fuller interpretation of these tonal disruptions requires that we read them in the context of the action they represent.[11]

The richest concentration of this alternative discourse occurs in chapter 6, when the court refuses to believe Tom's insistence that he is not the prince. Faced with the court's insistence that he *is*, Tom adopts the courtly style that he has learned to imitate from reading romantic adventure fiction. Significantly, Tom's role playing parallels Twain's own courtly narration in a similar charade to the one foisted upon Tom. And Twain calls our attention to his role playing by momentarily dropping the courtly mask and speaking in the voice and diction that in *Roughing It* and "Old Times on the Mississippi" helped publicize his frontier identity. By undermining his carefully constructed faux-Tudor dialect at precisely the moment when Tom insists on his true humble identity, only to be overruled and coerced by the force of law to assume the fictional royal status, Twain registers his own conflict between disparate narrative identities. Just as Tom fantasized a life of grandeur in reaction to his squalid existence, so too was Twain dissatisfied with his status among the literary peasantry of humorists; he longed, instead, for the power and prestige of legitimate authorship. That Twain deploys anachronistic metaphors in a tale ostensibly calculated to secure his legitimacy suggests his reluctance to leave the comfortable familiarity of the vernacular humorist for the demanding restrictions of a higher literary station. In other words, the disruptions in the narrative discourse reveal Twain's ambivalence about pandering to genteel taste, much as did the jest in his Whittier Birthday Dinner speech.[12] On the one hand, he desired the approval of the cultural establishment, but, on the other hand, he could not conform to the pressure of cultural authority without inflecting the tale with a touch of irreverence. His equivocation about assuming an authoritative role beyond that of vernacular humorist contributes psychological motivation for the divided structure, form, and theme of the text. In effect, Twain's authorial conflict makes *The Prince and the Pauper* not only a mistaken-identity tale but also a mistaken-identity text, split like a masquerader's identity between an ostensible persona outwardly projected by costume and an actual identity that lies half hidden behind it.

Of course, not all critics have complained that the text is entirely counterpoised to Twain's characteristic output. Walter Blair has cataloged many similarities between *The Adventures of Tom Sawyer, The Prince and the Pauper, Life on the Mississippi,* and *Adventures of Huckleberry Finn,* observing most notably that "Tom Canty is an amalgam of the characteristics of Huck Finn and Tom Sawyer" and that Prince Edward's travels with Hendon are a sixteenth-century version of Huck's picaresque excursion with Jim.[13] Indeed, *The Prince and the Pauper* binds together the attitudes toward authority held by Twain's more famous youthful protagonists as its own double premise. So instead of dismissing it for not stacking up to those other more notable books, we might more profitably view it as an interim project within the constellation of Twain's work that helped spur Twain's concern with history and historiography. When he resumed *Huckleberry Finn,* and later when he tried to confront the influence of history in *A Connecticut Yankee,* he would hone his concern with history writing to a critical edge. Since Twain composed *The Prince and the Pauper* in the middle of the frustrating yet productive period from 1874 to 1885, within the tangle of texts that yielded his two most successful books, we would have more reason to be surprised if *The Prince and the Pauper* shared nothing at all with them. Like *Life on the Mississippi,* also written during the period of *Huckleberry Finn*'s sporadic composition, *The Prince and the Pauper* was not only a diversion from compositional frustrations but also a bridge between *Tom Saw-*

yer and *Huckleberry Finn.* The intertextual correspondences between the Mississippi book and the two "boy books" carry over to Twain's historical fiction of displaced class identities as well. But intertextual correspondences between the more famous American boy books and Twain's English historical fiction seem to have swayed some critics to applaud what they see as *The Prince and the Pauper*'s "democratic thesis" without acknowledging its unsettling antithesis of progressivism and antiquarianism. According to Lears, the text's evasiveness was typical of the antimodernism of the day. Antimodernists promoted antiquarianism for the ethical purpose of renewing America's stalwart character, the kind of character that had fueled American republicanism in its heyday and, some hoped, could be inspired again. Since the early 1870s, a cult of the innocent child had sprung up around the literature of Louisa May Alcott, Thomas Bailey Aldrich, Horatio Alger, Jr., Frances Hodgson Burnett, Martha Finley, and Charlotte Yonge.[14] *The Adventures of Tom Sawyer* stands within this cultural trend honoring mischievous youths as potentially spunky citizens, as Judge Thatcher's prediction of Tom's prospects as a Senator indicates. In the postbellum era, the cult of youthful innocence lent itself to a cultural transformation that would honor the Middle Ages. Elizabeth Robin, writing in the *Atlantic Monthly*, extolled the virtue in the medieval propensity for "wanton playfulness – mischief for the sake of mischief."[15] Medieval societies were represented as embodying youthful vitality, and it was hoped that a salutary diet of medieval legends like Malory's *Morte D'Arthur* would reinvigorate America's youth. Accordingly, supporters of Twain's historical tale praised it as an important contribution to this ethical campaign. Howells declared it "a manual of republicanism which might fitly be introduced in the schools. It breathes throughout the spirit of humanity and the reason of democracy." The banner was carried in the twentieth century by John Macy, who praised the tale as "a democratic parable." And James M. Cox sees *The Prince and the Pauper* in complete conformity with the view of Twain as a democratic champion and interprets the tale of adventures of the two youthful social opposites in alien territories as a "democratic fable."[16]

To be sure, Tom's portion of the story, especially his early immersion in courtly life, supports the democratic thesis. For amidst the period details, these early episodes launch a critique of hereditary legitimacy. Consider, for example, the scene in which Henry VIII and his court officers refuse to believe Tom's admission that he is not the prince. They attribute his denial of royal identity to amnesia, a loss of self-knowledge – in their view, a form of insanity. This official dismissal of Tom's disclaimer ironically underscores the fact that it is the court's reason, not Tom's, that has become dislodged by blind devotion to the principle of legitimacy. The lawful speech of Henry VIII himself emphasizes the flawed logic of adhering to the legitimacy of blood rather than ability: "He is mad, but he is my son and England's heir – and mad or sane, still shall he reign!" (P&P, 36). The irony is twofold: the requirement that the king's heir will ascend the throne flatly ignores the question of whether or not he is equipped to govern, and the court's insistence on Tom's nobility exposes the fallacy of the legitimacy principle upon which monarchy rests. The authority of the court is exposed as a complex protocol of ceremonies, a system of pageantry so arbitrary as to misread appearance for substance. When Tom is clothed in the appropriate royal raiments, he *is* the authority, his lack of pedigree and education notwithstanding. Henry VIII's command that Tom conceal the fact of his illegitimacy is the crowning ironic touch: the king himself mandates the usurpation of the throne, deposing his own heir. Under royal sanction, Tom rationalizes his violation and owns, in his best approximation of courtly diction, that "[n]one may palter with the king's command, or fit it to his ease, where it doth chafe, with deft evasions. The king shall be obeyed" (41); Tom Sawyer couldn't have said it better. With the king's sudden passing, Tom assumes in life the authority he only imagined in play. But he is no ordinary usurper. Assured by the court that he is the king, Tom underscores the fictional basis of legitimacy with his first purposeful expression of power. He pardons Henry VIII's sworn enemy, the Duke of Norfolk, and declares, "Then shall the king's law be law of mercy, from this day, and never more be law of blood!" (83). Although this edict makes Tom's compassionate intention explicit, the text's ironic treatment of legitimacy shadows his decree. The ambiguity of the term "blood," signifying either cruelty or heredity, also allows his declaration to emphasize the fact that his accession to the throne terminates the genealogical legitimacy of the English monarchy. The usurpation may not have been Tom's idea, but he has taken the opportunity to subvert monarchical inheritance in this performative language.

Tom's accession to the throne is the crux of the democratic thesis, dramatizing the immediate context for Twain's composition of the tale. His "General Note" at the end of the text alludes to this context by virtually dedicating the historical narrative to *The True-Blue Laws of Connecticut and New Haven and the False Blue-Laws Invented by the Rev. Samuel Peters*, written by Twain's friend and neighbor, J. Hammond Trumbull. As Trumbull's title makes plain, his treatise was a response to an 1871 indictment of the Connecticut Blue-Laws by Samuel Peters, a Briton, as evidence that "majorities are more tyrannical than a hereditary ruling class." Reissued in 1876, Peters's book prompted Trumbull's rebuttal, which Twain cites as proof that American justice is superior to that of England. Louis Budd contends that Trumbull's text was more than the historical source that critics have often considered it to be; it was the impetus for the argument of *The Prince and the Pauper*.[17] Trumbull, who had contributed the epigraphs to *The Gilded Age*, not only provided several accounts of judicial atrocity to *The Prince and the Pauper* but also inspired its critique of absolute authority and aristocratic privilege in a barbed attack on the cruel reign of Henry VIII and the corruption and depravity that his tyranny bred. In a letter to Howells in March of 1880, Twain confirms his intention to refute Peters's Tory myths about the tyranny of democratic majorities when he described the rationale for his tale of displaced class affinities: "My idea is to afford a realizing sense of the exceeding severity of the laws of that day by inflicting some of their penalties upon the king himself & allowing him a chance to see the rest of them applied to others – all of which is to account for certain mildnesses which distinguished Edward VI's reign from those that preceded & followed it" (*MTHL*, 1:292). The implied comparison between the severity of monarchy and the liberality of democracy supports the critics who favor the democratic thesis.

But Twain's stated intention of offering an explanation for Edward's mild reign shifts the proportionate balance between the democratic thesis and the nostalgia thesis in the narrative's rhetorical scheme. The growing attention to Edward's adventures thematically recuperates the legitimacy principle, which resonates more harmoniously with Twain's own quest for legitimation than did the satire of legitimacy in the episodes of Tom's accession. So, despite the egalitarian appeal of vernacular style in Tom's portion of the narrative and the critical inclination toward the preferred image of Twain as a democratic champion, the narrative turns from the democratic thesis and focuses instead on the restoration of the rightful monarch. Consequently, the resolution to which Edward's experiences lead compromises the narrative's critique of authority and acquiesces in the tradition of genealogical legitimacy.

This is a far cry from the "democratic fable" that Tom's accession to the throne initiated. But the text's failure to make good on that promise has not deterred those committed to the democratic thesis. For example, with respect to Tom's role in helping to restore Edward, Cox places undue emphasis. He argues that the "fable discloses, through the device of mistaken identity, how the 'divine right' of monarchy comes from the capacity of the commoner to *remember* the action in his remote past by means of which the king transferred the power to him." But this reading construes the boys' relationship and Edward's actions in a manner not borne out by the text. The prince has not transferred power to the pauper, and they both know it. Far from entrusting the royal seal to Tom, Edward stores it in a safe place before he leaves to reprimand the castle guard who mistreated Tom. That act signifies Edward's respect and concern for the sign of royal authority. Edward's own words make clear that he is not transferring any power to Tom. The social cross dressing that the prince recommends is to be momentary, "a brief happiness" that they will enjoy "and change again before any come to molest" (18).

The entire scene, moreover, demonstrates how firmly the boys' identities are perhaps mistakable but far from exchangeable. The narrator comments that after having exchanged clothes "there did not seem to have been any change made!" – that is, their physiognomies are so similar that judging by appearances they seem not to have swapped clothes at all. But once the boys recover their voices, we learn that the narrator's use of the verb "seem" was ambiguous. The boys *have* exchanged clothes, and we know this because they *have not* exchanged stations. When the raggedly attired prince asks the regally attired pauper what he thinks of their appearances, Tom Canty demurs, "Ah, good your worship, require me not to answer.

It is not meet that one of my degree should utter such a thing"
(18). And although the prince claims that the clothing exchange
has induced a sentimental sympathy between him and the pauper,
his imperious determination to rebuke the guard who treated Tom
harshly is decidedly not an emotional response that a pauper would
act upon, if he were to have that response at all. To the contrary,
Tom exhibits appropriately common behavior when he dismisses his
injury: "Yes, but it is a slight thing, and your worship knoweth that
the poor man-at-arms–" (18). Despite his claim to sympathy with
Tom, Edward shows how accustomed he is to power, and how disin-
clined he is to relinquish any of it. He barks an order to silence
Tom's attempt to mollify princely indignation: " 'Peace! It was a
shameful thing and cruel!' cried the little prince stamping his bare
foot. 'If the king–stir not a step till I come again. It is a command!' "
His self-interruption suggests that Edward is unaware that such cruelty is *de rigueur* under his father's notorious reign. Indeed, his own
tyrannical confidence in stressing that his word is "a command!" also hints that abusive patterns of absolute authority are a
matter of training. Later Edward shows how little sympathy his
exchange of clothes has instilled in him. During his miserable wandering, he suspects "that the pauper lad, Tom Canty, had deliberately taken advantage of his stupendous opportunity and become a
usurper . . . He also made up his mind that Tom should be allowed
a reasonable time for spiritual preparation and then be hanged,
drawn, and quartered, according to the law and usage of the day, in
cases of high treason" (75). He will have to move farther along in
his cultural education as an involuntary exchange student before he
relinquishes his illusions about governmental benevolence and justice.

Of course, Cox finds the moral of his "democratic fable" at the
other end of the narrative, but the narrative resolution resists the
democratic thesis even more than the earlier stages do. When Cox
claims that " 'divine right' of monarchy comes from the capacity of
the commoner to *remember* the action in his remote past by means of
which the king transferred power to him," he overstates the nature
of Tom's instrumentality. Insofar as Tom has any "capacity" to validate Edward's legitimate claim, he does so as both a witness to Edward's action of safeguarding the seal and a prompt to Edward's
memory, which has been clouded by all he has endured in the inter-

vening episodes. More importantly, the function of Tom's instrumental role is, after all, to prove Edward's legitimate claim. Since Twain is writing in a democratic age and in a country where the notion of divine right has had no standing for more than a century, perhaps we could read Tom's "capacity" to validate Edward's legitimacy as the consent of the governed. But this consent, even if it omits divine right, still denies democratic government by perpetuating the rule of monarchy. Such consent looks less like the definition of a republic than like Gramsci's definition of hegemony. Twain renders this domination palatable for his audience because Edward's reign is enlightened, thereby appealing to genteel values. During Edward's travails, his eyes have been opened to the effects of his father's tyranny – revealing, in his words, that "[t]he world is made wrong; kings should go to school to their own laws, at times, and so learn mercy" (238). But his worldly education does not at any point encourage him to abdicate his power and convert England's monarchy to a democratic republic. Indeed, the final effect of the narrative diegesis is to restore the authority of legitimacy with a liberal face. Edward's accession and the restoration of Miles Hendon's legitimate seat in Hendon Hall, as well as the punishment of malefactors like John Canty and Hugh Hendon, Miles's usurping brother, put the various social pieces back in order.

The conservative resolution reveals that there are two forms of irony at work in the tale: the irony discrediting genealogical authority, in the episodes about Tom's experience at court, and its flip side supporting genealogical legitimacy, in the episodes about Edward's wandering career as a pauper. For example, the Prince of Wales is held in high esteem at all levels of the society. The motley society on London Bridge and the underclass criminal band Edward encounters while captive to John Canty both express their reverence for the authority of the title. And were Edward's actual identity recognized, there is little doubt that he would be treated with royal respect. But divested of his royal attire, he lacks the sign necessary to validate his claim.

Note, however, that this cultural respect for legitimacy indirectly ensures his survival. Edward makes his first escape from Canty's abusive paternal control when a "burly waterman" (74) among the teeming community on London Bridge takes offense at Canty's rude bustling through the crowd and refuses to let him pass until he has toasted the Prince of Wales. In order for Canty to drink to the royal heir – the very boy whose identity he has roughly denied and whom he manhandles at this moment – he must loosen his grip on Edward, and the unrecognized prince slips away amid the crowd. In the very next scene, a similar respect for royal authority secures Edward's safety once again. Outside Guildhall, Edward attempts to plead his case, "proclaim[ing] his rights and his wrong, denounc[ing] the impostor, and clamor[ing] for admission at the gates of Guildhall!" (79–80), which earns him no more than the mob's taunting mockery. His ensuing anger and Miles Hendon's gallant defense of the laughingstock prince inflame the crowd to violence. But just as the tension appears to be reaching a tragic climax, the passing of the king's messenger suspends the danger. With Edward's attackers distracted by their awe of the royal emissary, the prince and his protector take advantage of the diversion to make a narrow escape. Shifting quickly to the scene within Guildhall, the narrative conveys the situational irony of Edward's most recent escape by juxtaposing the messenger's unwitting contribution to Edward's survival with the announcement of Henry VIII's untimely death. This same messenger, having just saved Edward's life from the unruly mob, now prompts the noble throng within Guildhall to shout, "Long live the king!" (81). Thus, despite its initial subscription to the "democratic thesis," the historical tale's conservative thrust exposes its rhetorical attack on institutional authority as a screen that obscures an awkward fact from Twain's supportive critics: the narrative does not sustain the critical force that the democratic thesis requires.

And yet the text is divided in ways beyond its narrative plot about two boys displaced from their opposite social stations. The ideologically incompatible and mutually insufficient interpretations of the narrative as either a nostalgic romance of aristocratic tradition or a democratic fable of sentimental liberalism arise from formal problems reflecting the conflicted view of authority that both fueled and frustrated Twain's practice throughout his career. We are mistaken, though, if we stop short of considering how his authority crisis mirrors a similar conflict between the antimodernism of the period and the sense that American social development was adrift from history. The tale's rhetorical retreat to the principle of legitimacy is more than a symptom of Twain's own desire for literary legitimacy; it is the manifestation of a need to legitimize American culture within the trajectory of history.

The Ink of Fluid Prejudice

The critical appraisals of *The Prince and the Pauper* highlight a fundamental conflict between actual experience and textual experience as sources of authority. For critics like Goodman, the text's unfortunate indulgence in nostalgia is allied with a problematic departure from Twain's typical practice of writing from experience. Goodman, Twain's former editor at the Virginia City *Territorial Enterprise*, was a supporting presence when Twain was losing confidence in *Roughing It*.[18] The editor buoyed the sagging writer, for he saw much to praise in that memoir of the Far West. No doubt the missing element from *The Prince and the Pauper* was not simply "the wash of today"; Goodman had supported Twain's retrospective efforts in *Roughing It*. Some might justifiably argue that the difference between a decade and several centuries is no small matter, but the more significant difference between the two books was their sources: the memoir flowed from Twain's actual experience, and the historical tale was based on his reading of history. On the other hand, Howells's and Cox's approval of the historical tale emphasize its status as an instructional text, as a "manual" or a "fable." As a manual, Twain's tale joins a tradition of texts stressing the proper education for a monarch, such as book 5 of Gower's *Confessio Amantis* or the encyclopedic *Mirror for Magistrates*, or even Mason Weems's *Life of Washington*. As a fable, the text conveys a moral about legitimacy and humane justice, veering from Twain's typical course not simply in its conservativism but in its moralistic preaching. And yet this emphasis on the textual traditions behind the tales's genesis and reception points to a conceptual impasse. *The Prince and the Pauper* is a story generated by reading and produced to be read, but its discourse values experience over reading as a medium of moral education. The reform of English law under Edward VI occurs, Twain suggests, because Edward receives an education based on experience, not on books.

In two scenes, reading is even devalued as a corrupting influence. Because Tom has acquired a reputation for being enthralled with fabulous stories and for fantastically identifying with noble heroes, Tom's mother concludes that "foolish reading hath wrought its woful work" (67) when Edward, dressed in her son's rags, insists that he is the Prince of Wales. Similarly, Tom's confession to the court that he is not the Prince of Wales is taken as a sign of his madness, which the king attributes to "[o]verstudy . . . and somewhat too much confinement. Away with his books and teachers – see ye to it!" (36). Reading, they assume, is a dangerous activity.

One might be tempted to interpret all of this anxiety about textual experience as the legacy of the opposition to reading novels in early America. Eighteenth-century ministers, educators, and parents feared that novel reading would corrupt young minds. They supposed that young readers would be seduced via sentimental identification and risk falling from grace, like so many romantic heroines. Thus, as Cathy Davidson points out, not only were these stories *about* seduction, but the texts themselves were also considered to *be* a kind of seduction.[19]

In *The Prince and the Pauper*, however, the two different modes of experience do not generate a direct internal contest, nor does either boy have any difficulty in distinguishing textual fiction from actual fact. Indeed, the episodes where parents fret about reading ironize their assumptions about the unsettling influence of reading; it is not the boys' reading that is at fault but their parents' misreadings of the boys' appearances as the reliable signs of their identities. If anything, Tom's reading proves to be a benefit because it enables him to play along with the fraud that the court insists he maintain, which he inwardly recognizes: "Tis not for naught I have dwelt but among princes in my reading, and taught my tongue some slight trick of their broidered and gracious speech withal!" (45). And much of his early awkwardness in dealing with court protocols is alleviated by his discovery of a book of etiquette in the royal apartment. Granted, the first time he shakes off the misery of captivity within a royal identity, he "forget[s], for the moment, that he was but the false shadow of a king, not the substance" and impulsively command that some unfortunates who have been sentenced to death be brought before him. Relishing "a glow of pride and a renewed sense of the compensating advantages of the kingly office," Tom privately notes, "Truly it is like what I used to feel when I read the old priest's tales, and did imagine mine own self a prince, giving law and command to all, saying 'do this, do that,' whilst none durst offer let or hindrance to my will" (125). But although this appears to be closing in on the seduction of the sentimental reader that had generated so much fear of novels, it comes up short. In fact, the scene overturns any anticipation of the nightmare scenario that those fears inspired. For Tom's delight in living the life heretofore available to him only in tales doesn't interfere with his sentimental sympathy for the oppressed. Indeed, the text is explicit: "His concern [for the condemned] . . . made him forget" (125–6) that he holds royal power only by a fiction. And by nullifying the verdict against the convicted defendants he dispenses with protocols and antiquated superstitions. He understands these cases because of his common experience with the accused. The notable humanity he exhibits in his administration of justice comes from the common sense he has learned in a life of hardship, not from his familiarity with tales.

Like the pauper, the true Prince of Wales is almost entirely unsuccessful in persuading anyone that he is not who he appears to be. But the reversal of fortune in Edward VI's course is asymmetrical to Tom's because the prince's courtly reading and experience have not equipped him to assume a different station in life. His difficult transition from prince to peasant points to the inadequacy of available texts: the boys' experiences diverge into low and high, but the texts available to them have focused only on the lives of the privileged. Whereas these texts have instructed Tom how he should comport himself in order to maintain his imposture, they offer Edward little direction for the role he has assumed. Only his recollection of the story of King Alfred the Great's humble service provides a model for one instance of relatively successful imposture. Like Tom's compassion, the humane nobility that Edward acquires comes from having endured and witnessed the cruelty and corruption of his father's despotism, not from anything he learned from his tutored reading in his father's court.

The tale's hierarchy valuing actual experience over textual experience squares with Twain's customary stand. His authority in "Old Times on the Mississippi" rested on his experience as a pilot on the Mississippi. Although the *Atlantic* sketches made much of how a pilot learns to read the river, what one comes to know through actual experience (the real dangers of a shoal or snag) is opposed in the memoir with what one reads or, more accurately, misreads (the false impression of a bluff reef or wind reef). Twain's reliance on reading in the composition of *The Prince and the Pauper*, though, shows that his belief in experience as a basis for authority, at least for his own authority, was eroding. Given the period of the historical tale's composition – between "Old Times" and *Life on the Mississippi*, which, as I have argued, establishes the shift to a text-based writerly authority, and on the verge of his discovery of Huck's historically informed consciousness – *The Prince and the Pauper* is a pivot on which Twain's conception of authority turned. This shift signals Twain's attraction to the potential of the novel: a kind of writing in which invention and control of a textual world seems to promise relief from being controlled in the actual world.

Twain made no secret of the importance of textual authority to his composition of *The Prince and the Pauper*; to the contrary, he flaunted it, ostentatiously citing his historical sources – David Hume's *History of England* (1854), Leigh Hunt's *The Town: Its Memorable Characters and Events* (1859), John Timbs's *Curiosities of London* (1867), and Trumbull's *The True Blue-Laws of Connecticut* (1876) – in extensive notes. Even before the narrative gets under way, the book begins with a facsimile and transcription of a letter from Hugh Latimer, bishop of Worcester and adviser to Henry VIII, to Thomas Cromwell, lord privy seal and minister to the king, announcing the birth of Edward VI. In effect, these gestures to textual authority resituate the terms of the conflict within an altered hierarchy that discriminates, not between actual and textual experience but between different orders of textual authority.

For example, when Hendon considers in amazement the "history of [the prince's] recent misfortunes" (96), noting the uniqueness of what Hendon calls "this curious romaunt," his compassion for Edward's plight grows, in large part because Edward's account is not a conventionalized tale of misfortune. Hendon, nevertheless, classifies it as fiction. The disjunction implied between the narrator's term for Edward's story as a "history" and Hendon's reception of it as a "curious romaunt" ironizes Hendon's misunderstanding of the truth and thus signals that the problem with textual experience is not that it is essentially inadequate – at best, a mere simulacrum of the actual, at worst, a distortion of fact – rather, the problem with reading is interpretation – and, more accurately, misinterpretation, such as the misinterpretations, both low and high, of the boys' iden-

tities. But more importantly, in the new hierarchy of textual authority, history enjoys the position of reliability to which actual experience had been formerly assigned. History, in contrast to fiction, is
treated as an epistemologically stable transmission of the truth. Such
an assumption, however, reinscribes the dilemma that Twain faces
in composing this narrative. In the first place, by having initially
intended *The Prince and the Pauper* to serve as a rejoinder to the false
history that Trumbull accused the Reverend Peters of having "Invented," Twain allows that history is an interpretive field, subject to
the ideological biases of the interpreter. As such, the events of the
past are converted to a textual status as soon as they enter human
understanding through language as history. The accounts of these
events are subsumed within a larger cultural architecture that determines their relevance and meaning, and this architecture, in turn,
is itself shaped to some degree by those events and the various accounts of them.[20]

In the second place, *The Prince and the Pauper* hangs on a rather
unlikely interlude in history. So, although Twain's relationship to
textual authority appears to be growing more stable at this point in
his career, his assessment of the relationship between the various
forms of textual authority remains relatively unstable. The preface,
explaining the tale's source, flattens out the hierarchy between history and fiction by tracing the tale's transmission in a genealogy of
storytelling:

> I will set down a tale as it was told to me by one who had it of his
> father, which latter had it of *his* father, this last having in like
> manner had it of *his* father – and so on, back and still back, three
> hundred years and more, the fathers transmitting it to the sons
> and so preserving it. It may be history, it may be only a legend, a
> tradition. It may have happened, it may not have happened: but
> it *could* have happened. (xx)

The closing line stresses the importance of plausibility and ascribes
relative equality between fiction and fact even before the narrative
gets under way. Twain's deployment of a fictional narrative to ren-
der history corresponds to his interest in the picturesque over the
"dead facts." As one merely acquainted with a few facts of Tudor
history, and not overburdened, as were, say, the survivors of the
Vicksburg siege in *Life on the Mississippi*, he is able to tell a rousing

tale that, if not accurate in every particular, nonetheless dramatizes an historic moment – no matter that there is no evidence to support the exchange of identities in this case. Still, all of the gestures meant to certify the historical authority of his narrative suggest Twain's nervousness about the relative truth that the romanticized invention of an historic moment is supposed to convey. By including the facsimile and the transcription in late Middle English orthography, Twain looks to be calling upon the awe-inspiring spectacle of antiquity to puff the authenticity of the narrative, whereas in the preface he disregards history's claim to authority.

Twain's equivocation between the authority of history and the authority of art indicates his uneasy participation in the growing indictment of history by modern writers.[21] At the vanguard of the antihistorical movement was Friedrich Nietzsche, whose *Birth of Tragedy* (1872) helped to inaugurate it. A decade before Twain's complaint about the "dead facts" of history, Nietzsche argued that "[a] historical phenomenon, completely understood and reduced to an item of knowledge, is, in relation to the man who knows it, dead." Of course, even Nietzsche, whose suspicions about history ran deep, who saw human action arising from "unhistorical" motivations as yielding a happiness uncompromised by hypocrisy, and who saw historical consciousness as an inhibition on one's capacity to act, recognized some value in history. For "man can only become man," Nietzsche acknowledged, "by first suppressing this unhistorical element in his thoughts, comparisons, distinctions, and conclusions, letting a clear sudden light break through these misty clouds by his power of turning the past to the uses of the present." But Nietzsche's historical man, like Twain's overwrought Vicksburgers or his mnemonically capacious Mr. Brown, was hamstrung by "an excess of history" through which "life becomes maimed and degenerate, and is followed by the degeneration of history as well." The antidote to the stultifying excesses of historical consciousness, Nietzsche argued, was art. And likewise for Twain, fiction is the avenue to an historical imagination that fosters picturesque vitality and prevents the past from becoming, in Nietzsche's phrase, "reduced to an item of knowledge," an entry in history's catalog of "dead facts."[22]

What Nietzsche means by "turning the past to the uses of the present" can best be understood in relation to three of the forms of historiographical practice he describes in "The Use and Abuse of

History" – "monumental," "antiquarian," and "critical" – and the desires these forms serve. The critical historian attempts "to break up the past; and apply it too, in order to live. He must bring the past to the bar of judgment, interrogate it remorselessly, and finally condemn it."[23]

Critical history is the mode Twain first approached in the wry humor of *Innocents Abroad*. So, too, did he initially attempt a critique of history in *The Prince and the Pauper*, but he undermined this move by indulging in antiquarian history, an investigation by which one attempts to conserve the past in a state of reverence. The antiquarian inclination in *The Prince and the Pauper* is responsible for the emphasis on historical sources, calling up the reverential past with the apparent hope that some of that reverence might rub off. Unlike the fictional truth of the vernacular humorist's lies, antiquarianism attempts to embody a truth that is bred in tradition, appropriating the scholarly historian's legitimacy. Hence the importance of the preface. The account of the tale's genealogical transmission invokes a mode of ordinary storytelling that, as de Certeau observed, is opposed to historiographical discourse, while at the same time the genealogical transmission of power through patriarchy is the basis of legitimacy honored by antiquarian historiography. The one subverts historiography, the other supports it. This antithesis also fuels the tension between the uncertainty of "credit" that the preface cites as the absent history of the tale's reception and the virtual certainty of "credit" that the narrative urges us to extend to Edward in the closing lines of the tale: "The reign of Edward VI was a singularly merciful one for those harsh times. Now that we are taking leave of him, let us try to keep this in our minds, to his credit" (289). By soliciting our consent to the restoration of genealogical monarchy on the grounds of Edward's enlightened mercy, the text registers a desire for hegemonic complicity that pushes beyond Twain's personal desire for genteel appreciation. This narrative resolution attempts to bridge an historical gap that has separated the Old World from the New both in time and in social vision.

Furthermore, this call for homage to Edward marks a shift from antiquarian to monumental historiography, the practice of finding models on whom the man of action can pattern his course in his noble endeavors. Edward serves doubly well because he is not simply a monumental hero but also a practitioner of monumentalism himself. When asked to perform menial kitchen work by a farmer's widow who has taken him in during his journey back to the throne, Edward agrees, recalling that the legendary Alfred the Great had done no less when similarly called upon. And at the end of his misadventures, Edward interrupts Tom's coronation by bursting from the tomb of his namesake, Edward the Confessor, whose honesty and saintliness is thus monumentally reincarnated in the young claimant. This climactic moment recalls the hero's "resurrection" in *The Adventures of Tom Sawyer*, and the pattern overall anticipates the course of actions by which Huck Finn emulates legendary figures. But in Edward's case the emulation is entirely self-conscious and reinforces his sense of his own worth through identification with legendary heroes. Thus, although the tale may have begun in a critical mode, it backslides rather steadily into the historiographical modes that Nietzsche condemned.

The text's recession from critical, to antiquarian, and finally to monumental history creates another problem for Twain's project. For, inasmuch as monumentalism locates true greatness in vanished heroes of the past, this historiographical mode contradicts the ideal of cultural progress to which Twain subscribed. The dominant assumption underlying American historiography is that America is the realization of the Enlightenment ideal of progress. The late-nineteenth-century American acceptance of "cultural positivism," based on Herbert Spencer's deterministic social philosophy, conformed to this ideal. According to Lears, Spencer postulated that civilization was a process of "inexorable and beneficent" improvement, "from a warlike or militant stage of development to a pacific industrial stage" where "egoism and altruism were no longer at odds; in fact, they complemented one another." In America Spencer's theories were heralded as "a secular religion of progress, a social scientific version of the optimistic, liberal Protestantism which pervaded the educated bourgeoisie," and which informed the tradition of American exceptionalism.[24] As Sacvan Bercovitch has shown, exceptionalism was first ritualized in the tradition of the Puritan jeremiad and subsequently recast into secular, patriotic terms, initially to idealize the Revolution and afterward to urge a consensus at every stage of American political activity. Spencer's philosophy, then, found a ready audience in America and lent the credibility of "scientific" discourse to the modernization of the American cultural self-image.

Bercovitch's analysis of the jeremiad, moreover, helps to illuminate Twain's choice of setting. Puritan thought, Bercovitch argues, was originally a European construct, not an American one. The theological concept of an Old and New England anticipated the Great Migration, although America provided the geography for the actual exodus of these Chosen People. Analogously, *The Prince and the Pauper* pinpoints the rise of enlightened government in England prior to the English colonization of America, thus alluding to a similar continuity between the Old and New Worlds. Furthermore, Twain's choice of Henry VIII's reign as the moment to stage this historical suturing is significant because it was under Henry that the Protestant Reformation in England occurred.[25] Edward's reign, then, marks an historical turning point that connects English history to American history in ideological terms. This setting allusively acknowledges the Protestant and liberal roots of the American legacy. In his 1881 address to the New England Society of Philadelphia, "Plymouth Rock and the Pilgrims," Twain jested similarly about "The Mayflower tribe," who were the subject of oratorical veneration at that meeting. He acknowledges that "those ancestors of yours of 1620" may have been "better than their predecessors," but he finds nothing in that fact worthy of praise: "That is nothing. People always progress." This claim evokes the notion of history's course of evolutionary improvement. But he nonetheless finds reason to disdain the pilgrims for having "abolished everybody else's ancestors" (*CTSS&E*, 1:781–5). Of course, Twain intends the criticisms in this address to be humorous; he makes this clear in the hyperbole of claiming ancestry in all ethnic groups, including Indians and African slaves. Still, the concern that ancestry can be erased from the history of America's peoples resonates with the desire to reestablish the Anglo-American genealogy that had been minimized in Puritan historiography and the Revolutionary cultural identity that separated the United States irrevocably from England.

But whereas in Bercovitch's compelling interpretation the Puritan jeremiad leads to the American Revolution, Twain's tale hints at revolutionary change only in the episodes of Tom's accession to the throne. The retreat to the legitimacy of monarchy in Edward's half of the story emphasizes a more conservative evolutionary model, as if radically new formations were in a sense illegitimate because they bore no connection to the validating structure of history defined in patriarchal terms.[26] This doesn't flatly deny the notion of historical progression. But Twain's reinvention of English history, more than figuratively endorsing his own authorial legitimacy, posits Edward's liberal reign as the ancestral forerunner of the American republic to validate the liberal tradition that gave rise to the American system. In effect, such a narrative implication conservatively asserts American legitimacy by its genealogical tie to English monarchy, thereby evading the Revolution and, in turn, voiding the half of the paradox that defined American culture as a rebellious break from history.

The narrative denouement of Edward's return to the throne displays the text's affinity with the acquiescence of the romance and its aversion to the subversiveness of the novel; this resolution virtually traditionalizes, denovelizes, American liberalism by monumentally identifying it in a persona of noble worth from the past. That Twain should choose to turn the narrative in this direction is curious, since he had all of the necessary novelistic elements available to him from the outset. The revolutionary story of Tom's accession to the throne squares with Georg Lukács's definition of the historical novel, for Lukács claims "that the possibilities for . . . human upsurge and heroism are widespread among the popular masses, that endless numbers of people live out their lives quietly, without this upsurge, because no opportunity has come their way to evoke such an exertion of powers." In representing the common man's ability to govern with reason, *The Prince and the Pauper* declares its affinities with the Enlightenment, which Lukács credits with leading to the French Revolution and preparing "the social and ideological basis from which the historical novel was able to emerge." For "with . . . undaunted vigour the Enlightenment fought the historical legitimacy and continuity of feudal survivals." Herein lie the limits of Lukács's definition. He finds this Enlightenment perspective in Walter Scott, "a marked affinity with that resigned 'positivity' . . . observed in the great thinkers, scholars, and writers" of nineteenth-century Europe.[27] Twain, no doubt, would have protested Lukács's assessment of Scott as a progressive, but the same protest ought to be lodged against Twain's own historical fiction. For even though Tom's example and Edward's education steer a course of reform toward compassionate justice, neither the pretender nor the legitimate king abdicates to make way for democracy. Instead, the text represses its revolutionary tendencies and reverts to the accommodation available in romance. Tom Canty is a "mock king" throughout, and the story's conclusion maintains that his accession is a fraud. In the end, even after suggesting that paternal, social, judicial, and political powers are mere habits of cultural training, the narrative acquiesces in the traditional notion that authority is rooted in genealogy.

Granted, the plot development may not appear to be so much Twain's acquiescence as a function of the constraints of historical fiction, a genre in which the facts of history might be seen to determine the course of the plot. Certainly, adhering to the established chronology of fact in this case would prohibit the premature appearance of democratic government in the tale. But the historical pattern that determines Twain's narrative course specifies only the known outcome of events: Edward VI succeeded Henry VIII. Without violating the historical account of succession, a critical narrative – that is, a novel – might have sustained Tom's charade, conjecturing that the Edward who reigned with notable compassion and restraint after Henry VIII's tyranny was in fact a pauper who acceded to the throne by virtue of mistaken identity. This would have not only discredited the genealogical basis of legitimacy but also promoted the idea that the enlightened government that blazed the trail toward democracy was ruled by a commoner – a member of the *demos*, not the elite.

Instead, Twain's historical narrative avoids such a sly critique, opting to stand pat on a conservative desire for a benevolent *and* legitimate monarch, and thus accommodates existing institutions of power rather than subverts them. In terms of historical violation, the scene in which the boys exchange identities pales when compared to the recognition scene's public spectacle in which Edward is restored. The former could have occurred plausibly without the knowledge of any chronicler, whereas the latter is the one event in the tale that history would most certainly have recorded had it actually taken place. So, rather than a bar to Twain's fulfilling the democratic thesis, the genre's standard of historical reliability is a convention readily dismissed by the text's compulsion to dramatize the conservative rhetoric.

Such accommodation, I have argued, typifies the romance, not the novel. In fact, *The Prince and the Pauper* is the kind of romance for which Twain condemned Walter Scott. Lukács's praise notwithstanding, Scott came to represent everything that Twain distrusted about history. No doubt the composition of *The Prince and the Pauper* helped to focus that distrust. His heteroglot efforts in *Life on the Mississippi* and the confrontation with the historical unconscious in *Huckleberry Finn* shed a brighter and less flattering light on the topic of history. But Twain's bleakest conclusions about the restrictive authority of history did not emerge until his struggle with *A Connecticut Yankee in King Arthur's Court.*

Twain signaled *A Connecticut Yankee*'s fundamental difference from its predecessor when he shifted from the third-person narrator of *The Prince and the Pauper* and rendered the account of sixth-century England in the idiosyncratic voice emanating from Hank Morgan, much as he had done in the shift from *Tom Sawyer* to *Huckleberry Finn.* During his research of English history in preparation for *The Prince and the Pauper*, Twain had also turned to first-person narration in an unpublished burlesque of the legendary past, "1601 or Conversation as It Was by the Social Fireside in the Time of the Tudors." In this brief report from Queen Elizabeth's cupbearer, Twain fictionalizes the crudeness of revered royal and literary figures, offering a starkly different image from the mannerliness that Victorians expected of the highborn. As eyewitness accounts whose authority is direct, not filtered through the succession of patri-filial retellings that marked *The Prince and the Pauper*, both "1601" and *A Connecticut Yankee* attempt to cut through the distortions of sedimented historical knowledge, just as the *Personal Recollections of Joan of Arc* (1896) would attempt to do by rendering the narrative as the first-person account of Sieur Louis de Conte, Joan's lifelong friend and admirer. In the series of Adam and Eve diary sketches, Twain would go even farther in this regard by attempting to rewrite Genesis with authoritative first-person voices that supplant the authority of Moses.

Twain primarily intended "1601" to entertain his male friends in the Monday Evening Club, for whom he wrote it. The naughty indulgence of scatological and bawdy humor offered relief from the repression of genteel sensibilities. But to see it as merely a risqué joke is to overlook the critique of historiography it implies, a radical challenge that *A Connecticut Yankee* embodies as well. The unrefined image of the past offered in "1601" suggests that much of what passes for history is merely a distorted image of the past, romantically refracted through the ideology of a later era and therefore anachronistic. In the 1890s, Twain would reaffirm this in an aphorism: "The very ink with which all history is written is merely fluid prejudice" (*FE*, 2:392). Subsequently, in futuristic mock histories like the unpublished "Glances from History, Suppressed," "Outline of History," "The Stupendous Procession," and "The Secret History of Eddypus," he offers sharp satire, reflecting the erosion of his belief that America held a privileged place in history's march toward a perfect civilization as well as his continued disillusionment with literary falsifications of history.[28]

In contrast to *The Prince and the Pauper*, which begins with a facsimile document and a transcription of the Bishop of Worcester's letter announcing Edward VI's birth, in order to launch the tale's claim to historical validity, Hank Morgan's "Tale of the Lost Land" is written on a parchment palimpsest, a text effaced by the writing of other texts. The very form of the text corresponds to Morgan's own antihistorical tendencies; his text is, in effect, a new historical *tabula rasa* on which the Lockean ideal of a civil society can be written anew. But it is not an attempt to glorify the past or to validate the present as the fulfillment of the past. Unlike Nietzsche's practitioner of antiquarian history – one whose "virtues lie in . . . his instinctive correctness in reading the scribbled past, and understanding at once its palimpsests" – Morgan employs his palimpsestic text not to read through but to obliterate the stratified scribbling of the past. As the embodiment of the Enlightenment, he sees progress as an authoritative inscription of new truths blotting out old falsehoods, signifying his affinity for novelistic discourse, which is motivated by the same desire. He is, in his own words, "a new man!" (*CY*, 47) – and not simply in the clichéd sense he denotes in having escaped death by virtue of his memory of history, his theatricality, and his luck. Rather, he is an entirely new kind of man in contrast to the inhabitants of the sixth century, because of his practical outlook, knowledge, ingenuity, and desire to control the world in which he awakens. This desire to remake the world and to control it defines him as a figure of the novelist within the narrative, helping to underscore the origin of the novelist's license in the Enlightenment's support of the authoritative self.[29]

Morgan's unwavering dedication to innovation articulates the epistemology of novelistic discourse; his watchword is "novelty," denoting the fundamental principle encoded in the genre's name. Both Morgan and novelistic discourse value the "original" over the "regular," two categories that Michel Foucault claims have structured a similar hierarchy in the history of ideas. By elevating the original, the history of ideas "recounts the history of inventions, changes, transformations, it shows how truth freed itself from error, how consciousness awoke from its successive slumbers, how new forms rose up in turn to produce the landscape that we know today." Thus, the original is yet another aspect of the progressive ideal. Morgan does not, however, attempt "to rediscover . . . the continuous line of an evolution," as the historian of ideas would. Late-nineteenth-century civilization, especially American civilization, stands on its own merits, in Morgan's estimation. And he reverses the conventional "stadialist" model in which the past is plotted as a series of necessary stages in the march toward the present and future; instead, the present, for Morgan, is the model for remaking the past.[30]

In the starkest terms, Twain draws the distinction between innovation and tradition in the rivalry between Morgan and his nemesis Merlin. In the Fountain of the Valley of Holiness episode, Morgan underscores their differences, reporting that he went down into the well to inspect its physical condition, unlike Merlin, who "hadn't entered it himself. He did everything by incantations; he never worked his intellect . . . he was an old numbskull; a magician who believed in his own magic; and no magician can thrive who is handicapped with a superstition like that" (209). In his lack of resourcefulness, Merlin is a victim of the mental habits of the era. Such training becomes a cultural domination, inhibiting humanity's progress: "[F]or a man, in those days, to have had an idea that his ancestors hadn't had, would have brought him under suspicion of being illegitimate" (210). Thus in his opposition to Merlin, Morgan represents the challenge posed by empirical reasoning to the genealogical structure of traditional notions of legitimacy.

But Morgan's authority is more than that of an eyewitness; he is an active participant in the events of the distant past, which he makes plain at the outset. Morgan is amused at the nineteenth-century Windsor Castle tour guide's historically reasonable assumption that the curious bullet hole in Sir Sagramour's armor is of relatively recent vintage and mutters in Twain's hearing, "Wit ye well, *I saw it done*" and then adds the more startling admission, "I did it myself" (2). *The Prince and the Pauper* had received some mild criticism for its anachronism, but here Twain avails himself of the license that fiction affords him in order to foreground anachronism as an axiom of the text's constitution. In effect, Twain rewrites the notice that introduced *Huckleberry Finn*: anyone attempting to find conventional conceptions of historical consistency in this story will be prosecuted, banished, *and* shot. It did not have to be this way, of course. Twain might just as easily have claimed to have discovered an antique manuscript that denied mythologized history, much as he had in "1601" or would later do in "The Secret History of Eddypus." But Morgan's return to the sixth century enables Twain to return, at least fictionally, to the province of actual experience. This imaginative possibility offers the kind of authority that can directly criticize the past by contrast to the present and thus challenge the text-based authority of monumental historiography to which *The Prince and the Pauper* finally resorts.

Twain admits as much when he lays out his unconventional historical method in the preface to *A Connecticut Yankee*:

> It is not pretended that these laws and customs existed in England in the sixth century; no, it is only pretended that inasmuch as they existed in England and other civilizations of far later times, it is safe to consider that it is no libel upon the sixth century to suppose them to have been in practice in that day also. One is quite justified in inferring that wherever one of these laws or customs was lacking in that remote time, its place was competently filled by a worse one. (Unnumbered page)

On its face, such a method might seem vulnerable, since it does not deal with the facts of the past but makes inferences about "the ungentle laws and customs" of the past.[31] But by owning his assumption of historical progression, Twain makes explicit the axiom that has guided historiographical practice since the Enlightenment. By virtue of his frankness here and of his anachronistic approach to the historical tale overall, Twain implies that history, more often than not, is constructed according to the ideological desires of the present. Thus, to fault *A Connecticut Yankee* for not measuring up to a conventional standard of historical reliability is to misread the text's cues about how Twain intends it to be read.

The germ of the novel in Twain's notebook entry of 1884 contrasted the representations of knight-errantry in heroic legend to an experience-based account of the physical discomforts of knighthood: "No pockets in armor. No way to manage certain requirements of nature. Can't scratch. Cold in the head – can't blow – can't get at handkerchief, can't use iron sleeve. Iron gets red hot in the sun – leaks in the rain, gets white with frost & freezes me solid in winter. Suffer from lice & fleas. Make disagreeable clatter when I enter church. Can't dress or undress myself. Always getting struck by lightning. Fall down, can't get up" (*MTNJ*, 3:78–9). The development of this quick sketch into a full-length narrative goes well beyond the physical humor noted here. Throughout Morgan's tenure in King Arthur's England, his experience within that society runs against the grain of the textual representations that have customarily wrapped the era in the cloak of legend. During Morgan's quest with Alisande, whom Morgan dubs "Sandy" – a young noblewoman who petitions the court for a knight-errant to rescue her family and is assigned the Yankee as her champion – the couple encounter some of the very personages that populate her tiresome tales of adventure. These meetings emphasize the disparity between the characterological images projected in legend and Morgan's impressions of the people to whom those images correspond. Just as in Sir Kay's account, in which Morgan himself becomes " 'this prodigious giant,' and 'this horrible sky-towering monster,' and 'this tushed and taloned man-devouring ogre' " (31), Sandy's story of princesses taken captive by ogres is a fantastical rendering of pigs tended by swineherds (183). The source of these discrepancies is the primitive sixth-century mind, so unlike the nineteenth-century's cognitive temperament. The clearest index of this divergence is narrative style. Morgan suggests this, for example, in his critique of Sandy's storytelling, which lacks novelty, originality. And Twain's inclusion of Sir Thomas Malory's text in the framing device, which he reports he was reading when Morgan appears at his door, offers a similar representation of an archaic narrative mode.

Twain focused on literary fraud early in the composition of *Huckleberry Finn*, depicting Huck's irritation with Tom Sawyer's fantastical adventures. But not until *Life on the Mississippi* did his critique of literary falseness acquire an historical perspective. During the return trip to the river that informed the composition of part 2 of *Life on the Mississippi*, Twain observed differences between the cultures of the American North and South from which he drew his theory that the "Sir Walter disease" had caused the Civil War. George Washington Cable played an important role in tying these separate strands together, for it was Cable whom Twain had come to appreciate as a new sort of Southerner, one who had risen above the feudal shams of Scottism to embrace liberal views about race relations. Ironically, it was Cable who introduced Twain to Malory's *Morte D'Arthur* in December of 1884, during their "Twins of Genius" lecture tour. "You'll never lay it down until you have read it from cover to cover," Cable assured him. And for this advice, according to Cable, Twain would later name him the "godfather" of *A Connecticut Yankee*.[32]

But Twain appears to have felt differently about Malory's "enchanting book" (2). The text of his own fabulous tale of historical displacement not only dissolves the wonder of Malory's tales by their immersion in the vernacular humor of Morgan's account but also portrays Twain himself, in the framing device, as dozing off while reading the very book that Cable promised him would rivet his attention. Virtually contradicting Cable, he states flatly, just before Morgan is reintroduced in order to tell his tale, "As I laid the book down there was a knock at the door, and the stranger came in" (3). The introduction of Morgan's lively tale at precisely the moment when Twain's interest in Malory has hit bottom makes clear that *A Connecticut Yankee* is anything but a tribute to Arthurian legend. The differences between the medieval and the modern eras suggested a cultural discontinuity to Twain that apparently fascinated him. But the more crucial target of his concern was the disparity between actual experience and textual representation as exhibited in the discrepancy between Morgan's description of the court's demeanor and the nostalgic images popularized in historical romances. This critical intention transformed Twain's text from a mock historical romance to a jeremiad: it both warns against backsliding into medieval nostalgia, which had become popular in the decade that Twain's two historical tales bracket, and exhorts America to turn its attention to the industrial progress that was its destiny.

Critics have often noted the similarities between *A Connecticut Yankee*'s Camelot and the American South to support the conclusion that Twain had sighted southern backwardness in his novel's critical crosshairs. But in *Life on the Mississippi*, Twain had subtly assigned the blame to Scott. His primary target was not the society but the literature that had stunted that society's growth. In effect, he transformed a social problem into a literary one. For, unlike social problems, literary problems can be solved by literary solutions, the only means at his disposal. As a jeremiad, *A Connecticut Yankee* stands as Twain's attempt to rid the culture of the Sir Walter disease. But this treatment invests itself in a virtually magical cure, one that works by inverting the jeremiad's incantation. We can see this in Morgan's report of court behavior, distinguished like "1601" by its utter difference from the decorous medievalisms that Scott had made popular. Although Morgan has marveled at having been transported to this legendary era, he is nonplussed by the legendary figures before whom he is summoned. He disdainfully reports on the unabashedly indelicate speech of "the first ladies and gentlemen" in King Arthur's court, language that "would have made a Comanche blush." He continues,

> Indelicacy is too mild a term to convey the idea. However, I had read "Tom Jones" and "Roderick Ransom," and other books of that kind, and knew that the highest and first ladies and gentlemen in England had remained little or no cleaner in their talk, and in the morals and conduct which such talk implies, clear up to a hundred years ago; in fact clear into our own nineteenth-century – in which century, broadly speaking, the earliest samples of the real lady and real gentleman discoverable in English history – or in European history, for that matter – may be said to have made their appearance. Suppose Sir Walter, instead of putting the conversations into the mouths of his characters, had allowed the characters to speak for themselves? We should have talk from Rebecca and Ivanhoe and the soft Lady Rowena which would embarrass a tramp in our day. However, to the unconsciously indelicate, all things are delicate. King Arthur's people were not aware that they were indecent, and I had presence of mind enough not to mention it. (32–4)

Behind Morgan's approval of Sir Walter's decency, we should hear Twain's own ironic mocking of Scott and consider how this critique plays into Twain's vexed relationship to history.

Despite the text's obvious concern and engagement with history,

A Connecticut Yankee is an antihistorical book. To be sure, Morgan's plans are predicated on the Whig hypothesis of historical progress toward material abundance and political liberality. But as Morgan accelerates and streamlines the course of progress, the text also represents the erasure of thirteen centuries from history. By installing the industrial, social, and political mechanisms that encouraged nineteenth-century Americans to view their era as the culmination of Western civilization, Morgan converts the hypothesized evolution of history into a revolution against history.[33] This reversal of the historiographical process administers, albeit fictionally, a cure for the Sir Walter disease. By dispatching his practical mechanic to the Dark Ages, Twain electrifies prehistory with the scientific and political technology of the modern era and thus deprives Scott of the material from which he wove his historical fictions and infected the imaginations of an otherwise modern society. Anticipating Twain's own metaphor of Caesarean section, which he will use to describe his remedy for the problems of *Those Extraordinary Twins*, *A Connecticut Yankee* amounts to a sort of historical surgery. An extreme measure, to be sure – but in the absence of an effective cure for the cultural malaise that infected historical perspective, extreme measures would appear to have been Twain's only hope for maintaining the viability of the novel in which he had invested his professional identity.

There is something patently humorous about attempting to control history through such an absurd fictional gesture, just as there is in Twain's charging Scott with having caused the Civil War. In the unfinished tale "Tom Sawyer's Conspiracy," Twain exploits a similarly playful angle by having Huck credit Tom with the idea for the Civil War. In his role as narrator, Huck marvels at Tom's inventive anticipation and complains, "And it don't seem right and fair that Harriet Beacher Stow [*sic*] and all them other second-handers gets all the credit of starting that war and you never hear Tom Sawyer mentioned in the histories ransack them how you will, and yet he was the first one that thought of it" (*HF&TSAI*, 138). But the seriousness of this effort to overcome history emerges more clearly if we stand back and view this radical narrative within the dialectical course of Twain's career. Indeed, considering that Twain saw *A Connecticut Yankee* as the last he would write, the word "desperate" may better describe the project than either "humorous" or "serious."[34]

For, more than any other of Twain's texts, *A Connecticut Yankee* highlights the problem that the genre of the novel confronts. *The Prince and the Pauper* tries to reinvent history, but the record of Edward VI's coronation gives the lie to the narrative's veracity. *Life on the Mississippi* traces the progress of democratic culture, but in reversing its course upstream, it travels back to the river's headwaters – to the aboriginal legends that predate the history of United States culture – and looks back longingly to a simpler past. And *Huckleberry Finn* allusively figures the socializing influence of an historically informed cultural unconscious, preempting the naive hero's flight from "siviliz[ation]" and emptying Huck's promise of resuming his escape from the culture that formed him. So, after repeatedly bumping up against history in these narratives, Twain takes the radical approach in *A Connecticut Yankee* of using fiction – the novel's glaring weakness in the face of the actual – not merely to attack mythologized historiography but to circumvent history entirely. As *The American Claimant* and *Pudd'nhead Wilson* would show no less emphatically than the earlier texts, Twain viewed American society as hobbled by an infatuation with genealogical authority, which is but an institutionalized version of the Sir Walterish worship of the epic past. Thus, the implicit aim of *A Connecticut Yankee* is to free the present from the antiquarianism that interferes with the unfolding progress of America's novelistic destiny.

To be sure, Morgan tells us that American traces of "reverence for rank and title . . . had disappeared – at least to all intents and purposes" and that the "disease," having been reduced to a "remnant . . . restricted to dudes and dudesses," could "fairly be said to be out of the system" (67). But this observation merely helps to emphasize the differences between an author and a character too often assumed to be ideologically identical. Twain hints at the differences between them on this score by punctuating the Yankee's supposition of how Scott had improved his texts as a question rather than a statement in the imperative mood: "Suppose Sir Walter, instead of putting the conversations into the mouths of his characters, had allowed the characters to speak for themselves?" (34). Because there is no question about how Twain views Scott's historical fictions – they are nostalgic glosses elevating the past as an idyllic moment from which the present has presumably fallen, and such shams, in Twain's view, have tragic historical consequences – the question mark opens up ironic space between author and character. Morgan and Twain agree that caste distinctions were part of a feudal past anachronistic to American democracy, but unlike Morgan, Twain was aware that caste survived mythologically in American culture. His own writings attacked the pernicious chronic effects of this affliction. But if his writings before *A Connecticut Yankee* failed to dispel the nostalgia of historical romance that inhibited the critical imagination necessary for a novelistic culture, then the only way to eradicate the cultural pestilence plaguing the nineteenth century would be to return to the Middle Ages that Scott romanticized and not simply demystify them but preemptively modernize them. Using anachronism to inoculate against anachronism, *A Connecticut Yankee* epitomizes novelistic discourse.[35]

Back to the Future

If Twain's assault on the source material of Scottism signals his desperation, his recklessness is driven by a suspicion that novelistic authority is not just beyond rescue but perhaps unworthy of rescue. Henry Nash Smith has argued that the failure of Twain's "Fable of Progress," *A Connecticut Yankee*, is due to his protagonist's inadequacy. In Smith's view, Morgan is more of an American Adam than an American Prometheus and is, therefore, "an inadequate vehicle for depicting American industrial capitalism."[36] Smith portrays Twain as an antebellum consciousness, like Frederick Jackson Turner and Henry Adams, unable to grasp the complexities of technological innovation and economic modernization. This implies that in more competent hands the rhetorical project of *A Connecticut Yankee* would have turned out differently. But the failure of the novel could not have been prevented; rather, it is endemic to novelistic discourse, to the kind of authority that it attempts to assume. Accordingly, Morgan is not an ill-chosen cultural symbol but the most apt one to represent both a flawed ideal of social authority and its analogous literary form in novelistic discourse.

The power that Twain represented in Morgan is a very unsettling form of control. Ironically, traces of this invidious power appear in the Yankee's literary assessments of Scott. Morgan's approval of Scott's refinement reveals a troubling attitude about authority that goes a long way toward illuminating the dilemma that Twain discovered embedded within his novelistic enterprise. Although the Yankee's appreciation may be prompted by his sense of delicacy regarding sexual matters, Scott's literary policing – "putting the conversation into the mouths of his characters" rather than "allow[ing] them to speak for themselves" – is a form of authorial omnipotence with which Twain was continually uncomfortable. The total control that Morgan praises Scott for exercising is precisely the sort of authority that Twain questioned and then relinquished in *Life on the Mississippi*, even as he was establishing his own authority over abusive pilots like Bixby, Brown, and Sellers, and over a romancer like Scott. Similarly, Huck Finn's opening address to the reader in the story of his *Adventures* is a case in which a character isn't merely *allowed* to speak for himself but claims the authority to tell his own story rather than allow Mr. Mark Twain to tell it with "stretchers." More importantly, though, Morgan imagines Scott as a genteel censor who stifles the free speech of the characters. Morgan's sanguine view of such power foreshadows a crucial conflict lurking in the authority he exercises in remaking the backward world of King Arthur's England into a modern society. His scheme is aimed at remedying the political tyranny, superstitious ignorance, and economic inequality of the world into which he awakens. But in order to achieve this utopian state, he centralizes all power within himself, just as Scott had done in assuming complete authorial control over his characters. Despite the lip service Morgan pays to democratic reform, the kind of control he warrants tolerates no critique, challenge, or indifference to his authority. His admiration of Scott's censorship of free speech reveals his willingness to violate the democratic principles he espouses for the sake of fulfilling his teleological project.

Twain, on the other hand, was self-consciously circumspect about the authority of his own novelistic practice. In his explanation of his difficulty with *Pudd'nhead Wilson*, he credits his characters with wills of their own, not only saying things other than he wished them to but acting in ways that made the story something entirely other than what he had imagined it to be. *A Connecticut Yankee* posed a similar problem. In a letter dated August 3, 1887, Twain complained to his nephew and publisher Charles L. Webster that "the fun, which was abounding in the Yankee at Arthur's Court up to three days ago, has slumped into funereal seriousness, and this will not do – it will not answer at all. The very title of the book requires fun, and it must be furnished.''[37] Although suggesting his desire for autocratic control, the imperious tone in which Twain insists that the book must resume its humorous cast also reveals his anxiety about making the narrative conform to his design. The odd notion that the book's title dictates what it should be, rather than the other way around, indicates an inverted conception of the process, which the passive-voice construction – ''[F]un . . . must be furnished'' – reaffirms. In these remarks, Twain subtracts his own agency from the compositional process, as if he were merely observing the narrative events rather than inventing them, or even experiencing them as Morgan does. This conception of his relationship to his texts – as if he were not their creator and they not the medium of his ideas, but rather that the stories and their characters were the agents and he their medium – intimates Twain's uneasiness about the act of assuming novelistic authority over a fictional world created to relieve the constraining authority of historical interpretation.

Twain's struggle for control extends beyond a mimetic link between his compositional difficulties and the theme of conflicted authority. The Yankee's technological desire to control Arthurian England also mirrors Twain's disastrous investment in the Paige typesetter. The critical correlation between text and machine has yielded cumulative insight, but the biographical episode has still more to reveal about the dilemma of Twain's fascination with control.[38] If we locate the typesetter ordeal within the context of Twain's career, we can appreciate the magnitude of its value to Twain as an instrument for consolidating his power.

Paige's invention stands apart from the many get-rich-quick schemes Twain notoriously chased because it offered more than an investment opportunity; rather, this technology promised total control over the publishing enterprise in which Twain had become increasingly involved throughout his career. Having worked as a printer early on, he knew that the work of reproducing text would never afford him the power of authorship, nor would his wages ever rise very high in this manual trade. As a writer, Twain enjoyed the glamor and remuneration that his own mental labor brought through the sale of his books. But he also learned that his authorial function was not enough to guarantee success. After disappointing returns from some of his books, he blamed publishers like Elisha

Bliss, and James Osgood after Bliss, for failing to oversee the successful production and marketing of his work. So he entered the business of books as the owner and proprietor of the Charles L. Webster Publishing Company in order to assume greater control over the enterprise.[39]

The publishing venture allowed him to take control of his own work with broad power. In a letter to Howells, he jested about having "telegraphed orders to have [the printer's proofreader] shot without giving him time to pray" because the proofreader had dared to alter Twain's punctuation in A Connecticut Yankee (MTHL, 2:610). Moreover, as a publisher, Clemens stood to profit from the labor of other writers. He took great pride in the fact that the royalties he paid to Ulysses S. Grant's widow for her husband's Memoirs was "something like half a million dollars" (MTE, 186), a record sum at that date. Undoubtedly his own financial profit was also important, but apparently less so than the pride he took in rising from the status of "literary person" to businessman. His autobiographical dictation conveys this self-esteem in the suggestion that Twain had proved himself "a competent prophet" (MTE, 177) in predicting the success of Grant's book, in direct contrast to the general's impression that Twain's offer was foolishly inflated, proving the stereotype of "literary men" who are "flighty, romantic, unpractical, and in business matters don't know enough to come in when it rains or at any other time" (MTE, 185).

His investment in the Paige typesetter proceeded logically from this quest for control. By owning the technology that he assumed would be the means of production for every book printed in the foreseeable future, he would become the Boss of the publishing world, and not simply in books but in the voluminous production of journalism as well. In a fit of dizzy optimism, he projected that this stake would earn him in excess of $55 million per year. These prospects would clearly lift him to a new level of power among the elite industrialists like Andrew Carnegie and Henry H. Rogers with whom he had associated. It's no wonder that he thought of A Connecticut Yankee as his last book. He had always been a professional writer, in the sense of performing for money; when this ship came in, he wouldn't ever have to write again. Of course, the ship never did come in. Instead Paige's technological dream went the way of Hank Morgan's. As Twain was finishing A Connecticut Yankee, he grew increasingly aware that the technology in which he had invested both his fortune and his hopes for power was doomed to failure.

Twain had foreseen that his tale would end tragically from the very beginning. Early notebook entries indicate that he imagined that Morgan would finally find peace in suicide rather than earn the satisfaction of success. No other outcome for his utopian vision was feasible, given the actual trajectory of history. For if Hank Morgan were to have reshaped the sixth century in the image of nineteenth-century America, then the nineteenth-century America that would evolve from Morgan's newly constituted chain of history would not resemble the one from which he came and on which he modeled his revision of the sixth century. The text foregrounds its anachron-ismic obstacle when Morgan reports that he is about to dispatch an expedition to discover America. By having developed an Enlighten-ment utopia in Camelot, he has eliminated the ideological necessity for discovering America. Since America itself was an idea before there was a place to concretize it, Morgan's founding of that same idea in England absorbs the motivation for discovering America else-where. This doesn't deny the existence of the continent that stood between England and the Far East, but if Morgan's civilization suc-ceeds, that land mass to the west would be, conceptually, something other than America. As such, Morgan will have prevented both his own birth as a nineteenth-century Yankee and his subsequent return to an earlier time.[40] Despite the tale's antihistorical urge, it hangs on a preconditioned historical necessity.

Notwithstanding the premise that Morgan's plan must fail, the impending failure of the Paige typesetter secured the philosophical grounds of the novel's tragic ending. Twain's personal loss in this venture didn't simply darken his mood, suggesting the cataclysmic ending of "a man who is the victim of his own inventions," as Ken-neth Lynn suggests; rather, the failed machine and the text identi-fied with it give experiential and literary form to what Twain came to see as the inherent contradiction of Enlightenment progress. In other words, Twain didn't simply lose faith in business or the Ma-chine Age; he realized, as he watched the machine devour the for-tune he fed it, that even if the machine had succeeded, the power he had counted on was predicated on the assumption that it would eliminate workers from the process. Despite any justification that men would be freed from the drudgery of labor to pursue higher aims, profiteering at the expense of the unemployed must have gnawed at Twain's conscience, as Frederick Crews suggests. Either way, whether failed technology spelled Twain's personal economic disaster or technological efficiency eliminated human labor in a socioeconomic tragedy, the entire affair exposed the Enlightenment contradiction between freedom and control, leading both to the apocalyptic demise of Morgan's Enlightenment utopia and to Twain's cynicism about the founding premise of America itself.[41]

Regardless of his original tragic intentions, Twain hadn't expected his tale to reveal this philosophical crisis. He began rather optimistically, pursuing the assumptions of progress in the philosophical outlook he shared with the majority of Americans. So he turned to Morgan not as "the grotesque caricature of the Enlightenment" that Cox contends he is but as the essential persona of the Enlightenment.[42] For in order to take on the authority of history, Twain needed a character with the kind of reason and ingenuity that Morgan boasts. Given the narrative's absurd premise, he needed a narrator whose world view would recommend him as a credible witness. Who better than "The Yankee of Yankees" to underwrite this kind of credibility? The factory foreman strode to center stage, ready and willing to create a modern society out of a medieval one. His ability to adapt, to invent, to manipulate his environment in order to make it suit his needs is fundamental to the autonomy of the self to which the Enlightenment gave birth. In his own words, Morgan attests to his abilities as the ideal candidate for such an enterprise: "I could make anything a body wanted – anything in the world, it didn't make any difference what; and if there wasn't any quick, new-fangled way to make a thing, I could invent one – and do it as easy as rolling off a log" (4).

But the Enlightenment's empowerment of the individual has a countervailing influence as well. A desire for power over one's condition in the world is fundamental to the Enlightenment project. When this desire for power meets Morgan's self-assured arrogance, the product is a new version of despotism. Morgan has not even oriented himself in Camelot when he comes to a quick conclusion about the power he desires:

> I made up my mind to two things: if it was still the nineteenth
> century and I was among lunatics and couldn't get away, I would

presently boss that asylum or know the reason why; and if on the other hand it was really the sixth century, all right, I didn't want any softer thing: I would boss the whole country inside of three months; for I judged I would have the start of the best educated man in the kingdom by a matter of thirteen hundred years and upwards. (17)

By articulating these motives, Morgan reveals that the goal of the Enlightenment tradition is power: reason and knowledge are the means of attaining that goal.

As Morgan continues to advance in the society, his project emphatically reflects the primacy of power. For example, his plans to use the eclipse to intimidate the superstitious crowd will not only save his life but also afford him the advantage of prestige, since "in a business way it would be the making of me; I knew that" (45). Only after he has ascended to a position of power does he begin to feel disappointed in the quality of his life and to think about introducing improvements. He conceives of himself as "just another Robinson Crusoe cast away on an uninhabited island, with no society but some more or less tame animals, and if I wanted to make life bearable I must do as he did" (54). But Twain ironizes Morgan's colonialist ideology by representing some of the Yankee's improvements as insignificant – if not flat out anachronistically useless, like franchising stove-polish salesmen before there were stoves – when compared to the advantages of power he enjoys. Once he has "solidified [his] power," he begins to relish the opportunity that his own temporal displacement affords him, because he enjoys an even loftier status than he had as a foreman in the nineteenth century. He assesses Camelot as "[t]he grandest field that ever was; and all my own; not a competitor nor the shadow of a competitor; not a man who wasn't a baby to me in acquirements and capacities: whereas, what would I amount to in the twentieth century? I should be a foreman of a factory, that is about all" (62). This pathetic realization is riddled with anxiety about the unfolding history of industrialism. Acknowledging his sense of being squeezed out of the technological hierarchy of his own era, Morgan implies that industrialism is not about progress but about power. Because the sixth century offers a refuge from the realization of his own obsolescence in the late nineteenth century, the utopian model on which his plans for Camelot are founded implies prospectively that industrial America is a satisfying condition only for those who enjoy the privileges of power. From Morgan's vantage, the sixth century is utopian because it offers him those privileges. As a "Unique," who "could not be dislodged or challenged for thirteen centuries and a half, for sure" (63), Morgan has found himself in a version of America even better than the one he left behind because he doesn't have to share his power with others of equal or greater ability and fortune. For a monopolist like Morgan, Camelot is the ultimate American dream: all the opportunity without the competition.[43]

And yet this image of Camelot as Morgan's own private laboratory conflicts with Twain's critique of Scott in *Life on the Mississippi*. The disabling consequence of the Sir Walter disease was the imbalance of competition that it imposed between the realistically energized North and the romantically enervated South. A more balanced rivalry between sections would have led not to the Civil War but to a productive friction, the "all-pervading and restless activity" that Tocqueville found most promising in American democracy, "a superabundant force, and an energy which is unseparable from it and which may, however unfavourable the circumstances may be, produce wonders." In Morgan's view, though, competition didn't lead to a roundly shared vitality but tended to concentrate authority in the hands of an individual who could subject the many to his will. Unlike his prospects in nineteenth-century America, his opportunities in Camelot abound because he is poised to become that individual. Still, in achieving that status, Morgan embodies an aspect of power that Tocqueville theorized in his analysis of democracy, which Claude Lefort highlights in his reading of *L'Ancien Régime et la Revolution Française* and *Democracy in America*. According to Lefort, Tocqueville's "purpose is to demonstrate, using America as an example, that [modern society] is at its most vigorous when the illusion that its organization can be mastered is dispelled, when the activities and opinions of human beings escape state control." The power that Morgan wields is the product not of this kind of salutary political liberalism but of economic liberalism as formulated by the physiocrats. This economic liberalism, in Tocqueville's view, assumes a social power of such unforeseen domination that "the old words *despotism* and *tyranny*" are inadequate to express it. This dangerous domination perverts egalitarian ideals, turning democracy's impersonalized power into an alienating force. The sort of social power that Morgan assumes "is no longer content to demand obedience from all its citizens" but, as Lefort argues, "takes it upon itself to transform them or even to produce them."[44]

Morgan's "man-factories" clearly demonstrate this aspect of his social power. But they also concentrate the inherent dilemma of the Enlightenment. These "nurseries" for "training a crowd of ignorant folk into experts" are built on the same assumption that informs the aphorism Twain introduced in this text and used again in *Pudd'nhead Wilson* with a slightly different twist: "Training – training is everything; training is all there is to a person" (157). In acknowledging the influence of training, he shies away from the views of a Whig historian like David Hume (who, in his essay "Of National Characters," argues that the white race is innately superior and that this explains its preeminence in establishing "civilized" nations) and toward the democratic sentiments that Henry George elaborated in *Progress and Poverty*, attributing cultural differences to "education and habit" rather than upholding the traditional ethnographic hierarchy based on spurious biology. But despite Morgan's enlightened view, his "man-factories" are no more than training centers that update economic discrimination, retooling the superstitions of antiquity into mechanical skills that will undergird his power. Although he hopes to develop a progressive nation through these educational institutions, "to turn groping and grubbing automata into *men*," his technological applications threaten to reduce human beings to industrial-labor potential. Consider, for example, Morgan's harnessing of St. Stylite's ritual bowing to run a sewing machine: "I . . . got five years' good service out of him; in which time he turned out upwards of eighteen thousand first-rate tow-linen shirts, which was ten a day. I worked him Sundays and all; he was going, Sundays, same as week-days, and it was no use to waste the power . . . There was more money in the business than one knew what to do with" (214). Since capital power is his only concern, he continues to exploit St. Stylite until "I noticed that the motive power had taken to standing on one leg, and I found that there was something the matter with the other one; so I stocked the business and unloaded, taking Bors de Ganis into camp financially along with certain of his friends: for the works stopped within a year, and the good saint got him to his rest." Similarly, within a relatively short space of the narrative, Morgan can, on the one hand, revile the slavery that he witnesses in Camelot's starkly stratified aristocracy and, on the other hand, chuckle over his acquisition of knights during his travels with Sandy, comparing this windfall to cornering the market in pork futures. Such repeated intrusions of economic abuse undermine the democratic notions that Morgan alternately professes. Instead, his authoritarian arrogance motivates a transhistorical version of colonial domination.[45]

Of the many contrasting images that Morgan calls up to distinguish himself from the society – a "giant among pigmies, a man among children, a master intelligence among intellectual moles" (67) – the most resonant is his self-portrait as "just another Robinson Crusoe" (54). This literary model was a favorite of Twain's, mentioned explicitly in *Life on the Mississippi* and allusively in *Huckleberry Finn*. The difference here is that by identifying with Defoe's castaway, Morgan not only reaffirms the colonialist impulse for which America was an unanticipated by-product but also signals his own participation in novelistic discourse: "if I wanted to make life bearable I must do as he did – invent, contrive, create; reorganize things; set brain and hand to work, and keep them busy" (54). These processes are the active experiences that typically define both the American and the novelist. Through Morgan's identification, Twain acknowledges the link between the Enlightenment as the source of novelistic discourse and America as the geography where this discourse could be given experiential form.

In *A Connecticut Yankee*, Twain investigates this linkage and tests the novel's limits against its generic origins. The results show both the Enlightenment and novelistic discourse to be wanting. Even as Morgan speaks of his putative aims of freedom and knowledge, his programmatic march toward control of Camelot exposes itself as an authoritarian scheme that organizes all production and social practices under his power. Indeed, it is not those who resist his industrial democracy but Morgan himself who destroys the technological society he has built in anticipation of the climactic battle. Twain's historical fiction, then, anticipates the Frankfurt school critique of the Enlightenment as a flawed dialectic of freedom and control that generates totalitarianism. This is precisely the dialectic motivating Twain's double-crossed career, and the same flawed premises generate the dilemma of authority in novelistic discourse.[46] In the end, the text's radical circumvention of history equals the Enlightenment's aggressive control of history as a course of steady progress.

The paradoxical contradiction that Max Horkheimer and Theodor W. Adorno locate in what they call "the dialectic of the Enlightenment" and the "reversibility" that Lefort identifies at the root of Tocqueville's theory of democracy both emerge in *A Connecticut Yankee*'s idiosyncratic, paradoxical, and reversible form. This form depends not simply on the anachronism of time travel but permeates all levels of the narrative structure in contradictions, oppositions, and patterned reversals. This internally crossed narrative thwarts any attempt to construct a stable reading, but in that difficulty emerges a critique of the kind of control that Morgan represents, registering Twain's uneasiness about novelistic discourse and its relation to American ideology. As the vehicle for Twain's attack on the authority of history, *A Connecticut Yankee* is his discovery – perhaps dimly perceived, but no less astutely critical – that the novel is a project whose flaws go beyond its fictional status to the philosophical outlook that evoked it in the first place.

For example, on the local level, reversals arise in the mechanistic terms Morgan uses for describing processes that he endorses, such as his "man-factories," and others that he abhors, like the established church as a "political machine" (161). Similarly, Sandy's narrative defect arises from the mechanized form in which she tells stories: "She had a flow of talk that was steady as a mill . . . Her clack was going all day, and you would think something would surely happen to her works, by and by; but no, they never got out of order, and she never had to slack up for words; she could grind, and pump, and churn and buzz by the week, and never stop to oil up or blow out" (103). Sandy's fundamental storytelling flaw, though, is the lack of variety and inventiveness that the Yankee prefers. In his marveling at Morgan le Fay's "ingenious devilishness" in having "*invented*" narrative structures that would emotionally abuse her prisoners, the Boss shows his appreciation for a decidedly evil, though no less wondrous, form of creative machination (169). Hank Morgan's series of miracles continues the textual compulsion with reversal. In the eclipse episode, he pretends to turn noonday into night and hollowly threatens anyone who moves; "I will blast him with thunder, I will consume him with lightning!" (48). Later, when he destroys Merlin's tower, he makes good on his earlier threat to blast his enemies with lightning "that turned night to noonday" (59). His miracle of the Fountain of the Valley of Holiness also dazzles by its midnight spectacle "spreading a rainbowed noonday" and throws in an extra touch by mingling the opposing elements of fire and water: "a vast fountain of dazzling lances of fire vomited . . . with a hissing rush" and "in the uncanny glare . . . the freed water leaping forth!" (223). Morgan's own views of his technological project are often wildly divergent: he may at one moment proclaim his plan as a beautiful design for efficiency and progress and at another ponder its sublime potential, likening it to "any serene volcano, standing innocent with its smokeless summit in the blue sky and giving no sign of the rising hell in its bowels" (82).[47]

A more obvious pattern of narrative repetition and reversal operates much as in *Life on the Mississippi* and *Huckleberry Finn*, in which episodes on either side of a textual divide play off each other. For example, the restoration of the fountain stands as a central episode that divides two versions of Morgan's picaresque travels. In the first version, with Sandy, Morgan travels as a knight-errant and lampoons the social practice and classical form of legend that honored knight-errantry. In the second, Morgan and King Arthur travel as peasants, a form of slumming familiar from *The Prince and the Pauper*. But whereas Morgan's travels with Arthur may have started out as a means for Twain to address the injustices of aristocratic societies, as Edward and Hendon's journey had, the issue of slavery, which had emerged in *Huckleberry Finn*, assumes a higher profile in Morgan's second journey. The emergence of slavery as a topic in *A Connecticut Yankee* compromises Twain's plan to contrast the two eras because it exposes their similarity rather than their difference. As Morgan travels through the English landscape, he must confess that the English peasant "was just the twin of the Southern 'poor white' of the far future" (297), that the English ignorance of comparative monetary values recalls the economic disparity between North and South during the American Civil War, and that, contrary to his earlier claim that caste prejudice had died out in America, the law that remanded him and the king into slavery was the "same infernal law" that "had existed in our own South in my own time, more than thirteen hundred years later, and under it hundreds of free men who could not prove that they were freemen had been sold into life-long slavery, without the circumstance making any particular impression upon me" (303). And yet despite his vow to "be the death of slavery" (346) and his delight to hear Arthur promise that he will abolish slavery, there is a hollowness in the vow; much like Tom Sawyer, Morgan takes pride in inventing a "picturesque" plan to get free, one that "might delay us for months," but one that will be a fine "dramatic" show (353). Moreover, for all of the insight that Morgan is supposed to have gleaned from this experience, he shows not an inkling of critical perspective on his nineteenth-century model of utopia. Instead, in a head-over-heels version of Santayana's dictum, Morgan is destined to prefigure history because he has not learned its lessons.[48]

By attempting to remake the past in the image of the future, Morgan seeks to reverse social conditions as he found them. But his efforts do not so much circumvent the history of injustice leading to American slavery as accelerate the historical catastrophe that injustice brought on. In fact, Morgan's experience reads like a displacement of American history. He has, in effect, rediscovered America before the fact. We see this not only in his identification with Robinson Crusoe but also in his imitation of "Columbus, or Cortez, or one of those people" (40), using the eclipse to mystify the natives who threaten his life upon his arrival. At the story's other end, his defeat of English knight-errantry begins with a revolutionary battle in which he vows "to either destroy knight-errantry or be its victim" (384), paraphrasing Patrick Henry's choice between liberty or death. And the battle itself is marked by Morgan's own version of a shot heard round the world – the evidence of which is the pierced armor described by the Warwick Castle tour guide at the opening of Twain's framing device. But rather than leading comfortably to Morgan's glorious republic, this first shot echoes explosively in a resounding apocalyptic image of America's own mechanized Civil War.[49] Indeed, if Morgan's first battle with knight-errantry evokes the most famous line of Emerson's "Concord Hymn," then his last suggests the images of Melville's "Utilitarian View of the *Monitor's* Flight." As in Melville's poetic vision of technological warfare, the Battle of the Sand Belt replaces the romantic heroism of the glorious battlefield with the mechanical efficiency of an apocalyptic assembly line.

This anterior restaging of pivotal moments in American history calls attention both to Morgan's inability to improve civilization trans-historically and to the inability of novelistic discourse to circumvent history. In both cases, the dialectic of Enlightenment maps the unfolding course of history in which power struggles inevitably arise from the twin desires for freedom and control. In this way, *A Connecticut Yankee* stages historical inevitability differently from *Huckleberry Finn*. Where as Huck's narrative reveals the influence of culture on his consciousness as a process of recapitulation, Morgan's tale suggests that his cultural consciousness is conditioned not so much by historical content as by the epistemological form by which the Enlightenment has shaped the interpretation of events and given them meaning within cultural historiography. *A Connecticut Yankee* construes Morgan's experience in Camelot as a process of *pre*capitulation, the twisted fulfillment in advance of what another famous Yankee, Yogi Berra, has called "déjà vu all over again." In this precapitulation, the history of the Enlightenment is played out in miniature one thousand years before the Enlightenment will make its indelible mark on history. If the prevailing nineteenth-century cultural notion was, as Lears describes it, that "the pursuit of individual self-interest led . . . to Spencerian harmony as militant conflict gave way to industrial peace," then Twain's perception of the Enlightenment's dialectical paradox led him to the opposite conclusion. For Twain showed how Morgan's industrial expertise could undergird his quest for power with an unforeseen military capability.[50]

Still, Morgan's two martial encounters with knight-errantry do not allegorize the American Revolution and the Civil War as neatly as they might, because sandwiched between them is another version of the Civil War. This interim battle arises from a rivalry prompted by aggressive stock speculation and pits two factions of knights against each other. Although this fictionally represents the kind of market manipulation in which Twain was involved, albeit unsuccessfully, in his hope of enticing investors to support the Paige typesetter, it allegorizes the fratricidal tension that crystallized the horror of the Civil War. And just as Twain was absent from the Civil War, Morgan also misses this war between the knights, having been sent abroad, on doctor's orders, to care for his sick child. In this we can read the echo of Twain's "Private History of a Campaign That Failed." In that fictionalized reminiscence, he recalls, "I was not rightly equipped for this awful business; that war was intended for men, and I for a child's nurse" (*CTSS&E*, 1:880). In this admission lies the motivation for projecting two images of the Civil War. The first is the war for which he was unequipped and from which he is absent, like Morgan nursing his sick child. The second is the war of the novelist's fiction, a war in which he imagines himself unmatched by any power, just as Ambrose Bierce shows the inventiveness of the doomed Peyton Fahrquar effecting a miraculous romantic escape, against all realistic odds, in "An Occurrence at Owl Creek Bridge." In this climactic war, Twain vents his frustration at the authority of history by wielding the only power he has at his disposal: authorial power.

The entire sequence, though, mythologizes Western history even as the Enlightenment is portrayed as a means of extinguishing myth. These military engagements depict an America that inverts the national portrait Twain had already detailed in *Life on the Mississippi*. In the Mississippi book Twain claimed that romanticized medievalism caused the American Civil War, launching the modern era; but in *A Connecticut Yankee*, he imagines that the greed of modern capitalism causes this civil war between the knights and ushers in a regressive dimness that Morgan thought he had illuminated away forever.

Having remade the Middle Ages in the image of the Gilded Age, Twain has administered his antidote for the Sir Walter disease. But does this make any difference? The answer is the text's salient point. Given the informing dialectic of the Enlightenment, the historical consequences are immutable. Western history and Twain's text are both structurally compromised. The collision of forces in the last throes of *A Connecticut Yankee*'s plot hastily stages the terms of the impasse. Morgan's antagonism toward the Roman Catholic Church goes beyond establishing the premise of Enlightenment, because the plot that Twain develops in Morgan's absence also shows the complexity of that antagonism as a dialectical struggle. The Yankee's industrialized market economy doesn't simply defeat the forces of superstition; rather, the new system reveals, as Horkheimer and Adorno contend, that "the unleashed market economy was both the actual form of reason and the power which destroyed reason . . . The Catholic counterrevolution proved itself right as against the Enlightenment, just as the Enlightenment had shown itself to be right in regard to Catholicism."[51] Twain represents the struggle in precisely these terms: Morgan's empirical reason initially defeats the Church's superstitious oppression, only to be overthrown by the Church's interdict when the market economy destroys reason in the war among the stock board's speculators. When Morgan returns to his paralyzed utopia, he reaffirms his opposition to the Church, the knights who have fallen in line behind its authority, and all but fifty-three of the English population.

As the dynamic contest intensifies into the conclusion's frenzied pace, philosophical oppositions are rapidly synthesized, giving literary form to the later words of the Frankfurt critics; "[S]urvival as affirmed by reason – the reified drive of the individual bourgeois – [is] revealed as destructive natural power, no longer to be distinguished from self-destruction. The two [are] now indissolubly blended."[52] Morgan's self-preservational motive in the eclipse episode has evolved into a self-destructive authoritarianism bent on controlling this world by destroying it. In all of his significant actions, he reveals that the Enlightenment comes under the "mythic curse" that Horkheimer and Adorno see as its dialectical flaw: "It wishes to extricate itself from the process of fate and retribution, while exercising retribution on that process." Morgan pays out his retribution in the climactic battle, judging no one except his fifty-two worthy of being saved. The admiration he once expressed for the nation of common citizens has evaporated, for now "even the very men who had lately been slaves were in the 'righteous cause,' and glorifying it, praying for it, sentimentally slobbering over it, just like all the commoners. Imagine such human muck as this; conceive of this folly!" (427). In this contempt for the willingness of former slaves to resubmit to the insidious authority from which they have been freed, we should note a shift from the rhetorical emphasis with which he concluded *Huckleberry Finn*. Whereas that text portrayed Tom Sawyer as a self-serving villain who would reenslave Jim while pretending to free him, even if it should take eighty years to do it, *A Connecticut Yankee* lays a share of the blame on the former slaves themselves. This later stance conforms with Twain's invective against the South's voting *en bloc* for the Democratic Party in the wake of Reconstruction, but it simplistically ignores more complex factors, such as the Jim Crow legislation that abrogated black voting rights in the South.

If this rhetorical turn signals his disillusionment with the American Enlightenment, it also registers his frustration with his own novelistic enterprise. For insofar as his creative act formalizes his own urge to mythologize, it mirrors a contradiction embedded in the Enlightenment, an epistemological movement founded on reason in rejection of mythology but which cannot escape mythologizing itself. The critical impulse of novelistic discourse labors under the same conceptual impasse. On the one hand, this revolutionary genre born of the Enlightenment breaks from the constraints of the past to enable a literary freedom of the imagination. But on the other hand, since the author controls all that happens in this image of the world, the authority of novelistic discourse is as totalitarian as the philosophical revolution from which it arose. Furthermore, because this novel's attempt to create a fictional world relies on replacing the facts of history with disruptive possibilities, its alternative is, in part, an anti-Enlightenment project in which fiction, a mythologizing practice, substitutes for empiricism. Thus the double-cross of novelistic discourse inheres in its own split identity between reason and enchantment.

Horkheimer and Adorno liken an artist's work to the magician's: the work of art "posits its own self-enclosed area, which is withdrawn from the context of profane existence, and in which special laws apply. Just as in the ceremony the magician first of all marked out the limits of the area where the sacred powers were to come into play, so every work of art describes its own circumference which closes it off from actuality."[53] The structure of Twain's text clearly marks it off from the world of actual events. One of the chief effects of Twain's framing device is to show Morgan's narrative as a kind of enchantment under whose spell Twain himself has come. But we nonetheless know that the first and final enchanter at work here is Twain. Despite his attempt to separate his own realistic practice from Morgan's enchantment, the motivation of Twain's novelistic discourse is not fundamentally different from that of his hero's project. Both resort to the linguistic arena after their efforts in technology have foundered. For Morgan, this means abandoning bustling industrial creativity upon his return to the shambles of his once booming civilization. Heretofore his plans have succeeded to the degree that they involved active construction. Morgan is by his own definition a man of action, and on several occasions he distinguishes between the reality of experience and the mere images of language. In the last stage of his civilization, though, his actions are increasingly verbal ones, many of them written: the Proclamation of his Republic (423); his "Tale of the Lost Land," which he will place in Twain's hands in the next millennium; sentimental letters to Sandy and their daughter, Hello Central; a "congratulatory proclamation" (432) to his stalwart fifty-two; and an implied ultimatum to the army of knights who are poised for a second futile strike against his impregnable stronghold (434), recalling his engraved challenge of "[P]ut up or shut up" after his revolutionary victory in the lists (396–7). He even imagines that his letters to Sandy and Hello Central are "almost like having us all together again," despite acknowledging that his writing was "a habit . . . kept up . . . for love of it and her, though I couldn't do anything with the letters after I had written them" (426–7). In this observation, Morgan crystallizes the problem of writing, as Twain has come to understand it. It is mere habit, and one without much useful impact, since "[w]ords are only painted fire" (357). "Words realize nothing, vivify nothing to you, unless you have suffered in your own person the thing which the words try to describe" (278–9). But when faced with the failure of their technological dreams, both Morgan and Twain have only words for consolation.

Although David Sewell makes a case for the colonializing force of the Yankee's language, citing Tzvetan Todorov's argument in *The Conquest of America*, Morgan's voice finally lacks the authority to transcend the course of unfolding events. The material form in which Morgan's narrative comes into Twain's hands suggests this lack of authority. Morgan's palimpsestic text cannot entirely erase the traces of history; instead, from beneath Morgan's writing, "traces of a penmanship which was older and dimmer still – Latin words and sentences: fragments from old monkish legends, evidently" (7) – endure, despite the Yankee's attempts to obliterate the past with his own story.[54] Likewise, Twain's efforts in novelistic discourse are also exposed as a kind of "painted fire," unmatched to the task of circumventing historical and ideological forces that he hopes to transcend. We see this pointedly in the language of the preface: "It is not *pretended* . . . ; it is only *pretended* . . . , it is safe *to consider . . . to suppose* . . . One is quite justified in *inferring* . . ." All of the verbs suggest the mythologizing impulse of fiction. And the profusion of impersonal constructions suggests Twain's circumspection about the efficacy of his enterprise even before it gets going. Since novelistic discourse is itself conditioned by history and ideology, even Twain's radical version cannot escape its own double-cross of trying to control or even deny history while remaining always subject to and within history.

And so, while taking on the nostalgic mythology of Scott's literary shams, Twain tests his own confidence in Enlightenment progress and recognizes that much of what has been offered as the greatness of Western civilization is the illusion of what Herbert Marcuse skeptically termed the "affirmative character of culture."[55] In trying to subvert the authority of history by way of a radical version of novelistic discourse, Twain discovered historical inevitability not as a cultural repetition compulsion in the manner of *Huckleberry Finn* but as a dominating philosophical double bind. This epistemological impasse had foredoomed his attempt to short-circuit the pathway of oppression because the Enlightenment's promise of freedom was already compromised by the impulse to dominate.

In the failure of *A Connecticut Yankee*, Twain confronted the scandal that caste-based oppression persisted in the ostensibly enlightened atmosphere of American culture. As Viscount Berkeley, in *The American Claimant*, realizes, "[T]here is an aristocracy of position here, and an aristocracy of prosperity, and . . . an aristocracy of the ins as opposed to the outs . . . Plainly there all kinds of castes here" (*AC*, 108–9). In the last dialectical stage of Twain's novelistic career, he attempted to expose those assumptions of caste that had conditioned his own consciousness no less than that of any American.

4

TWAINING IS EVERYTHING

THE AMERICAN CLAIMANT *AND* PUDD'NHEAD WILSON

The law is usually supposed to be a stern mistress, not to be lightly wooed, and yielding only to the most ardent pursuit. But even law, like love, sits more easily on some natures than on others.

Paul Laurence Dunbar, "The Scapegoat"

Like Hank Morgan, Mark Twain returned to the nineteenth century in the aftermath of *A Connecticut Yankee*. Beyond returning to a familiar era and the familiar geography of the United States, he also returned to the character Colonel Mulberry Sellers, whose harebrained scheming and good-natured idiocies had helped initiate Twain's first attempt at book-length narrative fiction in partnership with Charles Dudley Warner. Sellers was the only element of *The Gilded Age* that continued to occupy Twain's imagination. John T. Raymond's successful portrayal of Sellers in a stage adaptation had reinvigorated Twain's interest in writing a sequel featuring the madcap opportunist. But the play entitled *Colonel Sellers as a Scientist,* which Twain wrote in collaboration with Howells in 1883, lay dormant because Howells was embarrassed by the farce.[1] In 1884, around the same time that the initial idea for *A Connecticut Yankee* emerged, Twain decided to convert the Sellers play into a novel.[2] But with *A Connecticut Yankee* absorbing his literary energy during the 1880s, he didn't get around to this conversion until 1891.

After betting on the subversive critical energy of the novel against the authority of history in *A Connecticut Yankee* and losing, Twain found the Sellers farce an attractive mode. He mustered a desperate and cynical stand in this last complete dialectical stage. Morgan's story had shown him that caste traditions persisted even in a culture presumed to have broken from genealogical privilege. This awareness concentrated Twain's turmoil over authority and gave rise to *The American Claimant* and subsequently *Pudd'nhead Wilson*, in which his concern for caste reemerges. This pair of narratives registers the extreme degree of Twain's conflict over control in the divided structure of each text: both narratives started as farces, but *The American Claimant* ends as a romance comedy and *Pudd'nhead Wilson* as a novelistic tragedy. The confusion of modes in both reflects the representational crisis that Twain had reached.

Twain's alteration of the Sellers play benefited by his experience in writing Morgan's antihistorical, dystopian novel. Twain altered *Colonel Sellers as a Scientist* by adding the story of Lord Berkeley, an idealistic English heir to an earldom who forsakes his legacy on democratic principles. The story of his trials in America, however, exposes the shallowness of his principles and the contorted logic of their application within American society generally. By the addition of this counterstory to that of Sellers's claim to aristocratic title, Twain's composition of *The American Claimant* resembles his practice in *Life on the Mississippi*, in which material composed earlier is altered by the addition of new material that bears a strikingly different rhetorical orientation. But the critical perspective achieved in the Mississippi book by that method of construction is denied here. Instead, the critical potential of Berkeley's story to expose the compromise of American ideals by caste consciousness is dissipated by the comic resolution that, in one stroke, secures Berkeley's title, his marriage to Sellers's daughter, and Sellers's own dream of nobility.

Twain's second, critically novelistic effort in *Pudd'nhead Wilson* deserves more of our attention. For the novel's troublesome instabilities reveal more about the unsettling politics of authority in a society where the individual is pitted against the system or the mob, and thus, as Toni Morrison has observed, where "individualism fuses with the prototype of Americans as solitary, alienated, and malcontent."[3] The subversive critique that Twain launches in a second-effort text like *Pudd'nhead Wilson* bears its own notorious formal problems as the stress marks of the bolder effort it embodies. In those formal difficulties, *Pudd'nhead Wilson* tips its hand about the enticing but insurmountable challenge that the American paradox of freedom and control poses to the novelist. Set in the Mississippi valley where Twain first discovered the conflict between freedom and control, his last explicitly American novel concentrates that conflict to an even greater degree by its foregrounding of the caste distinctions in America's racial consciousness.

Gene-illogical Authority

Colonel Mulberry Sellers had a strong humorous appeal for Twain. After Morgan's failure to remake sixth-century England in the image of nineteenth-century America, Twain no doubt found Sellers to be the kind of character who would ease the burden of the authoritarian reality he had stumbled upon. Sellers's foolish pretensions to noble genealogy enabled Twain to bring his trademark broad humor to the kind of story that Hawthorne had attempted to treat with gothic seriousness.[4] Although *A Connecticut Yankee* revealed to Twain that authoritarian control in some form was endemic to the American utopia, it was surely a great relief to ridicule caste prejudices as embodied in Sellers.

The linkage between *The American Claimant* and *A Connecticut Yankee* precedes this development, though. Sellers's technical inclinations align him with Hank Morgan but whereas Sellers imagines himself a technological genius on the order of Morgan, his schemes reveal him to be anything but a "practical" man, "barren of sentiment" (*CY*, 4). None of his schemes approaches the scope of Morgan's enterprises. With the exception of Sellers's only marketable invention – a simple though intriguing child's puzzle – most of his ideas are not just impractical; they are ludicrous misconceptions. His major scheme is "materialization," a process by which he claims to be able to revivify corpses, allowing them to perform living tasks without the ordinary bodily demands of mortals. As the owner of these reanimated bodies, he anticipates possessing a monopoly on cheap labor: "Within three days I shall have completed my method, and then – let the world stand aghast, for it shall see marvels . . . [W]ithin three days – ten at the outside – you shall see me call the dead of any century, and they will arise and walk. Walk? – they shall walk forever, and never die again" (44). He imagines staffing the New York City Police, the United States Army, even the Congress, replacing "these practically dead people . . . with the genuine article" (46). And, for his trouble, he imagines reaping billions. In this scheme, we should see the inverse of Morgan's "man-factories" combined with his slaughter of English knights. Rather than turning automatons into men, as Morgan had proposed to do with his "man-factories," Sellers plans to turn corpses into automatons, to bring back to life "ten thousand veterans drawn from the victorious legions of all the ages – soldiers who will chase Indians year in and year out on materialized horses, and cost never a cent for rations or repairs" (45). Sellers's claim that he is an earl whose title has been usurped is a family gag ridiculing Twain's own relative, Jesse Leathers, who made a similarly preposterous claim. But we should also read Sellers's materializing process as a moment of Twain's self-mockery for having invested in a machine like the Paige typesetter, which was expected to cut labor costs of printing houses to a fraction and from which Twain had calculated, in the inflationary fashion of Sellers, that he would earn $55 million annually.

Sellers even imagines answering a need for control of domestic labor with his materializing process. He finds it nothing but "trouble" to have "old house-servants that were your slaves once and have been your personal friends always" (81). For domestics such as these become "members of the family . . . They do just about as they please, they chip into a conversation whenever they want to, and the plain fact is they ought to be killed." This last expostulation becomes the stimulus of a new brainstorm: "When I've got the materializing down to a certainty, I will get Hawkins to kill them, and after that they will be under better control. Without a doubt a materialized negro could easily be hypnotized into a state resembling silence" (82). Exposing a dark authoritarian side to his otherwise humorous characterization, this burlesque of Sellers's desire for control points ahead to the racial theme of *Pudd'nhead Wilson*.

Twain doesn't follow up on the Jim Crow application of Sellers's process. Instead, the colonel devotes his materializing efforts to a less ambitious goal: by bringing back to life a bank robber who has died in a hotel fire, he hopes to earn the reward that has been posted for apprehension of the thief. This is where Sellers and the British Disclaimant cross paths. Lord Berkeley, the son of the earl whom Sellers claims has usurped his rightful title, believes in social equality. When he learns that Sellers's claim is valid, Berkeley repudiates all ties with the aristocratic fraud of English society and sails for America, where he hopes to realize his true human value. The perfect Americanizing opportunity arrives after he is presumed to have died gloriously in an act of heroism during the same fire that claims the bank robber's life. Contrary to the newspaper myths of Berkeley's fatal heroism, the viscount escapes safely, managing to grab only the clothing of the criminal, whom Sellers will plan to materialize back into a zombielike state. Berkeley's identity is burned up along with his introductory letters of credit, and he glows with the spirit of American individualism derived from starting afresh:

> Yes, nothing could be better than the way matters have turned out. I have only to furnish myself with a new name, and take my new start in life totally untrammelled. Now I breathe my first breath of real freedom; and how fresh and breezy and inspiring it is! At last I am a man! a man on equal terms with my neighbor; and by my manhood, and by it alone, I shall rise and be seen of the world, or I shall sink from sight and deserve it. This *is* the gladdest day, and the proudest, that ever poured its sun upon my head! (76)

Berkeley's condition recalls the terms in which Edward Said has defined the authority of the novel: The young man is starting over with the invigorating sense of power to chart his own life. Contrast this with Sellers's romantic desire for validation through aristocratic recognition. But despite the suggestive opposition, the chance intertwining of their courses casts doubt on Berkeley's idealism. His metaphoric rebirth from aristocratic fraud is rhetorically undermined by juxtaposition to Sellers's absurdly literal resurrection of dead people as materialized zombies.

Sellers believes that Berkeley, who has rechristened himself "Howard Tracy," is the one-armed bandit, materialized through the colonel's fantastical process, though the materializee's two arms and English accent are a puzzler. Attempting to put it all right, Sellers explains that the materialization has been incomplete, stopping a century shy of the incarnation he had targeted. In an absurd literalization of Morgan's notion that the human mind is produced by training, by inherited ideas, Sellers believes that "*Every man is made up of heredities*, long-descended atoms and particles of his ancestors" (193). Consequently, he concludes that Tracy "is nothing but a damned ancestor" of the wanted man he was trying to summon back from the dead. This shortfall in Sellers's plan to transform the deceased bandit into a born-again zombie parallels Berkeley's own emerging self-doubt as his fortunes fail to materialize as expected. The confidence with which he had declared himself a new man ebbs away when he comes up short of the potential he believed himself to possess.

For example, as a new arrival, he flushes with pride when a critic at the Mechanics' Debating Society rebuts Matthew Arnold's attack on the disrespectful American press, leading Berkeley to denounce the "innumerable slaveries imposed by misplaced reverence!" (99). But it isn't long before he is taken aback at the titles of address that Americans bandy about and rankled more deeply by the familiarity that Americans assume with him. He writes in his diary, "The thing I miss most, and most severely, is the respect, the deference, with which I was treated all my life in England, which seems to be somehow necessary to me" (128). Contrary to his first impressions of the vast "material development" (99) of America, "a land where there was 'work and bread for all' " (104), he comes to recognize that the America he has discovered is far from the ideal democracy he had expected to find: "[T]here is an aristocracy of position here, and an aristocracy of prosperity, and apparently there is also an aristocracy of the ins as opposed to the outs, . . . [T]here are all kinds of castes here, and only one that I belong to – the outcasts" (130–1). His anticipation of utter poverty makes him shudder at the naive optimism he finds when he reads his early diary entries. Clearly, America is not the ideal society he desired, but more vexing is the realization that he is not the stalwart idealist he had pretended to be. He sends a cablegram informing his father of his new identity, with the implied hope that the Earl of Rossmore might bail him out of his idealistic folly. In a daydream, "the sumptuous appointments of his father's castle [rise] before him without rebuke. Even the plushed flunky, that walking symbol of a sham inequality, had not been unpleasant to his dreaming view" (143). In contrast to this reverie, he shudders with shame at the thought of returning to the Mechanics' Debating Society, where, in the company of men with true conviction, his unregenerate aristocratic temperament is exposed all the more starkly to him. Like Sellers's incomplete materialization of the bank robber, Berkeley's incomplete remaking of himself has left him no better than one of his ancestors.

His conscience is soothed, however, when his one friend – a well-read, republican chair-maker named Barrows – explains that "the factor of human nature" (147) reveals the foolishness of absolute rubrics of equality in American society. Barrows persuades Berkeley that any American would accept aristocratic privilege without hesitation if it were offered. He argues pragmatically that to pass up such an advantage would be foolish if to do so were to have no impact on the social system. The only ones to blame are the citizens of a nation who would put up with hereditary privilege when they are excluded from the benefits of rank and title. Barrows's rationalizing eases Berkeley's troubled mind. As his former reluctance to acknowledge his title dissolves, Berkeley represents the same ideological mechanism that characterizes the romance genre, a capitulation to the authority that had been targeted for critique.

Berkeley has no intention of flaunting his rank but when situations appear to call for him to reveal it, he does so readily. Twice he admits that he is the son of the Earl of Rossmore, but in neither case does that information serve his circumstances as he expects. In the first instance, he has been robbed of his little remaining money and his board is overdue. His claim to noble birth and his expectation that he will shortly be receiving money from his father by cablegram are seen as lies or mad delusions, making him the butt of waggish humor and the object of pity. When the cablegram does arrive, its failure to corroborate his claim appears to confirm the skepticism of his critics and his pitiers. Having sunk to a new low, he resolves not to "play earl's son again before a doubtful audience" (171). Of course, he does do it again, and this time the consequences are more humorously absurd. The question of his identity propels the narrative into a drawing-room farce.

Berkeley and Sellers's daughter, Sally, have fallen in love. With this turn, the narrative transfers the power to instill human virtue from idealistic political rhetoric to an equally idealized representation of love. The sense of fulfillment that overcomes Sally in this relationship changes her irrevocably: "[S]he was become a new being; a being of a far higher and worthier sort than she had been such a little while before; an earnest being, in place of a dreamer; and supplied with a reason for her presence in the world, where merely a wistful and troubled curiosity about it had existed before" (227). But as the narrative winds on about her altered state in the glow of her acknowledged and requited desire, it inflates the account of her alteration well beyond proportion:

> So great and so comprehensive was the change which had been wrought that she seemed to herself to be a real person who had lately been a shadow; a something, which had lately been a nothing; a purpose, which had lately been a fancy; a finished temple, with the altar-fires lit and the voice of worship ascending, where before had been but an architect's confusion of arid working plans, unintelligible to the passing eye and prophesying nothing. (227–8)

The hyperbolic prose points to the narrative's own confusion, which Sally herself approximates by equivocating, after ostensibly having become fulfilled. Berkeley's former dilemma about the incompleteness of his transformation from aristocrat to democrat is transferred to Sally, who wavers in her belief that Berkeley's love is genuine.

Sally's sense of fulfillment prompts her to throw off all traces of admiration for the aristocratic shams that had formerly enthralled her: she refuses to answer to the name "Lady Gwendolen," which her father has conferred on her to fit their newly acquired nobility, and presumably she intends to withdraw from Ivanhoe-Rowena College, "the selectest and most aristocratic seat of learning for young ladies," replete with "[c]astellated college-buildings – towers and turrets and imitation moat – and everything about the place named out of Sir Walter Scott's books" (53–4). Love, it appears, has cured her of the "Sir Walter disease" before her case has reached the terminal stage. With this turn in the narrative, Twain parodies the sort of conventional marriage plot he loathed in Jane Austen's novels by predicating the success of the courtship on the democratic repudiation of aristocratic privilege.[5]

But despite her resolve, Sally is soon plagued by alternating desire for and doubt about Berkeley, and she therefore alternately ignites and extinguishes their courtship. Her denunciations of aristocratic privilege make Berkeley fear that if she were to know of his true identity as a viscount and heir to an earlship she would reject him. Sally, in turn, reads his uneasiness as a lack of sincerity, fearing that perhaps he is more interested in her title than in her. Finally he confides his secret to her: "Your rank *couldn't* ever have been an enticement. I am son and heir to an English earl!" (242). The startling claim does put her off, but not because of her distaste for rank; rather, she simply doesn't believe him, and, just as in the boarding-house scene, he can produce no proof of his claim.

After several more turns to the spiral of acceptance and rejection, Berkeley is finally bailed out, by none other than his father – and not by a cablegram or money but by a personal appearance. Arriving at the Sellers residence, the Earl of Rossmore puts everything right by his interview with and approval of Sally. Sally accepts Berkeley; Sellers accepts Rossmore, "the two earls [being] such opposites in nature that they fraternized at once" (269), and the comedy ends as it should, with a wedding and a complete reconciliation of both social and narrative orders. Quite simply, the narrative cops out, as do the characters, and accepts the status quo without the slightest hint of uneasiness. As in all of Twain's romances, he initiated an inquiry into the structure of social authority – caste, in this case – only to step back from the critique that his examination seemed to promise at the outset.

Those Extraordinary Twins began with precisely the same concern with genealogical authority, as the impending arrival of the Italian counts, Siamese twins joined at the waist, sets the town of Dawson's Landing astir. In its broad representation of the social rise of Mrs. Patsy Cooper and her daughter Rowena, who bask in the limelight for having the noble freaks residing under their roof, this story replicates the burlesque of aristocratic privilege that Twain had flirted with in *The American Claimant.* In backwater Missouri, even thread-bare vestiges of aristocratic grandeur confer prestige. But as Susan Gillman suggests, the twins' aristocratic signification gives way to a "cultural mythology that arose around Siamese twins" and to a cultural anxiety about racial mixture.[6] For this nearly hopeless and highly frustrating narrative has a dark mystery of miscegenation and murder growing within it. This tangled double narrative in which Twain explores both aristocratic and racial prejudice inhabits a text divided against itself. The dark strand of the narrative finally prevailed when Twain extricated it from the manuscript of *Those Extraordinary Twins* and published it as *Pudd'nhead Wilson.* The novel, in contrast to the farce from which it sprang, sustained Twain's interest because it explores the ways in which genealogically based social discriminations intersect with race and gender issues.

Pudd'nhead Wilson tests the rules governing society by focusing on

the lives of the marginal and displaced: David Wilson, Roxana, and
Tom Driscoll. Each represents a different version of exclusion. Wilson, a freethinker and newcomer to Dawson's Landing, finds his
plans for self-made success foreclosed by the town's misunderstanding of his ironic wit and eccentric hobbies – palmistry, fingerprinting, and making maxims for a witty calendar. Twain adopts some of
these maxims as chapter epigraphs; one of them – "Training is
everything" – thematically underscores the American belief that education and diligent industry lead to individual excellence, a principle that Wilson comes to personify, albeit perversely. The marginality that Roxana endures differs from Wilson's, because as a mulatto
slave woman she is institutionally denied access to the ideal of self-making. Within her excluded position, though, she subverts genealogical privilege and racial oppression by exchanging her master's
infant son with her own. Tom Driscoll's marginality is different still,
masked by the displacement that thrusts him into the social center.
As Roxana's erstwhile slave child, transformed, like Tom Canty, by a
change of clothing into a patrician, Tom unwittingly mocks the system of genealogical privilege. But his place is also fragile. Although
he grows up with the benefits of aristocratic training and falsely
inherited status that his mother's subversion enables, he is prone to
vice. Tom's career in crime escalates from gambling to stealing in
order to pay his gambling debts and culminates with the murder of
his adoptive father, his uncle, Judge Driscoll, who has caught Tom
in the act of stealing. Knowing that discovery would mean being
disinherited, Tom opts for murder to maintain his secret and to
secure his fortune. Wilson's and Tom's opposite mobilities on either
side of Roxana's fixed status reveal the true distinction between
birth and training in terms of race and gender. These inequities
compromising American social ideals appear as loose threads in the
tangled detective plot that Twain weaves around the lives of this trio.

Because this complex double mystery of miscegenation and murder emerged, in a sense, unauthorized from Twain's problematic
farce about Siamese twins, the story's genesis raises questions about
the issue of legitimacy that is its central theme. The fact that the
knotted issues of genealogy, genre, and race evolved nearly unconsciously out of a farce about freaks demonstrates that these triangulated concerns profoundly influenced his fascination with authority,
perhaps more persuasively than if he had actively sought to repre-

sent them. Indeed, it is often difficult to ascertain how much of this confused narrative Twain consciously intended. Twain's difficulty in controlling both the narrative convolutions that he clearly intended and those that appear to have escaped his awareness reveals the conflicted authority that shaped his career as a whole.

Beginning with Twain's formal and thematic difficulties in controlling his texts, both the published novel and the longer farce from which it sprang, we can trace Twain's ambivalence toward this genealogical complex through three stages. For the source theme, Twain reached back to an idea he had explored some twenty years earlier in "Personal Habits of the Siamese Twins" (1869), a burlesque in which Siamese twins frustrate conventional systems of authority and invite chaos in the society's controlling logic. However, when Twain redeployed the topic in 1890, he hadn't counted on the narrative confusion that his text would generate. Much like the twins' contrary temperaments, the text's bizarre fusion of farce and tragedy was a dilemma that Twain attempted to solve by reduction. After editing *Pudd'nhead Wilson* from the inner turmoil of a narrative stylistically divided, he ended up with a text that amounts to slightly more than half the length of the original project. Consequently, Twain's compositional method in his last American novel is the reverse of the one that he used to build *Life on the Mississippi*, where he joined thematically compatible but generically dissimilar narratives into a book something more than twice the length of "Old Times on the Mississippi." Twain's surgical remedy for *Those Extraordinary Twins* does not, however, sufficiently untangle the double text's confusion. Instead, the repressed doubleness returns in *Pudd'nhead Wilson*, deconstructing Twain's intention to bring order to the narrative.

Twain's repression of doubleness in *Those Extraordinary Twins* yields his double identifications with Roxana and Wilson. As opposite agents of narrative control in *Pudd'nhead Wilson*, they dramatize Twain's ambivalent desire both to subvert authority and to contain the threat of that subversion. Roxana's subversion lends the text a critical perspective on gender and race in American culture, but her plot finally exceeds the degree of subversion that Twain is willing to entertain. Wilson, the canny detective who unravels the mystery, imposes Twain's needed closure on Roxana's plot, stabilizing the social chaos that ensues from her subversive gesture. But Wilson's narrative resolution reflects a kind of racist repression, casting a shadow across Twain's image as a liberal with respect to race relations. This double representation of narrative control indicates the kind of authorial ambivalence that haunts Twain's enterprise. And the vicissitudes of his conflicted identifications require a double interpretation.

The portrait of Tom as a mulatto murderer suggests Twain's susceptibility to the cultural training of racial stereotypes, lending ironic credence to Wilson's maxim on training. Yet Twain's identification with the detective Wilson ultimately exploits the reversibility of racial stereotypes to express his anxiety of literary influence. In this light, *Pudd'nhead Wilson* appears finally as a parody of the genre Edgar Allan Poe invented. As always for Twain, problems of literary authority are inseparable from problems of social authority. Thus, when Twain mocks genealogy as a literary institution by satirizing Poe's paternal relation to the detective tale, he creates a mongrel text that enlists the "signifying" play of the African-American narrative tradition, symbolically subjecting Poe to the racial oppression that his anxious aristocratic affinities represent to Twain.

The Siamese Text

Although Twain edited *Pudd'nhead Wilson* from *Those Extraordinary Twins* to achieve narrative coherence, he ultimately included the rest of the original *Twins* fragment in *Pudd'nhead* under the subtitle "The Suppressed Farce." In reuniting the finished text with the fragment from which it had emerged, Twain was no doubt responding to a marketing requirement for a long book. But he exploits the opportunity afforded by the joint publication of his now separate and unequal twin texts to burlesque his haphazard compositional methods, thus illustrating how "a man born without the novel-writing gift" goes about trying "to build a novel" (*PW*, 119). In the preface to "The Suppressed Farce" Twain recounts the evolution of *Pudd'nhead Wilson* from *Those Extraordinary Twins*, describing himself as a "jack-leg" novelist, self-made not born; that is, the product of training, not genius. When this kind of writer sits down to write, Twain tells us,

> He has no clear idea of his story; in fact he has no story. He merely has some people in his mind, and an incident or two, also

a locality . . . [I]n the beginning he is only proposing to tell a little
tale; a very little tale; a six-page tale. But as it is a tale which he is
not acquainted with, and can only find out what it is by listening
as it goes along telling itself, it is more than apt to go on and on
and on till it spreads itself into a book. I know about this, because
it has happened to me so many times.

And I have noticed another thing: that as the short tale grows
into the long tale, the original intention (or motif) is apt to get
abolished and find itself superseded by a quite different one.

Hershel Parker has instructed readers of *Pudd'nhead Wilson* to ignore
what Twain says about its composition because his account is misleading.[7] In at least one respect, Parker is correct; the "six-page
tale" that Twain sat down to write was not *Those Extraordinary Twins*
but "Personal Habits of the Siamese Twins," which exceeds the six-
page target by only about five lines. When he came to his second
attempt, *Those Extraordinary Twins*, his aim was clearly to fulfill the
ambition that he momentarily entertained in "Personal Habits" but
checked in his penultimate remark in that tale: "I could say more
of an instructive nature about those interesting beings, but let what
I have written suffice" (*CTSS&E*, 1:229). Clearly, Twain was unable
"to let what" he had written "about those interesting beings . . .
suffice." *Those Extraordinary Twins* was an attempt to write not a six-
page tale but a full-length narrative that would satisfy that ambition
to "say more."

But Parker is wrong to discount everything in this preface.
Twain's account tells us a lot about the "instructive nature" of that
interesting being, the jack-leg novelist, by implying an analogy between the evolution of a novel and the evolution of American society. For example, when Twain observes that as the tale grows "the
original intention . . . is apt to get *abolished*" his carefully chosen language casts the growth of a narrative in terms of the nation's development, focusing particularly on the pivotal issue in the nineteenth
century, the abolition of slavery. The slavery debate in antebellum
America turned on rival interpretations of the founding fathers'
original intentions with respect to the "peculiar institution." Both
southern slavery apologists and northern abolitionists in favor of
disunion viewed secession in light of the revolutionary doctrine in
the Declaration of Independence, whereas the unionist view held to
Constitutional principles of national integrity. However, as abolition-

ist sentiment escalated, George Fredrickson points out, the authority of original intention became even more ambiguous.[8] And just as ideological confusion ultimately rendered original intention irrelevant in the evolving national conflict, narrative confusion sets aside Twain's original intention in his conflicted novel.

Twain appears to have discovered the parallels between society building and narrative building, and specifically the abolition of original intention, sometime after he had begun his full-length burlesque of Siamese twins. Although this discovery was not part of his original intention, it nonetheless reflects the way that Twain's conception of his authority evolved to encompass the history of American culture through the several stages of Siamese twins texts. In the "Personal Habits" burlesque, Twain drew on the immediate background of the Civil War, depicting the twins as "strong partizans [sic]" (CTSS&E, 1:296) on opposite sides in the national conflict and playing generally on the uncomfortable fusion between two such different temperaments as a dilemma that pits union against independence. By 1890, though, Twain employed many of the same irreconcilable differences sketched in "Personal Habits" to make Those Extraordinary Twins a parody of contemporary politics.

For example, after the town grows accustomed to the freaks and comes to know the twins in their diametrically opposed personalities, each twin attracts a staunch faction of supporters, oppositionally aligned with the Democratic and Whig Parties, who nominate the twins to stand against each other in the election for alderman. The farce in this plot segment depends, of course, on the fact that they inhabit one body. The original edition graphically hammers the punchline home by including an illustration of two campaign posters, one for Luigi's Democratic candidacy and one for Angelo's as a Whig, but both posters prominently display the same portrait of the two-headed candidate.[9] The twins' idea of alternately delegating control of their single body weekly to one or the other of their very different heads suggests a burlesque of the oscillating control over the American body politic exercised by the Democrats or the Republicans, rather like Hawthorne's account of political turnabout in "The Customs House" preface to The Scarlet Letter.

Several years before Those Extraordinary Twins, Twain's frustration with the two-party system reached such a peak that he became an avowed mugwump in the 1884 election. Twain lectured publicly, fervently urging Americans to free themselves from their slavish obedience to the dictates of political machines. Though he resided abroad during most of the political struggles of the 1890s, he reconfirmed his mugwumpery upon returning to the United States in 1900 and declared himself "the only living representative" of the mugwumps shortly thereafter. But for all of Twain's idealistic rhetoric, the word "mugwump" indicates its own ambivalent genealogy. Originating from the Algonquian word meaning "leader" or "great man," as Alfred Holt reports, the label was later seized upon by detractors as a metaphor for political straddling: the mugwump was said to have "his mug on one side of the fence and his wump on the other." One of the illustrations that Twain approved for "Those Extraordinary Twins" anticipates this joke by portraying the twins in exactly this metaphoric posture. So the twins not only emblematize a body politic run by a two-headed party system but also an ambivalence attributed to mugwumpery, regardless of Twain's high-minded profession of the temperament that animated his political independence.[10]

Furthermore, despite Twain's commitment to mugwumpery, it has little bearing on his concern for violated original intention in the narrative or the nation. Machine politics occupied Twain's satiric imagination initially, but the twins' unusual partnership prods Twain toward a sweeping critique of social control that cannot avoid the culture's growing concern about race.

The most extended burlesque episode in "Those Extraordinary Twins" focuses on another object of Twain's scorn, the judicial system, but also includes the issue of race within its scope. Here we can detect Twain's emerging awareness of the ways in which social control and narrative control elude the exclusive grasp of an independent authority figure. In the twins' trial for assault, the court is frustrated by Luigi's and Angelo's alternating control of their mutual body. Consequently, the issue at stake in their trial is the authority not simply of either twin over the actions committed by their body but also of the court to administer justice. To resolve the dilemma that the freaks have inflicted on the court, the presiding justice, Judge Robinson, declares that the twins will stand trial separately. When Wilson, counsel for the Siamese defendants, objects, on the grounds that such a motion lacks precedent "[i]n the courts of this or any other State" or "the oldest and highest courts in Europe," (149), Judge Robinson sets him straight. Although he admits that he is "not acquainted with other courts," he adamantly refuses to have his "judicial liberty hampered by trying to conform to the caprices of other courts." The judge insists that the court's authority resides in its autonomy. And his insistence is all the more emphatic when he repudiates the idea of a "European plan." Robinson's confidence in the court's independence defines the Americanness of his court. The gallery applause that punctuates his speech testifies to his oration's populist appeal. And the narrator reinforces the American identity of this posture by figuring his authority as "the sturdy jurist's revolutionary hand" (153). The trope of revolution historicizes this assertion of freedom from traditional authority, invoking an American tradition of subversion for the sake of liberty.

But although the judge pronounces anterior models of authority unnecessary because this court "has a plan of its own" (149), subordinate only to "His [God's] approval" (which the judge is confident "this court continues to have"), Robinson's authoritarian ideal of justice is countermanded in this scene. He expects the twins to be convicted; the jury interprets divine authority differently and, unable to decide which twin was at fault, finds that "justice has been defeated by the dispensation of God" (153). Here, Robinson's lack of judicial control anticipates the lack of textual control to which Twain admits in his preface to "The Suppressed Farce." Judge and author expect to preside over their court and text, respectively, as autonomous authorities, but their original intentions are intruded on by others. In both instances the intrusions foreground the issue of race.

For Robinson, Wilson's savvy defense of the twins introduces the kind of justice that antebellum slavery apologists and postbellum radical racists gloomily predicted. Resenting the invalidation of his authority, Robinson rebukes the jury for their decision in precisely the same racephobic rhetoric, foreseeing the same evil consequences:

> You little realize what far-reaching harm has just been wrought here under the fickle forms of law . . . You have set adrift, unadmonished, in this community, two men endowed with an awful and mysterious gift, a hidden and grisly power for evil – a power

by which each in his turn may commit crime after crime of the most heinous character . . . Look to your homes – look to your property – look to your lives – for you have need! (153–4)

As Parker reminds us, Twain did not explicitly intend to concern himself with race at this stage of the composition. But to ignore the racial implications in Judge Robinson's apprehensive rhetoric would be a crucial misreading. In the context of the racially hostile social climate of the 1890s when Twain was writing, the "awful and mysterious gift," the "hidden and grisly power for evil" Robinson fears, refers to the paranoid racist notion of the mulatto's hidden blackness, his ability to pass among whites without attracting suspicion of his criminal motives. Thus, conscious intentions notwithstanding, Twain's burlesque of judicial authority implicitly represents the dominant culture's fear of the mobility of free blacks in post-Reconstruction America.[11]

The Siamese twins themselves suggest a racially mixed message. Upon arriving in Dawson's Landing, Angelo's recitation of his and Luigi's joint autobiography is a kind of slave narrative in which he describes their indenture as freaks in a cheap Berlin museum. Moreover, the Siamese twins embody Tocqueville's observation about race relations in American society, "[T]he two races are fastened to each other without intermingling; and they are alike unable to separate entirely or combine," yielding "the most formidable of all the ills that threaten the future of the Union." In his autobiography, Twain recalls an aspect of his youth similarly: "All the negroes were friends of ours and with those of our own age we were . . . comrades, and yet not comrades; color and condition interposed a subtle line which both parties were conscious of and which rendered complete fusion impossible" (*MTA*, 1:100). The fusion of races that both Tocqueville and Twain deem impossible fuels the thematic transition that Twain achieves between *Those Extraordinary Twins* and *Pudd'nhead Wilson* by discovering that Tom is a mulatto.[12]

The impossibility, in the farce, of determining which of the twins committed the criminal assault translates into the equally frustrating dilemma of determining the motivation for Tom's antisocial behavior in the novel: Is it his aristocratic training that spurs him to his ultimate barbarism, as antebellum northern vilifiers of the South postulated? Or is the motivating factor his one drop of Negro blood, as the racebaiters insisted?[13] Although the line between white and black was presumed to be very clear, the fact that similar behaviors simultaneously convey such opposite stereotypes demonstrates the ambivalence in nineteenth-century American consciousness of race.

Indeed, Judge Robinson's fear that the twins' acquittal will set a precedent appears justified, if not judicially then at least textually. His final cry of alarm predicts the plot of the novel that Twain discovered "kept spreading along and spreading along" until

> other people got to intruding themselves and taking up more and more room with their talk and their affairs. Among them came a stranger named Pudd'nhead Wilson, and a woman named Roxana; and presently the doings of these two pushed up into prominence a young fellow named Tom Driscoll, whose proper place was away in the obscure background. Before the book was half finished those three were taking things almost entirely into their own hands and working the whole tale as a private venture of their own – a tale which they had nothing to do with, by rights. (121)

As the twins' defense counsel and one of the characters who took to "working the tale as a private venture," Wilson upsets the order of both trial and text. A distinction remains, however, because Roxana, and Tom to a lesser degree, not Wilson, activates the race issue, thus decentering the social coherence of Dawson's Landing and unraveling the formal coherence of the farce Twain thought he had embarked upon. So when Twain complains that Wilson, Roxana, and Tom abrogate his rights over his narrative, he twists the facts. Certainly, Wilson's presence in the twins' assault trial subverts community standards. But Wilson's defense of the twins compromises Judge Robinson's authority without interfering with Twain's plot about the Siamese twins. Roxana, on the other hand, inserts her own plot into the narrative and overwhelms Twain's original intention to write a farce. Indeed, her subversive cradle swap thwarts not only the slave owner's control over his human property but also Twain's control over his narrative property.

Roxana announces the slave's perilous condition as a theme by her attempt to do something about it. And just as abolitionism brought the Negro to the foreground of nineteenth-century American consciousness, so too does Roxana's subversive action "push into prominence a young fellow named Tom Driscoll, whose proper place," Twain tells us, "was away in the obscure background." What Twain doesn't specify is that because Tom is legally a slave, and therefore excluded from public life, his proper place is marginal, not only in relation to Twain's authorial intention but also within American society. Roxana's act changes everything – for Tom and the narrative; she turns a slave into an aristocrat and a farce into a tragedy. This unplanned alteration was, Twain tells us, "a most embarrassing circumstance. But what was a great deal worse was, that it was not one story, but two stories tangled together; and they obstructed and interrupted each other at every turn and created no end of confusion and annoyance" (119). Thus, what started as a topic – two people tangled together who obstruct and interrupt each other at every turn – becomes a formal feature of the text, when Roxana's plot overtakes the Siamese twins farce. The formal congruity between object of representation and authorial performance reveals that Twain's ambivalence toward authority expresses itself in the content he actively chooses, in the content that insinuates itself into the story, and in the conflicted assertion of his own authority over the text.

When Twain constructs an adversarial relation between himself and his characters who insolently usurp his authorial rights, he obscures the aspects of his own identity that he invested in his characters. Examining Twain's identifications with the novel's subversive characters, Roxana and Wilson, explains his sensitivity to the culture's racial crisis, while at the same time it gauges the difficulty of escaping the cultural training that conditioned nineteenth-century consciousness.

Reconstructing Authorhood

Twain's depiction of Roxana as an intruder who wrests control of his narrative recalls Georg Lukács's praise of realism in the novels of Balzac. Lukács measures the achievement of the French realist in the ability of his "characters . . . once conceived in the vision of their creator, [to] live an independent life of their own: their comings and goings, their development, their destiny is dictated by the inner dialectic of their social and individual existence." And he proclaims confidently that "[n]o writer is a true realist – or even a truly good writer, if he can direct the evolution of his own characters at will.''[14] Oddly, Lukács's litmus test of a realist's greatness is precisely the same criterion that determines for Twain his status as a second-rate – that is, a "jack-leg" – novelist; his inability to control his narrative and its characters distinguishes him from the "expert." Value judgments aside, the truth of Roxana's independent control of the story versus Twain's control of Roxana lies somewhere between his self-disparagement and Lukács's criterion of novelistic greatness. For even though Roxana's actions threaten social order well beyond what Twain had bargained for when he began, and to some degree beyond her own intentions and control, Twain ultimately reestablishes control by ironizing Roxana's control and by reinvesting the authorial role in Wilson.

Roxana's gender and race qualify her as the most radical of subversive agents in Twain's major fiction. But it is her actions within that role that afford a range of critique unavailable to him in any other of his characters. We can gauge the daring and the danger of this representation in the way that Roxana challenges nineteenth-century cult notions of maternity and "woman's sphere."[15] Praised as the most fully realized female character in Twain's novels, Roxana has attracted comparisons to other notable mothers in American fiction. James Cox names Hester Prynne, Kenneth Lynn chooses Cassy from *Uncle Tom's Cabin*, and Frederick Anderson cites Aunt Rachel from Twain's own "True Story" as analogues.[16] Additionally, the tragic mullata is a common figure in nineteenth-century sentimental literature, beginning with William Wells Brown's *Clotelle*, one of the first African-American novels in which ostensibly white, female beauty is enslaved for its taint of black blood. Metta Victor's popular dime novel, *Maum Guinea*, features as its title character a mulatto who projects a characterological complexity similar to Roxana's. Still, we find perhaps the most interesting model for Roxana in nonfiction. Linda Brent, in Harriet Jacobs's autobiographical *Incidents in the Life of a Slave Girl*, emphatically anticipates Roxana's maternal power. She protects her children by subverting the economy that makes the slave woman the sexual object of her owner, a victimization which determines her value according to her ability to increase the slaveholder's stock. But Roxana's subversion even exceeds Brent's, because rather than manipulate the sale of her son from one cruel owner to another who intends his manumission, as

Brent does, she makes her son a master, endowing him with all of the advantages of aristocracy by exchanging his coarse tow-linen shirt for his patrician counterpart's soft muslin gown. In one stroke, Roxana's act turns the slavery system's assumptions about genealogical hierarchy on their heads and complicates the theme of maternal power within the cult of true womanhood. The aggressiveness of her act goes well beyond even the "sustained narrative dissection of the conventions of true womanhood" that Hazel Carby credits to Linda Brent.[17]

Moreover, Roxana's treachery hints at Twain's uneasiness with maternal power – even as he represents it in a putatively sympathetic light – and exposes anxieties not overtly manifested in the popular idealization of motherhood. Playing on Roxana's maternal power as a subversion of his own authorial control, Twain shows how her exchange of the infants alters his plan. In the opening of chapter 4, even the narrator must comply with the terms of Roxana's subversion: "This history must henceforth accommodate itself to the change which Roxana has consummated, and call the real heir 'Chambers' and the usurping little slave 'Thomas à Beckett' – shortening this latter name to 'Tom,' for daily use, as the people about him did" (17).

The exchange also forces Roxana to accommodate herself to Tom's status. For "by the fiction created by herself," Tom does not become an agent of vengeance on the slave system as much as "her master." The effects of Roxana's fiction become "automatic and unconscious; . . . deceptions grew into self-deceptions" until Roxana becomes "the dupe of her own deceptions" (19), no longer even superintending her fiction. The self-subordinating flaw in Roxana's gesture of maternal authority undercuts the "omnipotent quality of maternal influence" that Lydia Huntley Sigourney, in the widely popular *Letters to Mothers*, exhorted nineteenth-century women to exercise:

> How entire and perfect is this dominion over the unformed character of your infant. Write what you will upon the printless tablet with your wand of love. Hitherto your influence over your dearest friend, your most submissive servant, has known bounds and obstructions. Now you have over a new-born immortal almost that degree of power which the mind exercises over the body.[18]

Twain was surely familiar with the popular ideal, even if he didn't know Sigourney's text.[19] Indeed, the figures that Sigourney assembles in this short passage are so germane to the representation of maternity in *Pudd'nhead Wilson* that Twain's depiction of Roxana's subversion seems a rather pointedly ironic response to Sigourney's rallying cry. Usurping Twain's text, Roxana embodies Sigourney's conception of maternal influence as a kind of writing. The identity that Roxana reinscribes on Tom, however, contradicts Sigourney's terms by turning maternal mastery over her child into absolute subservience to him. Thus, Roxana's attempt to combat slavery is informed by nineteenth-century sentimentalism, which prescribed in popular literature like *Uncle Tom's Cabin* the ideal of maternal love as the cure for such social ills as slavery. But due to his apparent uneasiness with the sentimental ideal of motherhood, Twain complicates the resolution formulated in the antecedent texts when he embodies the ideal in Roxana.

Still, Twain does not simply invert the ideal closure of sentimentalism, sentencing Roxana to irredeemable victimization. Rather, he dichotomizes her character between devoted maternal vulnerability and independent resourcefulness. Upon the death of her master and Tom's ostensible father, Percy Driscoll, she gains her manumission from master and son. She leaves Dawson's Landing to work as a chambermaid on a steamboat, vowing to "be independent of the human race thenceforth forevermore if hard work and economy could accomplish it" (33). But after financial ruin frustrates her plans for a comfortable retirement, she returns to Dawson's Landing to solicit Tom's support. When Tom abuses her in time of need, she rises up indignantly and asserts her power over him by revealing the secret of his birth. Heretofore, Tom's wanton behavior has only temporarily jeopardized his stake in the Driscoll patrimony, his uncle's sentimentality always getting the better of his outrage. But in her double identity as Tom's mother and the author of his aristocratic place, Roxana has the power to disinherit him permanently unless he complies with the terms of her extortion. Although this power satisfies her need for "something or somebody to rule over" (46), her attitude toward Tom softens as he begins to show her the maternal respect she demands. Returning to the self-sacrificing maternal devotion that gave rise to her original plot, Roxana later proposes that Tom sell her into slavery to save him from exposure by his creditors. She underscores the selfless love motivating her plan in echoes of the maternal ideology that bolstered abolitionism in the nineteenth century. But again, Twain challenges the ideal which optimistically assumes that the offspring of devoted mothers will be grateful. Roxana's devotional sacrifice does not move Tom; instead, he betrays her maternal love and sells her down the river.

The reorienting feature of Roxana's condition that locates her beyond the conventions of maternal sentimentality is, of course, her race – and Tom's hatred of the racial identity that Roxana reminds him he shares. Twain foregrounds the racial issue when Roxana escapes and tracks down her betrayer in St. Louis. Dressed in man's clothing and having blackened her skin, Roxana assumes a disguise that reverses her sex but also confirms what her white skin has kept hidden all of her life. Her blackened face emphasizes the fact that originally potentiated Roxana's subversive power well before the infant exchange that actuated it. In a seigneurial system that confers power only on white males with distinguished ancestry, Roxana can assume power only as the "other." When the local personages of this system are first introduced, the narrative alludes to the unsanctioned turn of events that will ensue. Among the distinguished members of Dawson's Landing society, one gets short shrift: "Then there was Colonel Cecil Burleigh Essex, another F.F.V. [First Families of Virginia] of formidable caliber – however, with him we have no concern" (4). When we learn later that Essex is Tom's father, his understated dismissal might at first appear an instance of Twain's irony. But in a society that places value on pedigree, Tom's half a pedigree is wholly worthless. The narrator is emphatically correct: "we have no concern" with Essex, because Roxana's race negates his ability to transmit genealogical authority to Tom. Twain underscores this paradox of Roxana's power in an electoral metaphor: "[T]he one-sixteenth of her which was black out-voted the other fifteen parts and made her a negro" (8–9). In assigning veto power to the fraction of her heritage that had no Constitutional right of suffrage, Twain ironizes the contorted logic of genealogical privilege which recognizes the power of black heritage to negate social status far beyond the power of white heritage to endow it.

As a slave, Roxana is excluded from the rights and privileges that defined the "cult of true womanhood" and thus stands opposed to the kind of women Twain enlisted to dictate the genteel standards with which his vernacular method tensely competed – even as he submitted to their censorship. The challenge to the maternal ideal that Twain personifies in Roxana is an ambivalent one. In two personal appeals to feminine influence, he enlisted Mrs. Fairbanks and, later, his wife, Olivia, not simply as literary censors but as maternal governesses of his mischievous impulses: he referred to Fairbanks as "Mother," and one of Olivia's pet names for him was "Youth." As the personalities behind the formation of a Freudian superego, these two women instilled in him an internal, if irregularly heeded, censor. In a meditation on authorship, Twain describes how this faculty operates to inform a writer's style

> by an automatically-working taste – a taste which selects and rejects without asking you for any help, and patiently and steadily improves itself without troubling you to approve or applaud. Yes, and likely enough when the structure is at last pretty well up, and attracts attention, *you* feel complimented, whereas *you* didn't build it, and didn't even consciously superintend. Yes; *one* notices, for instance that long, involved sentences confuse *him*, and that *he* is obliged to re-read them to get the sense. Unconsciously, then, *he* rejects that brick. Unconsciously *he* accustoms *himself* to writing short sentences as a rule.[20] (Emphasis is added.)

The shift from second-person to third-person pronouns illustrates Twain's perception of the consciousness of the "other" operating in the creative process, as we might expect from a writer who had fashioned a divided identity for himself by assuming the literary persona "Mark Twain."

But Twain's novelistic effort was not the process of conforming regularity he describes here; rather, his work within that discourse was more akin to the impish perversity that he describes in "The Facts Concerning the Recent Carnival of Crime in Connecticut" (1876). With regard to Roxana's subversiveness, his practice in *Pudd'nhead Wilson* initially follows this submission to waywardness. Indeed, Twain not only allies Roxana more with the vernacular tradition from which he sprang but also projects his own authorial identity in her role as a storyteller. For example, upon returning to Dawson's Landing after her career as a chambermaid on a steamboat, she enjoys such celebrity for the stories she tells about her life on the Mississippi that "she was obliged to confess to herself that if there was anything better in this world than steamboating, it was the glory to be got by telling about it" (34). Clearly, this same revelation had informed Twain's career as a writer, and in casting Roxana's return to Dawson's Landing in this manner, Twain forges an identity between himself and his tragic mulatto heroine. This identity suggests that Roxana's subversion of Twain's original narrative intention is really an extension of Twain's own desire to subvert institutions of social control.

The identity between the author and his maternal character is further reinforced by the ambivalence toward authority that both experience. Immediately after being struck by the idea to exchange infant slave for infant master, Roxana reveals her inner turmoil by minimizing the revolutionary force of her subversion. Concocting a distorted precedent, in a rather convoluted and erroneous justification of her baby exchange, she assures herself, " 'Tain't no sin – *white* folks has done it! It ain't no sin, glory to goodness it ain't no sin! *Dey's* done it – yes, en dey was de biggest quality in de whole bilin', too – *Kings*!'" (15). She then dredges from her memory "dim particulars of some tale that she heard some time or other," oddly interweaving the Moses story and Twain's own *The Prince and the Pauper* to assuage her sense of wrongdoing. All the more important, and peculiar, is the fact that Roxana fails to attribute the deed to white folks when she re-authors English history. Instead, in her recollection of the precedent, "one o' de niggers roun' 'bout de place dat was mos' white" exchanges her slave child for the heir to the English throne. Thus, rather than the "minstrel version" of *The Prince and the Pauper* that Evan Carton sees in it, Roxana's justification story reveals her attempts to repress her programmed consent to slavery's principles.[21] Unable to repress completely here, Roxana narrates herself into the justification story as the culpable agent of a historically sanctioned precedent. Moreover, her use of *The Prince and the Pauper* follows Twain's own pattern of retreat from subversion to accommodation in his romances.

Roxana exhibits a similar ambivalence during Tom's unruly childhood. Her accommodation to the consequences of having substituted her own child for the master's becomes "automatic and unconscious" and corresponds to the internalized "automatically-working" censor that Twain described in his meditation on authorship – except in Roxana's case, the results are far from salutary.

The project that she didn't "consciously superintend" has made her the slave to the child over whom she should have maternal control.

Roxana's uncertain relationship to authority even extends to the slavery system against which her subversive action is aimed. At several critical moments, she embraces the assumptions of slavery, despite knowing the slave's vulnerability to the caprices of the master. For example, subscribing to the patriarchal ideal of genealogical authority, she proudly informs Tom that Essex is his father and boasts, "Dey ain't another nigger in dis town dat's as high-bawn as you is" (43). Later, with equal pride in the noble blood that runs in her own veins, she declares herself a descendant of Captain John Smith.

But unbeknownst to her, the narrative has already implicitly undercut her claim to this distinctive lineage in the description of Wilson's fingerprinting procedures. On each glass slide of "faint greaseprints," we are told, Wilson "would write a record on the strip of white paper thus: 'JOHN SMITH, *right hand*'" (7). By citing the absolute ordinariness and virtual anonymity of this hypothetical John Smith, the narrative foreshadows and negates the illustrious nobility that Roxana attaches to the name of her ostensible ancestor, emptying the name of all significance. This subtle narrative gesture implicitly countermands Twain's complaint of Roxana's intrusive authority over his Siamese twins farce and signals, instead, his ironic authority over her.

Twain's willingness to indulge the subversion that his identification with Roxana affords is limited, especially when it encroaches on his own narrative control. Twain crosses the threshold from indulgence to repression and dramatically ironizes her power at the one moment when Roxana dramatizes her ability to tell stories about her familiarity with steamboats. After escaping from the downriver plantation to which Tom had sold her, Roxana confronts him with the story of her bondage and her freedom, which culminates with the nostalgic description of her voyage north on the *Grand Mogul*, the steamboat aboard which she had worked for eight years during her independence:

> So I . . . went up on de biler deck en 'way back aft to de ladies'
> cabin guard, en sot down dah in de same cheer dat I'd sot in mos'
> a hund'd million times, I reckon; en it 'uz jist home agin, I tell
> you!

> In 'bout an hour I heard de ready-bell jingle, en den dat racket
> begin. Putty soon I hear de gong strike. "Set her back on de
> outside," I says to myself – "I reckon I knows dat music!" I hear
> de gong agin. "Come ahead on de inside," I says. Gong agin.
> "Stop de outside." Gong agin. "Come ahead on de outside – now
> we's pinted for Sent Louis, en I's outer de woods en ain't got to
> drown myself at all." (87)

Here, Twain signs his appropriation of the slave-narrative genre with
the kind of dialect flourishes that built much of his reputation. And
insofar as he registers the narrative authority of a dialect speaker
here, we might read this as sustaining the power of vernacular. But
to the contrary, Twain uses Roxana's narrative to reveal that her
power is itself a fiction. Her familiarity with the discourse of steamboat navigation allows her to call out commands. But in this case,
familiarity translates not into mastery but into its illusion. As Roxana
utters the syllables of authority, the actual voice of authority speaks
above deck in the pilothouse. The entire episode provides a figure
that asserts Twain's ultimate control of the text. Just as Roxana's
commands from outside the ladies' cabin aft – a significantly subordinate and gendered position – give the illusion that she navigates
the steamboat, her actions in the plot of Twain's story give the illusion that she controls it. And just as there is a pilot directing the
Grand Mogul's course in a voice we can't hear, Twain, too, stands
above the deck on which the narrative action unfolds, controlling its
course unseen.

Twain's deconstruction of Roxana's feminine control of the creative process by his own technical mastery as steamboat pilot turned
author requires us to reconsider his preface to "The Suppressed
Farce." For if Roxana represents authorial subversion and maternal
power, Twain's account of how he solved the text's two-story dilemma offers preliminary insight into the text's fusion of motherhood and problematic narrative control. He tells us that after he
discovered "where the difficulty" of his story "lay . . . I had no further trouble. I pulled one of the stories out by the roots, and left the
other one – a kind of literary Caesarian operation" (119). Like the
narrative he claims to have remedied, his treatment also suffers from
the confusion revealed in the mixed metaphor. Cox has noted the
sleight of hand in Twain's figuring the novel *Pudd'nhead Wilson* as
the mother from whom he surgically removed the stillborn farce,

which contradicts Twain's explicit acknowledgment that *Those Extraordinary Twins* came before the novel. Indeed, Cox's attention to this peculiar dramatization of the act of writing is well-founded, because Twain's decision to figure himself as an obstetric surgeon signifies his uneasy relationship to his literary production.[22] In light of the paternal connotation in the word "author," Twain's decision to assume a less personally invested role seems odd. Had he called the rival stories his fractious textual children – a readily available figure, given the bickering siblings he began with – rather than textual mother and child, he could have have easily assumed the more conventional role of literary father.

Instead, he avoids the metaphorical genetic relation to these texts, just as he specifically disavowed paternalized responsibility for the practice of his craft in his 1890 meditation on authorship: "[D]oubtless I have methods, but they begot themselves, in which case I am only their proprietor, not their father." Corresponding to his reluctance to claim literary paternity, the obstetric-surgeon metaphor might seem to distance Twain from the creative act by aligning the process of literary production with maternity, to which he serves as technical assistant. But the ironic effect of Roxana's steamboat narrative reveals the invisible but unmistakable control that Twain equates with technical expertise. The obstetric metaphor, then, doesn't so much distance him from the creative act as allow him to assert full control over it, just as the surgeon usurps control over the act of giving birth with his scalpel. Thus, Twain defines the creative process as a masculine act of violence inflicted on the body of the feminized text. Although he indulges an identity with a female figure in the plot and invests her with power to combat the social injustice inflicted on her gender and caste, he exerts a violent mastery over her and the female text in the performance of his authorial role.

Still, Twain's control from without is not sufficient to restore the order that Roxana's action has unseated; the narrative consequences that the identification between white male author and mulatto slave mother create in the plot must be stemmed within the plot. To achieve that internal control, Twain invests an equal share of his authoritative identity in his other insolent character, the stranger Pudd'nhead Wilson.

Readers have readily perceived Wilson as Twain's persona because the eponymous ne'er-do-well mirrors his author's own ironic temperament and fascination with newfangled notions, scientific and pseudoscientific. The fact that Wilson is explicitly acknowledged as an "author" (47), the writer of "Pudd'nhead Wilson's Calendar," helps insure the identification and imbues Wilson's ability to represent Twain with appropriate ambiguity. As a wanderer who comes west to Dawson's Landing to make his fortune, a freethinker, a writer of calendar maxims, Wilson is a Franklinesque figure, as Cox has observed. And although Twain also followed a Franklinesque path, he resented Franklin for having subjected American boys to the prudent correctives of Poor Richard. Wilson's calendar entries turn Poor Richardisms into cynical nuggets of irony, applying Twainian torque to the Franklin association.[23]

Furthermore, Wilson's role as a calendar writer is reflected generally in the story's opening self-description as a "chronicle" (3) – that is, a record of events in succession, one thing after another, as on a calendar. But a chronicle is supposed to record, as Hayden White notes, "the life of an individual, town, or region, some great undertaking, such as a war or crusade, or some institution, such as monarchy, episcopacy, or monastery," without interpreting them.[24] In contrast, Twain's narratorial comment offers wry interpretive analysis similar to that in Wilson's maxims. Indeed, not only are Wilson's aphorisms included as chapter epigraphs of Twain's novel, but the narration often assumes an aphoristic inflection as well, as if it has absorbed Wilson's tone by the technique of indirect free style. For example, after describing the misfiring of Judge Driscoll's well-intentioned attempt to elevate Wilson in the town's estimation, the narrator axiomatically comments, "That is just the way, in this world; an enemy can partly ruin a man, but it takes a good-natured injudicious friend to complete the thing and make it perfect" (25).

And yet Wilson's ultimate control of the narrative depends not on his ability as a writer but on his function as a reader. The opening dramatic action of the narrative presents Wilson "at work over a set of tangled account books in his work-room" (7). This image of Wilson as an untangler of confused accounts recalls Twain's own role as a reviser of the text that he described as "two stories tangled together" which he "read and studied over . . . on shipboard" (119) during several Atlantic crossings. And it is in Wilson's capacity as a reader that he stands opposed to Roxana and embodies a turn in

Twain's own temperament. Whereas Roxana resembles the early Twain, converting a steamboat career into engaging stories for the reward of notoriety and daily bread, Wilson assumes the role of the older Twain, reading and rereading confused records of transactions to discover a way to bring coherence to an account. In their resemblances to opposite points of Twain's career they approximate their functions in this tale: that is, Roxana, as the story's motivator, is the agent of "narratability," to recall D. A. Miller's term – "the instances of disequilibrium, suspense, and general insufficiency from which a given narrative appears to arise"; and Wilson, as the one who restores order to the violated society, is the agent of closure.[25]

By enlisting a detective to straighten out his tangled story, Twain also attempts to cash in on the increasing popularity of detective fiction in order to restore his own sagging readership and squandered fortune. What's more, this shift to a reader-based authority becomes a way for Twain to reread his career and redefine its shape. For example, by relying, finally, on Wilson's authority as a reader who detects meaning by scrupulous study, Twain inverts the evolution of authority documented in *Life on the Mississippi*. Wilson's control rehabilitates the kind of exclusive authority that the pilot's careful scrutiny of the river represented in "Old Times," which Twain discredits in the Mississippi book and replaces with the inclusive authority of the storyteller, who creates rather than detects meaning. Employing Wilson to check Roxana's subversion amounts to regression as well as repression because Wilson reinstates a kind of control that signifies Twain's retreat from the democratic textuality of heteroglossia. Thus, ten years after *Life on the Mississippi*, Twain appears uncomfortable with the pluralism he endorsed and retreats from the Mississippi book's swirling current of language to impose a more narrowly conforming model of authoritative action.

To control the perceived threat of social chaos unleashed by Roxana's plot, Twain not only *reinvests* his identity in Wilson but also *reinvents* him. In *Those Extraordinary Twins* Twain employed Wilson as his subversive identity to burlesque the legal system. By converting Wilson from agent of subversion there to agent of order in *Pudd'nhead Wilson*, Twain implies his alternating desire for individual integrity and social acceptance. In the novel Wilson seems content to endure his marginal status for the sake of critical individualism, but, like Tom Sawyer, his opposition to social convention gives way to the desire of the impresario to stage a spectacle for his own social advantage. But whereas Tom Sawyer manipulates Huck's needless subversion of the slave code by obscuring the fact that Jim is already free, Wilson manipulates Roxana's plot by revealing the fact that Tom is actually a slave. The distinction that Twain draws between the two texts revolves around the culture's anxious realization in the 1890s that race is not always easily discernible. In the world of *Huckleberry Finn*, race is not an issue; slavery is. In the world of *Pudd'nhead Wilson*, however, racial illegibility has become such a problem that a Negro may be taken for an aristocrat and an aristocrat may even be taken for a Negro. By identifying with a slave mother, Twain makes illegibility an ironic feature of the text's authority. Because his identification with Roxana has lingered in a critical blind spot, Twain has pulled off a cultural satire so subtle as to have gone undetected by literary critics. Still, even for the author of the satire, the anxiety of that subversive identity was enough to warrant him to find a less disturbing persona, one who shares his race and gender. Thus, in the identity of David Wilson, Twain not only retreats from his subversive identification with a slave woman to the stable order of convention but also redresses the violations that he committed in his subversive identity.

Twain's deployment of his Wilson persona significantly revises the vernacular roots of his career by reinterpreting his earliest literary effort. The eastern traveler who frames "Jim Smiley and the Jumping Frog" arrives in Dawson's Landing reinvented as the misunderstood genius of *Pudd'nhead Wilson*. The contrast between Wilson and the unnamed narrator of Twain's inaugural text reveals the degree to which Twain revised vernacular from a discourse that humorously vents frustration to one that threatens social stability.

In "The Jumping Frog," Simon Wheeler exploits the Easterner's ignorance of vernacular method and makes him the captive victim of a rambling tale about an obsessive gambler, Jim Smiley. We may also recall that in addition to Smiley's celebrated frog, Wheeler digresses with the history of Smiley's notorious dog, Andrew Jackson. This unimpressive-looking pup attracted lucrative wagers for Smiley against Andrew Jackson's chances in dog fights. The success of the ventures rested on Andrew Jackson's tenacious ability to clamp his jaws on his opponent's hind leg "and hang on till they throwed up the sponge, if it was a year" (*CTSS&E*, 1:171). Smiley's comeuppance arrives when he engages Andrew Jackson in a fight with a dog who had lost his hind legs to a circular saw. His winning strategy neutralized, Andrew Jackson loses and, heartbroken, limps off to die. The point of all this in relation to *Pudd'nhead Wilson* is the nameless and hind-leg-less dog – a half of a dog, we might say. Wilson earns his unflattering nickname because of another half of a dog. Shortly after Wilson arrives in Dawson's Landing, one of his first opportunities to socialize is frustrated by a dog whose incessant barking interrupts his conversation. Wilson wryly expresses a wish to own half of the dog. And when asked why, he delivers the punchline, "Because, I would kill my half" (5). Failing to grasp his humor, the community concludes that Wilson is a fool.[26]

The significance of the relationship between the two tales consists not merely in the coincidence of two half dogs but in Wilson's appropriation of vernacular conventions. His half-dog joke was among the very stock in which vernacular humor of the region and period traded.[27] But Twain restructures the relation of teller to audience on the occasion of Wilson's wisecrack and radically inverts the conditions of vernacular. The Easterner in the "Jumping Frog" is a vernacular storyteller's victim, partly by virtue of a half dog's triumph over a wily vernacular character; Wilson, conversely, is an Easterner, bothered not by a storyteller but by a half dog itself. And he becomes a victim not because he is ignorant of vernacular but because he masters the idiom's propensity for irony in the midst of a frontier community unwilling to perceive his mastery as anything other than eccentricity. As an unpedigreed newcomer from the Northeast, Wilson's primary social responsibility is to conform, to let the frontier characters tell the jokes at his expense. Here, Wilson's fatal vernacular mastery confirms Twain's ebbing faith in vernacular subversion. He converts the vernacular mode that gave public life to "Mark Twain" from a discourse in which the low abuses the cultural elite, out of envy and in order to compensate for cultural powerlessness, to a linguistic expression of tension between margin and center in which the violation of the cultural standard is not celebrated but feared and repressed.

Once the town has foreclosed Wilson's future, he can regenerate his status in the society only by satisfying their desire for stability, which translates in narrative terms into acting as the agent of closure. After twenty-three years, Wilson achieves redemption not only by solving the mystery behind Judge Driscoll's murder but also by detecting the truth behind Roxana's plot. In his success, too, Wilson inverts the conditions of vernacular. As a New Yorker who makes his mark in the frontier and thus becomes "a made man for good," Wilson demonstrates the antithesis of what Twain wrote to the *Alta California* upon arriving in New York as a vernacular humorist in 1866: "Make your mark in New York, and you are a made man. With a New York endorsement you may travel the country over, without fear – but without it you are speculating upon a dangerous issue."[28] Wilson's New York endorsement does him more harm than good, and his career is finally made by speculating upon the most dangerous issue of cultural anxiety – racial identity.

Yet Wilson's triumph of genius over ignorance, and order over subversion, does not, in fact, provide the stable closure that it might seem to establish. Even the narrator implies this. He notes the dilemma of the true heir, who by virtue of his aristocratic heritage can no longer enjoy the comfort of the kitchen, and by virtue of his slave training can find no comfort in the parlor where he is now installed, and then adds, "But we cannot follow his curious fate further – that would be a long story." The shorter story of Tom's fate, which abruptly ends the novel, is another matter, however:

> The false heir made a full confession and was sentenced to imprisonment for life. But now a complication came up. The Percy Driscoll estate was in such crippled shape when its owner died that it could pay only sixty per cent of its great indebtedness, and was settled at that rate. But the creditors came forward, now, and complained that inasmuch as through an error for which *they* were in no way to blame the false heir was not inventoried at that time with the rest of the property, great wrong and loss had thereby been inflicted upon them. They rightly claimed that "Tom" was lawfully their property and had been so for eight years; that they had already lost sufficiently in being deprived of his services during that long period, and ought not to be required to add anything to that loss; that if he had been delivered up to them in the first place they would have sold him and he could not have murdered Judge Driscoll, therefore it was not he that had really committed the murder, the guilt lay with the erroneous inventory. Everybody saw that there was reason in this. Everybody granted that if "Tom" were white and free it would be unquestionably

right to punish him – it would be no loss to anybody; but to shut up a valuable slave for life – that was quite another matter.

As soon as the Governor understood the case, he pardoned Tom at once, and the creditors sold him down the river. (114–15)

The community's inability to appreciate irony explains its blindness to the double standard invoked here. But Wilson, who embraces the doubleness of irony, participates wittingly in the restoration of Tom's slave status in a manner that infects the story's ethical tone as well. The narrative discourse, which has elsewhere echoed Wilson's aphoristic irony, assumes in this passage the kind of monological assurance of certitude that characterizes the tone of the legal language it describes. Divorcing itself from the ambiguity revealed by Roxana's subversion, the narrative reverses its earlier accommodation with regard to the false name that Roxana had given to her child and now de-"accommodates itself" here from the terms of her exchange by placing quotation marks around the word "Tom."

But despite the narrator's assurance of the creditor's rightful claim, "Tom" is not legally the property of the Percy Driscoll estate. Judge Driscoll had purchased the slave Valet de Chambre from his brother shortly before Percy died (22). Therefore, Wilson's role as agent of closure is peculiarly double as well. By revealing Judge Driscoll's murderer, Wilson honorably upholds justice, but by revealing the secret of Tom's birth and allowing him to be sold, under the pretense of satisfying the creditors' unjust claims, he subscribes to the injustice wrought by slavery. Even Tom Sawyer has the decency to reveal that Jim has been freed by the widow Douglas when justice is in jeopardy, but Wilson's detective genius is morally deficient. He becomes a bona fide member of the community because he patches up the threadbare justice that Roxana's plot has exposed. Thus, the cycle of the entire production turns inside out. Wilson, first cast as a decentering agent in the Siamese twins farce to indulge Twain's fascination with subversion, reemerges as a recentering agent in the detective story to repress the disorder of Roxana's plot and invoke "justice." In the end, Wilson serves justice only by applying his detective mastery selectively, for the critical truth of his solution to the mystery threatens to unravel the social fabric as much as it undoes Roxana's attack on the slaveholding aristocracy. To paraphrase the electoral metaphor in which Twain describes Roxana's heritage, we might say that Wilson's ability to shun the truth outvotes his insight, making him Dawson's Landing's leading citizen. Having languished on the low rung of society as a putative freethinker, Wilson is finally a "made man for good" by virtue of his training among the slave society.[29]

This interpretation of the novel's ending does not entirely square with Twain's ostensible intention to condemn the barbaric reality behind the genteel disguise of aristocratic privilege and to celebrate the self-made man's rise to the vanguard of society through his perspicacity and native intelligence. The community does finally recognize Wilson as more than a mere pudd'nhead. But in rising to prominence Wilson compromises his humanitarian virtue for the sake of obtaining status within the community. In this compromise, *Pudd'nhead Wilson* becomes the tragedy that emerged from Twain's attempt to write an extravagant fantasy about Siamese twins. Twain's shifting identification from Roxana to Wilson also suggests that the tragedy extends beyond the text, that Twain's liberal consciousness was tragically flawed as well.

"Signifying" and Negrifying; or, Puttin' on Ole Massa

In 1896, about the time *Tom Sawyer, Detective* was published, Mark Twain observed that the detective story is "a curious thing." Then he asked this intriguing question: "And was there ever one that the author needn't be ashamed of, except the 'Murders in the Rue Morgue'?"[30] It is not difficult to see why Twain might have been ashamed of *Tom Sawyer, Detective*. But since he makes no exception for his first full-length work in that genre, *Pudd'nhead Wilson*, presumably he also assigned this relatively successful, yet nonetheless troublesome, work to the double category of the curious and shameful. If Twain's novel is curious and shameful, it may be because its depiction of race reflects discriminatory prejudice. If so, Twain's admission of shame becomes a curious form of self-humiliation before the patriarch of the detective story, as a means of atoning for the declension the genre had suffered after Poe. But Twain's genealogical derivation of detective fiction from Poe is itself curious for Twain traces this ancestry without mentioning that his text's representation of race reflects its descent from Poe's detective tale. In this series of implied statements and silences, Poe's founding of the genre becomes both a standard to live up to and a stigma to live down. *Pudd'nhead Wilson* articulates Twain's misgivings about this genealogical dilemma and becomes a sly attack on Poe and the genre he initiated by exploiting racial fears.

All of this emphasis on kinship bears directly on *Pudd'nhead Wilson*; this detective novel's payoff turns on a genealogical puzzle. The murder mystery that Twain's eponymous detective solves is bound together with a tale of miscegenation in which an aristocrat is revealed to be a mulatto slave. The miscegenation theme motivating the story is widely regarded as Twain's way of exposing the double standards of slavery and genealogical privilege in a nation designed to promote individual opportunity. Yet there's a problem with this reading. Although Twain does challenge the arbitrary racial distinctions of color by dramatizing a mulatto's ability to live undetected as an aristocrat for twenty years, the criminal's mulatto identity appears to invalidate the notion that "training is everything" (*PW*, 21) by playing right into the negrophobic rhetoric of the 1890s that sounded the alarm about the dangers of miscegenation. In this light, Twain's celebrated irony begins to look like a self-incriminating gesture: rather than dispelling racist dogma, *Pudd'nhead Wilson* appears to subscribe to the fear of "passing" that contributed to the climate of racial hysteria in the wake of Reconstruction. If the novel is complicit in this racist atmosphere, then it unsettles Twain's reputation as a liberal humanitarian, an honor he has enjoyed ever since Huck Finn was willing to damn himself to hell in order to save Jim. And although a reversal of Twain's reputation could be viewed as yet another facet of Twain's own peculiar doubleness, we cannot measure the impact of racial bias in *Pudd'nhead Wilson* by simply invoking it as a hallmark of his genius. Rather, "Twainishness," the characteristic doubleness that led to the split of Twain's persona into Roxana and Wilson, can be adequately understood only in terms of history and genealogy; that is, by examining the text first in the context of the racially tense time in which Twain wrote it and second as a detective tale anxious about its genealogical connection to the racially peculiar genius of Poe.[31]

If, as Roxana sees it, Tom's "vicious nature" – that is, his Negro blood – motivates his murder of Judge Driscoll, then Twain's plot undermines Wilson's maxim "Training is everything." But paradoxically, Twain's construction of the plot attests to the cultural training he received. A son of the South, who grew up in a slaveholding community and a slaveholding household, Twain struggled throughout his life with the racial prejudice he had learned as a boy. In his 1890 biographical sketch of his mother, Twain recalls her tender affection for animals and her unquestioning acceptance of slavery in such close proximity that his interjected repudiation of slavery as a "bald, grotesque, and unwarrantable usurpation" seems mitigated by his insistence that the slaves of his community and household were "convinced and content" (*HF&TSAI*, 87–8). Twain notes that "training and association can accomplish strange miracles," inducing the kind inhabitants of Hannibal – especially his mother, with her "large nature and liberal sympathies" (86) – to overlook the injustice of slavery. But the distanced observations beg the question, How did having spent his own formative years in this environment affect him?[32]

Given Twain's nostalgia for his antebellum hometown, it would be a mistake to ignore the influence of this training manifesting itself in his portrait of Tom Driscoll. From this angle, Tom's pampered childhood, fine clothes, and Yale education cannot check the ineradicable influence of his drop of Negro blood. Ultimately he lashes out against Judge Driscoll, his surrogate father and unwitting master, fulfilling white America's racist nightmare. Granted, Tom's bloody insurgency occurs after he learns the truth of his birth, so that we could construe his act as a fulfillment of the racist assumptions that informed his own aristocratic training. In other words, he acts as he thinks a Negro would. These assumptions of the master class have also informed the race ideology of his slave mother, Roxana. When Tom refuses to avenge an insult by dueling, for example, she lays the cause of this cowardice to his Negro blood. But to highlight internalized white assumptions of Negro characters in order to exonerate Twain from the charge of having subscribed to racist imagery calls more attention to the likelihood that the author himself was influenced to some degree by those same assumptions. Finally, even before Tom learns who his mother is, Twain offers us an exhibit of white stereotypes of Negro behavior in all the incidentals of Tom's character. He gambles, steals, and drinks, and well before Roxana confronts him with the fact of his slave birth, he even stabs his loyal boyhood slave – the true heir, Chambers – foreshadowing his murder of Judge Driscoll.[33]

Such irresponsible and "vicious" acts as Tom's were commonly attributed to blacks, supporting assumptions that informed race consciousness in white America of Twain's day and beyond. Wilson, Judge Driscoll, and Roxana pejoratively refer to Tom as a "dog," a "hound," and a "cur," figures of speech that register prevalent racial stereotypes. For example, in Metta Victor's popular dime novel *Maum Guinea*, when the runaway slave Hyperion learns that his master has called him "an ungrateful dog," he is quick to correct, "Ungrateful son, he means, 'stead of dog," indicating the same miscegenate relationship of master-father to slave-son that Twain had planned for Judge Driscoll and Tom in an early draft. Elsewhere, in an influential tract on the origin of slavery, Louisiana slaveholder George Sawyer relied on this clichéd portrait of the Negro as a dog: "the very many instances of remarkable fidelity and attachment to their masters, a characteristic quite common among them, are founded not so much upon any high intellectual and refined sentiment of gratitude, as upon instinctive impulse, possessed to an even higher degree by some of the canine species." Typical of the ambiguity of such generalizations, Sawyer's rhetoric complicates his depiction of the Negro's instinctive compliance toward domestication with the complementary assertion that "lust and beastly cruelty" rather than "emotion of parental and kindred attachment glow in the negro's bosom."[34]

In his similar characterization of Tom, Twain appears to subscribe as much to these genetic character theories as to his stated belief in the degenerate training of the South's slaveocracy. The text of *Pudd'nhead Wilson*, then, may suggest to us – much as Wilson's palmistry demonstration confirmed to Tom – that "A man's own hand is his deadliest enemy" and "keeps a record of the deepest and fatalest secrets of his life" (52). In the 1870s, Twain recalled the overtly racist notions that he had held two decades earlier and judged that "ignorance, intolerance, egotism, self-assertion, opaque perception, dense & pitiful chuckle-headedness – and an almost pathetic unconsciousness of it all" were his qualities at twenty, a judgment that, he contends, sums up "what the average Southerner is at 60 today." But the racial stereotyping in his detective novel prevents us from readily concluding that he had rid himself of all prejudice.[35]

Still, as compelling as this evidence of Twain's subjection to cultural training appears, such a conclusion is too simple. Racial attitudes in American culture were more complex than this argument allows, as the double representation of the Negro as both docile child and violent savage and as the intersection of stereotypes to represent either the degenerate southern aristocrat or the slave attest. With a writer as absorbed in doubles and irony as Twain and a text as saturated in double images and structures as *Pudd'nhead Wilson*, we can hardly overlook this complexity.[36] Twain's equivocating temperament was so sensitized to cultural crosscurrents that it prevented him from dominating his text with an exclusive bias. Moreover, to detect racial prejudice in *Pudd'nhead Wilson* does not invalidate Twain's critique of America's racism. Rather, the ambiguous representations of race in Twain's detective tale unwittingly underscore the problems of the detective genre, while also revealing the complex interpenetration of the social and the literary within his self-made identity.

For an ironist like Twain, who delights in seemingly endless double-play, detective fiction is a distinctly unsuitable genre. Detective fiction confronts linguistic indeterminacy, restoring the stability of the law, in order to bolster what the genre portrays as an inherent truthfulness of language. The detective's closure, D. A. Miller argues, "consists in a *depletion* of the signifiers generated by the crime and accumulated in the course of inquest," making all signs appear to lead to the inescapable solution of the mystery, as if the relation between sign and referent were fundamentally stable.[37] Certainly, Wilson's solution imposes a repressive closure by upholding slave law. And though Twain explicitly undercuts the morality of Wilson's closure by designating the slave system early on as "a fiction of law and custom" (9), he also mitigates the larger social truth by invoking the slanted fiction of racial stereotypes that depict the criminal as a Negro beast. However, *Pudd'nhead Wilson* invokes racial stereotypes not to endorse them as the stable language of truth but to illuminate the breakdown of the master–slave opposition in the portrait of Tom. The theme of doubling in this narrative is not, then, simply some Twainian quirk but an ambiguity inherent in the reversible stereotypes of aristocrat and Negro that Tom embodies.

Twain's detective fiction also appears troubled structurally insofar as the reader is denied the opportunity to identify with the detective in the act of decoding the clues. Dramatizing Wilson "at work over a set of tangled account books" (7) at the outset, Twain foregrounds the fact that the genre of detective fiction, as Miller notes, "conceives reading and detection as fully analogous, often overlapping, at times perfectly identical activities."[38] Conventionally, the force of that analogy urges the reader to identify with the detective and to try to solve the mystery itself or the parallel mystery surrounding the detective's method of deriving a solution. But Tom's identity as mulatto and murderer is never a mystery to us, nor is Wilson's mode of solving it a surprise. We know early on that fingerprinting will reveal the hidden facts of the case.

Furthermore, if the reader is supposed to identify with the detective, then the writer, having left a web of clues that the reader is to decode, assumes the role of the criminal. Yet Twain's description of Wilson "at work over a set of tangled account books" is a compensatory self-portrait to the one he projected in Roxana. As a careful reader, Twain discovered that his Siamese twins farce "was not one story, but two stories tangled together" (119) and then separated them to create *Pudd'nhead Wilson*. But if Twain denies the writer's identification with the criminal by allying himself with the reader's detective role, then who, we might ask, is the criminal? As Jacques Lacan has suggested in his reading of Poe's "Purloined Letter," criminal and detective can share an identity. However, because Twain exploits the instability of class stereotypes and thus denies the secure closure of detective fiction, he holds open another possibility. Tom's status as aristocrat and slave coupled with Twain's personal anxiety about the literary genealogy of detective fiction give us cause to speculate that there is another mystery in the text, a meta-narrative mystery. Like the one in the plot, this mystery also concerns the identity of Tom Driscoll, and in decoding this mystery the reader assumes the role of detective.[39]

What I am about to suggest may seem rather extravagant, but no more so than it would have to the townspeople of Dawson's Landing if at the outset of his case David Wilson had flatly identified Roxana as the author of Tom Driscoll's aristocratic position. For although Wilson proves that Roxana, by the cradle exchange, has represented Tom as an aristocrat, I suggest that Twain, by allusive literary invention, represents the mulatto murderer as the fictional embodiment of Edgar Allan Poe, who inaugurated detective fiction

on the pervasive, negrophobic stereotype of a murderous orangutan. As we might expect from Twain, this metanarrative mystery itself
has a double edge. But before examining Twain's motives in and
the effects of the metanarrative mystery, let us consider, first, the
evidence for such an outlandish claim.

Poe was one of the most notable authors in Twain's personal
library, a collection distinguished for its haphazardness and largely
forgotten writers. A number of Poe's tales, which appear in volumes
that Twain owned, serve as analogues for the murder scene in
Pudd'nhead Wilson.[40] For example, Tom's stealthy intrusion into his
uncle's office and his unconsciously intentional disturbance of his
sleeping uncle recall the action of Poe's deranged narrator in "The
Tell-Tale Heart." In Poe, the maniac's desire to murder his uncle
can be satisfied only if he bungles the cunning concealment of his
presence in his uncle's bedroom, because attracting the gaze that
incites his murderous impulse requires clumsiness, rather than
stealth, to awaken his victim. Tom's attack on his uncle must also be
incited, if not by his uncle's gaze then by his arresting grasp. Later,
Tom's admiration of "the shrewd ingenuities by which he had insured himself against detection" (102) reinforces his resemblance
to "The Tell-Tale Heart" narrator, who boasts that his crime and its
concealment were executed "so cunningly that no human eye . . .
could have detected anything wrong." And when Tom goes to ridicule Wilson on the eve of the trial's final day, carelessly giving the
hopeless detective the evidence he needs to untangle the mystery,
he resembles Poe's narrator in "The Black Cat," whose arrogant
"phrenzy of bravado" prompts the irresistible and perverse urge to
mock the investigators by tapping on the very wall behind which he
has concealed the victim's corpse. In each case, the criminal's hubris
is his downfall, drawing attention to incriminating evidence in an
otherwise inscrutable crime.[41]

"The Murders in the Rue Morgue" also figures prominently in
Pudd'nhead Wilson – not surprisingly, given Twain's recognition of
Poe's mastery of the genre in its debut. For example, the murderous
ape and his master in Poe's tale escape only a moment before the
victims' neighbors arrive; likewise, Tom flees from the scene of his
crime just as "the stillness of the night was broken by the sound of
urgent footsteps approaching the house" (95). Responding
promptly to Judge Driscoll's cry for help, the Italian twins arrive first

on the scene, only to give the obvious impression of their guilt. The fact that their habitual "long stroll in the veiled moonlight" (93) has placed them in the neighborhood alludes further to Poe's detective tale. In their habit of venturing out only "late at night, when the streets were deserted" (84), the twins resemble Dupin and his narrator-companion, who remain in "perfect seclusion . . . until warned by the clock of the advent of the true Darkness," at which time they "sallied forth into the streets, arm in arm."[42]

When Tom blackens his face with burnt cork and arms himself with the twins' knife before entering the den of his sleeping uncle, he imitates Roxana, who, in her escape from the slavery into which he had sold her, hunts him down wielding a knife and disguised as a black man. But Tom's imitative gesture also plays on Poe's use of the orangutan in "Murders in the Rue Morgue." In Poe's story, the orangutan's master confesses that he had returned home on the fateful day to find the ape imitating him, standing before a mirror with a razor in hand. Startled, the beast escapes with the razor that becomes the murder weapon. Tom's imitation, then, is a double reflection of racial stereotypes; it implies the racial character of his criminal actions both directly in his exposing masquerade – by blackening his face, Tom is not so much assuming a disguise as asserting his racial identity; the dark pigmentation and knife are the signs of his, and Twain's, indulgence in racial stereotyping – and indirectly in the allusions to the racial terror implied in "Rue Morgue."

Twain reinforces the racial dilemma in his story with another Poe allusion in his depiction of Tom's anxiety upon discovering that he is in fact a slave. When Judge Driscoll, noting the change in Tom's behavior, declares that his putative nephew is acting "as meek as a nigger," Tom recoils, feeling "as secret murderers are said to feel when the accuser says 'Thou art the man!' " (45). Although the internal irony of this narrative detail is difficult to miss, further irony lies half exposed in the fact that the proverbial accuser's words are the title of a Poe mystery in which a nephew is framed for his uncle's murder. In Twain's text, not only is the nephew the murderer but also the arresting accusation with which Poe's detective narrator confronts the actual killer is for Tom an internal echo of a racial epithet that rings all too true.

Finally, even Wilson's innovative technique for solving the Dawson's Landing mysteries recalls an aspect of the deductive method of Poe's original literary sleuth. Critics have often noted that Wilson's use of fingerprinting to solve the double mystery came to Twain from reading Francis Galton's study of the technique, which established it as a forensic science in 1892. But Wilson's conclusive evidence is also clearly prefigured in "Murders in the Rue Morgue." Just as Dupin demonstrates that the murderer is an orangutan by drawing a facsimile of the pattern of bruises made by the beast's oversized fingers on one victim's throat, Wilson proves his case with the aid of enlarged pantograph drawings of the fingerprints he has collected over the years.[43]

As compelling as this series of allusive details from Poe's macabre and detective stories is, the case for Poe's incriminating presence cannot and does not rest solely on them. If these were the only evidence, the only warranted speculation would be a case of influence, plain and simple. But Twain's text complements its allusions to Poe's tales by weaving strands of Poe's biography into its fabric. Behind the interpretation that Tom's behavior generally illustrates southern aristocratic degeneration lies the actual degeneracy of Poe's life. Like Tom, Poe was the foster child of a Virginia aristocrat, Mr. John Allan, from whom Poe adopted his middle name. Furthermore, the particulars of Poe's waywardness and aristocratic pretensions, as documented by Rufus Griswold, strikingly anticipate Twain's mulatto antagonist. Griswold's description of Poe's "proud, nervous irritability" and his account of how this "nature was fostered by his guardian's well-meant but ill-judged indulgence" foreshadow what Twain tells us about Judge and Mrs. Driscoll's blissfully lenient parenting: "Tom was petted and indulged and spoiled to his entire content – or nearly that" (23). Indeed, Griswold's account of Allan's insistence that "[n]othing was permitted which could 'break [Poe's] spirit.' He must be master of his masters or not have any" is a plausible target of flat-out irony in Twain's portrait of Tom.[44]

Finally, the derisive, aristocratic portraits of Tom and Poe coincide most strongly in the dissolute habits they share. According to Griswold, Poe picked up "gambling, intemperance and other vices" at the University at Charlottesville, behaviors that "induced his expulsion." Tom, similarly, returns with these habits after his two years of futility at Yale. For both, these dishonorable behaviors led to their disinheritance by their aristocratic foster-fathers.[45]

Naming Poe as the murderer's final identity might seem a difficult charge to make stick, since portraying degenerate aristocrats as villains was a cliché evoked widely in sentimental literature without any specific connection to Poe. But the intersecting allusions in Twain's text both to Poe's tales and to his biography align the identification on two axes that bring it into clear focus. Moreover, of the sentimental literature that features the pampered, no-good aristocrat, there is one notable exception – coincidentally, the very first American detective novel – which alludes to Poe's texts and reflects Griswold's characterization of Poe, thus setting a precedent for Twain's representative act. Metta Victor, under the pseudonym "Seeley Regester," sketches the murderer James Argyle as a likeness of Poe in *The Dead Letter* (1867). Argyle, a cunning and self-possessed villain who gambles heavily and steals from his uncle – a wealthy lawyer – to defray his gambling losses, arranges the murder of his cousin's fiancé in the hope that she will then marry him and thus secure his place in his uncle's law firm and estate. Despite the gambling, the marital designs on a cousin, and Dupinesque similarities in the story, the murderer's portrait itself is hardly specific enough to warrant reading Poe in it. But the gaming-club scene, in which the first-person narrator discovers Argyle's Poeish vices, opens with a strikingly encoded passage that confirms Victor's intention to implicate Poe in the crime. Before entering the card parlor where he witnesses Argyle's run of bad luck and the villain's promise to square his debt when he marries his cousin, the narrator observes a servant whose smile prompts him to imagine that the servant

> . . . had probably been *usher* to the *maelstrom* long enough to know that those whose feet were once caught in the slow delightful waltz of circling waters never withdrew them, after the circle grew narrow and swift, and the rush of the whirlpool sounded up from the *bottomless pit*.[46] (Emphasis added.)

"Usher," "maelstrom," "bottomless pit": in one sentence Victor clearly fingers the literary-biographical villain of this mystery.[47] We do not yet know that Twain had ever read *The Dead Letter*, but his library contained another of Victor's novels, and it seems quite conceivable that someone as interested in the success of the detective genre as Twain was would have acquainted himself with the first book-length tale in that genre. Whether he knew of Victor's fictional incrimination of Poe or not, Twain went a step beyond her tale by taking a cue from Poe himself and attaching a racial stigma to criminality. Twain's metanarrative mystery transforms Victor's literary commentary on Poe's indelicacy into a broader social critique that reveals the artificial line between aristocrat and Negro.

The master–slave opposition breaks down because the stereotype of degeneracy cuts two ways. Twain alludes to this ambiguity when Tom blackens his face with burnt cork before entering the scene of his crime. On the one hand, Tom's blackface confirms his crime's racial motivation; on the other, however, it reenacts a theory that some black leaders defensively adopted in the 1890s during the frenzy of rape accusations against black men. Joel Williamson reports that these black leaders didn't deny the occurrences of the crimes but "gave birth to the idea that many of the rapes had actually been perpetrated by white men who disguised themselves with burnt cork to sate their sexual appetites and blame black men."[48] Whether influenced by Twain's novel or the phenomenon described by the black leaders, Charles Chesnutt, in his novel *The Marrow of Tradition* (1901), depicted his degenerate aristocrat villain in precisely this act. Tom Delamere blackens his face with burnt cork and disguises himself as his grandfather's faithful Negro servant in a burglary intended to eliminate his gambling debts. The criminal's target in this theft is not a patriarch but the grand dame of the North Carolina town, yet, like Tom Driscoll's crime, Delamere's ends in murder.

In Twain's novel, the ambiguity of his villain's gesture – as either a disguise of his white skin or a confirmation of his black blood – foregrounds the lack of distinction between the stereotypes of aristocrat and slave. Of course, the ambiguity that we perceive here is not a problem for the community. Although Tom's identity appears to us as a critical rent in the social fabric, the community unconsciously patches over the damage by repressing disquieting interpretations. The ambiguity of Tom's identity is easily resolved for them. He is first and foremost a Negro "by a fiction of law and custom" (9). On the textual level, however, the law and custom of fiction prevail. Twain's text is not the kind of detective fiction that fixes meaning by censoring the signs that disrupt the stable closure of the law but rather a parody of detective fiction – one that turns the oppression of a fraudulent truth like racism against itself. The authority of Twain's parody empowers him to mock institutions of law and custom in a satire that negrifies Poe along the way.

The question of Twain's motives still remains. Surely he could have parodied detective fiction and mocked social injustice without having cast Poe as a mulatto criminal. So why would Twain make Poe his satiric victim? The answer that I propose requires that we view this portrait of Poe in *Pudd'nhead Wilson* as a rather elaborate double-edged joke on the father of detective fiction. In the logic of this joke lies the motive for Twain's satire of Poe.

The joke's leading edge offers a brand of poetic justice: it punishes Poe for racism by transposing his biography onto a genealogically anxious murderer, exposed as a mulatto and sold down the river. The parody generates its force first by maintaining the insidious logic that rules Tom a slave, not for black skin but for his disqualifying genealogy, and then by exploiting Poe's own genealogical anxieties in a fiction that refutes Poe's affectations of pedigree by labeling him a Negro. Twain's duplicitous version of racial stereotyping finally plays on a racist nightmare as deeply embedded in the consciousness of white America as the fear of Negro violence: the fear of "passing," or invisible blackness. Twain maximizes this fear of undetected blackness by turning the difficulty of reading the mulatto's race into the most extreme horror for Tom. After having knelt to Roxana, still ignorant of his blood tie to her, Tom consoles himself, " 'I've struck bottom this time; there's nothing lower.' But," the narrator corrects, "that was a hasty conclusion" (40). Even lower than self-abasement to a Negro is recognizing oneself as the racial other and the fear that one may be so recognized by society. Thus formulated, invisible blackness does not merely threaten the discriminatory standards of social purity to which Poe subscribed but also, more intimately, fictionally challenges Poe's presumptions about his own racial integrity. As an orphan, Poe endured a kind of disenfranchisement approaching that endured by blacks. Twain's parody suggests that Poe's desire for legitimation ironically emblematizes a fear of the genealogical stigma that his orphanhood makes possible.[49]

In the second edge of the joke, Twain offers a literary critique, suggesting an oedipal conflict in his creative identity. By exercising his own authority in revenge for the social inequities Poe endorsed as a journalist and encoded in the first two of his detective tales, Twain thus exerts his mastery in the genre of which Poe is the father and from whom its authority descends.[50] But, his attempts to out-master Poe notwithstanding, Twain's subordinate role in the gene-alogy he implicitly acknowledged in his notebook entry fuels the conflict that yields Twain's ambivalence toward his literary forebear. This ambivalence is keenly demonstrated in the respectful authorial kinship Twain implied between himself and Poe in the notebook, and in the name he chose for his detective persona; David Wilson is, in effect, a distant cousin of William Wilson, Poe's most extreme character of double identity and genealogical anxiety. But in per-ceiving Poe's shadow looming over all detective stories after "Rue Morgue," Twain implies his misgivings about working in the shadow of Poe's mastery. Twain's only escape from literary slavery to the conventions that Poe instituted is to turn to a negrifying parody of the master. Twain's implied oedipality in his contortion of the genre multiplies like so many fingerprints indicating his presence at the scene of a crime.

In his derisive nickname for the founder of Christian Science – "Mary Baker Eddypus," around which he built another satire – Twain indicates his knowledge of the Oedipus myth.[51] But in *Pudd'nhead Wilson*, he demonstrates an even deeper sense of the myth as a story of violated authority and detection. The surface of Twain's tale is fraught with a number of correspondences to the Oedipus myth, manifesting the strain of Twain's oedipality without the least indication of his awareness of it. For example, Roxana as-sumes a Jocasta-like role in her attempt to save her son from his foretold tragic destiny. Judge Driscoll assumes a double role, as the slain father and as Tiresias figure. As the latter, he employs oracular language in his election-day stump speech to impugn the character of his opponents, the Italian twins. Later, when they appear to be his red-handed murderers, the judge's ambiguous pronouncement assumes the force of veiled prophecy, fulfilled to the satisfaction of nearly everyone until the climax of the trial.

The role of Oedipus in Twain's detective story is a trickier matter. It is split between Tom, the outcast who commits the vile crime of patricide, and Wilson, the stranger who saves the community by solv-ing the double riddle of Tom's crime and birth. Initially, this divided role implies the opposition between Twain and Poe in their personae as detective and criminal. However, this opposition collapses when scrutinized from either of two perspectives. First, by splitting the oedipal role, Twain distinguishes between criminal and detective rather than merging the identities. Second, having drawn his narrative from the tradition of the Oedipus myth, Twain virtually announces the identity he has meant to repress in the opposition's structure. For by casting Poe as an oedipal patricide, Twain – if not symbolically slaying Poe as the father of detective fiction – at least fictionally enslaves him to the rule of slave law within a parody of the genre he created. The presence of the Oedipus myth in *Pudd'nhead Wilson* may have prompted Twain to subtitle the novel "A Tragedy." However, his manipulation of the mythic allusions into an intense parody of detective fiction mocks as well the tragic mode.

Twain's use of parody as a way of putting on the master of detective fiction involves a further ironic jab by evoking a fundamental trope of black narrative discourse known as "signifying."[52] Indeed, Twain's joke on Poe "signifies" doubly, by both undermining the master's authority and revising it against him within the idiom of the disenfranchised community to which Poe, as Tom, is reenslaved at the close of *Pudd'nhead Wilson.* However, in Twain's text we see this signifying not as an exclusively black phenomenon but as a vernacular expression of class tension, a phenomenon whereby the members of any group express their resentment of someone who assumes superiority over them. For example, when Tom returns from Yale, he takes great pleasure in strutting through town with all of the affectations of an eastern dandy. His annoyed contemporaries in Dawson's Landing vent their "anguish" in a version of signifying. They "set a tailor to work," so that "when Tom started out on his parade next morning he found the old deformed negro bellringer straddling along in his wake tricked out in a flamboyant curtain-calico exaggeration of his finery, and imitating his fancy eastern graces as well as he could" (24). This negrified parody of Tom's behavior unwittingly ironizes Tom's actual status as a slave, but more importantly, it is an emblem of the relation of Twain's text to Poe, because it deconstructs aristocracy with the "deformed" Negro it resembled. But if this is analogous to Twain's negrification of Poe, then that critique registers again the persistence of Twain's racial prejudice, because to objectify the Negro as an intrinsically degraded image shames the satirist no less than his target. Thus, by treating the Negro as a scandalizing identity, Twain reveals the durability of his cultural training; indeed, perhaps training *is* everything.

Twain's detective story is, finally, even more of "a curious thing" than he realized. Although he may have started out to try his hand at a popular genre that attempts to stabilize the indeterminacy of language, Twain subverts the genre's motivation and turns his text into a signifying parody that destabilizes the literary and social discrimination at the source of the genre's genealogy. Confronting this source, Twain's detective novel, like Wilson's offstage dog – like Tom – is a mongrel, without pedigree.[53] Thus, Twain's attack on the ancestry of the genre seems to be an attempt to compensate for the prejudices that his text fails to shrug off. Ultimately, *Pudd'nhead Wilson*'s mongrel status certifies it as a novel that is fundamentally American, a parodic mirror of the complex tensions in a diverse and competitive society. Precisely because it is an untrained mongrel, the novel is also an elaborate signifying text, but one that confirms both Twain's sensitivity to racial injustice and his internalized racial bias. Although *Pudd'nhead Wilson* appears to celebrate the triumph of training over birthright, the text's genealogy reveals otherwise. Despite Twain's attempt to train his text into a stable narrative that could bear the name "tragedy," his imagination was too diverse, too untrainable, to construct a homogeneous narrative. He began with *Those Extraordinary Twins*, an uncooperative dog of a text that failed to learn any new tricks. Instead, it begged to please with linguistic parodies of electoral rhetoric, slave narratives, Latinate medical jargon, and the stiff vocabulary of the legal profession. Even killing off half of that dog wasn't enough; the half that remained howled when the racial biases Twain thought he had trained out of himself turned up against his better intentions. Twain may have been merely trying "to tell a little tale; a very little tale," but plagued by an incurable conflict with authority, he produced a text that was destined to chase its own tail.

EPILOGUE

AFTER THE DOUBLE-CROSS

═══════════

> Doesn't a thought which introduces constraint of the system
> and discontinuity in the history of the mind remove all basis
> for progressive political intervention? Does it not lead to the
> following dilemma:
> – either the acceptance of the system,
> – or the appeal to an uncontrolled event of upsetting the
> system?
>
> — The editors of *Esprit* to Michel Foucault
> "History, Discourse and Discontinuity"

Some six years after *Pudd'nhead Wilson,* Twain would reinvestigate
the master–slave opposition in an unfinished narrative entitled
"Which Was It?" In this text, he rotates the roles, depicting a slave,
Jasper, as the detective who discovers a white man's act of murder.
Although still maintaining the appearance of the slave system, Jasper
subverts it by extorting subservience from the criminal, George Harrison, by threatening to expose Harrison's crime. Kenneth Lynn has
observed the similarities between this tale and Melville's "Benito
Cereno"; and the reversal of racial power and the public charades
of the status quo performed by Jasper and Melville's slave character
Babo are certainly remarkable.[1] However, the means by which the
power roles are reversed in the two narratives are distinctly different.
In Melville's story, the slaves become masters by physical force; they
become renegades from the slavery system who use the threat of
violence against the agents of that system. In Twain's story, on the
other hand, Jasper maintains his mastery of Harrison through
knowledge of the truth and the threat of subjecting him to the sys-

tem of justice whose discovery he has eluded. Despite the replication of the conditions of *Pudd'nhead Wilson*, the exchanged racial identities of criminal and detective make all the difference. Jasper cannot shake off his social stigma and rise to prominence, as David Wilson does. Because of the inequities of slavery, Jasper's only recourse is to dictate a private form of retributive justice. His vengeful leverage over Harrison is no less self-serving than Wilson's repression of the social critique embedded in his solution of the Dawson's Landing mysteries. But in contrast to Wilson's implicit assent, Jasper's privately controlled justice underscores the rigid circumscription of the slave's status. Consequently, the tale represents Twain's attempt to redress the racism in the genealogy of detective fiction beyond his oedipal rivalry with Poe in the metanarrative of *Pudd'nhead Wilson*. Twain uses "Which Was It?" to penetrate the surface of social conventions and to expose the racial guilt buried in the American unconscious.

However, having conceived "Which Was It?" as a dream tale, Twain signals his skepticism about achieving justice of this magnitude in reality. More importantly, the fact that he never finished the tale suggests the limits of his ability to overcome the repression enacted in *Pudd'nhead Wilson*. Nearly all of Twain's later work is distinguished by these two features: a pursuit of the surreal, either in dreams, gothic adventures, science fiction, or futuristic discoveries of historical manuscripts; and a difficulty that prevented him from bringing most of it to a close. Indeed, it's often noted that he left more unfinished than finished work. There are exceptions: *Joan of Arc* and *Following the Equator* as well as the thinner efforts of *Tom Sawyer Abroad* and *Tom Sawyer, Detective*. But none of these later published works have the sustained critical edge of novels.

Critics have commonly viewed the diminished quality and quantity of Twain's published work as the effect of age and philosophical bitterness brought on by personal grief. But this explanation seems insufficient on two fronts. First, the problem of finishing manuscripts had haunted Twain throughout his career. Although it's true that the problem became more exaggerated toward the end of his career, that was not because he lacked creative energy. Twain turned to writing all the more in his later years as an outlet. In an 1897 letter to Howells he confides, "I couldn't get along without work now. I bury myself in it up to the ears. Long hours – 8 & 9 on a stretch, sometimes. And all the days, Sundays included" (*MTHL*; 2: 670). These are not the words of a desiccated has-been, as the standard portrait of Twain's later career suggests. But Twain's problem wasn't generating stories or ideas for them. And if we bear in mind Edward Said's definition of the novel as a "new beginning," we might think of Twain's unfinished work as a continuing series of projects in which he starts over. In this light, his effort in these projects would correspond to the etymology of "author" that Said emphasizes: "a person who originates or gives existence to something, a begetter, beginner, father."[2] Twain's encounter with the double-cross of novelistic discourse had revealed to him the difficulty of completing a project or, perhaps worse, the futility of doing so. He may well have taken heart in that part of the process that sanctioned him to start over without worrying about what he knew would never satisfy. This interpretation still accounts for the tragedies that beset him in later life. Indeed, his more focused commitment to beginning, to fathering as it were, occurred at that time of life when the emotionally devastating illnesses and deaths of his wife and two of his three daughters would have made him aware all the more powerfully of his role within his family.

Still, Richard Sennett reminds us of another etymology of "author," derived from the Latin *auctor*: "The Roman auctor was, in one of his guises, the giver of guarantees."[3] It was precisely in this function of authority that Twain sensed how novelistic discourse comes up short. Unable to give any guarantees that would extend beyond fiction, Twain found it ever more difficult to complete, to control, or to imagine he was controlling his fictional challenges to the world that had turned so grim. In the generally private and unfinished later work, he directed his attention toward more experimental fiction spurred by his awareness of the double-cross of novelistic discourse.

I want to stress, however, that these late developments are of a piece with his career overall. As I have argued throughout my analysis of his dialectical career, Twain found sustaining the critical discourse of the novel an ever-present difficulty that became perhaps worse in degree yet not in kind. The succession of Twain's texts reveals that his artistic difficulties were not a matter of something going wrong late in life but stem from his awareness that something was wrong from the beginning. In his attempts to inveigh against social control, he continually rediscovered authority's double bind in the "something wrong" that his own texts exhibited. As much as he tried to resolve it, the double-cross of the novel was always there. With each successive failure, his awareness of it grew more acute.

Twain's evolving awareness of both the potential and the limits of the genre is what warrants us to consider him a representative American novelist. Although no other writer projects the dialectical oscillation between romance and novel that distinguish his career, many – Melville and Faulkner perhaps most notably – labored with the sense that, despite their sometimes prodigious efforts, failure was inevitable. Charles Chesnutt articulates his lack of confidence in fictive representation when his narrator describes the fate of the villainous Captain McBane in *The Marrow of Tradition*: "McBane had lived a life of violence and cruelty. As a man sows, so shall he reap. In works of fiction, such men are sometimes converted. More often, in real life, they do not change their natures until they are converted into dust. One does well to distrust a tamed tiger."[4] Any interpretation for the ending of Chesnutt's story, in which a white aristocratic southern woman promises to rise above her prejudice and acknowledge her mulatto half sister, must account for Chesnutt's jaundiced view of fictional resolutions to social problems.

Beyond the personal impact on individual authors, I suggest that Twain's representative texts show us how American narratives can be assigned to one or the other category with critical profit. The genre categorizations that I propose highlight new distinctions between a group of texts that include *Letters from an American Farmer*, *The Coquette*, *Typee*, *The Scarlet Letter*, *The Awakening*, and *Invisible Man* and another group that include *The Power of Sympathy*, *The Last of the Mohicans*, *Uncle Tom's Cabin*, *The Red Badge of Courage*, and *Their Eyes Were Watching God*. My point is not to discriminate hierarchically but to show how these texts work differently. Consider, for example, William Hill Brown's *The Power of Sympathy* and Hannah Foster's *The Coquette*. In Hill Brown's romance, the freedom of the new literary form anxiously represents the immorality that arises when liberty – political or literary – turns into license, in which the disregard for order by the generation of revolutionary fathers leads to the near horror of incest. The rhetoric of the romance shuns the revolutionary impulse and calls instead for a return to the order that the political activism and the ideologically parallel literary form sought to undermine. Foster's novel, on the other hand, questions the gender inequities that conditioned the exercise of freedom both in social relations and in fictional narratives. *The Coquette* criticizes the hypocrisy of a society that perpetuates gender discrimination while also striking a blow for humanitarian self-determination and implicitly recognizes the inability of literary fiction to influence the state of affairs. Although both narratives are based on actual events, they couldn't take more opposite positions on the prospects of American freedom. Thus, although I agree with Cathy Davidson's alignment of the new literary genre and the political efforts of the American Revolution, the novel represents more than a literary echo of Enlightenment idealism. The novel is distinctive for its textual awareness of the limitations of fiction to generate active challenges to the status quo.[5]

In part, I seek to moderate new historicist claims that exaggerate the political influence of fictional narratives. Although I agree that critics must recover the cultural context in which these texts were produced in order to understand their rhetorical intentions, I'm deeply suspicious of the ability of fiction to perform much of the cultural work that Philip Fisher, in *Hard Facts*, and Jane Tompkins, in *Sentimental Designs*, for example, have ascribed to it. When it comes to fiction, political intentions are usually a far cry from political effects.[6] Fictional narratives may question and reconfigure the ideological assumptions of the culture within their representations, but the fictional image is not the real thing, and to confuse the two is to suffer from quixotic delusion. In short, *Uncle Tom's Cabin* did not start the Civil War, as President Lincoln's often quoted, flattering remark to Harriet Beecher Stowe seems to suggest. Indeed, Twain implies the foolishness of such an idea, first, when he names Sir Walter Scott as the cause of the war in *Life on the Mississippi*, and later, in "Tom Sawyer's Conspiracy," when he has Huck dispute Stowe's credit by insisting that Tom Sawyer originated the idea for the Civil War.

So why do authors write novels, and why do we read them? Surely, some authors write fictional narratives with the hope, if not the expectation, that their wishful representations will transform reality. But most such texts, like the utopian *Looking Backward* by Edward Bellamy (1888) or the paranoid *Turner Diaries* by William Pierce under the pseudonym "Andrea Macdonald" (1978), are works of fanaticism of one kind or another. In all cases, though, the articulation of a desire for a hypothetical alternative in fiction serves as a coping mechanism for both writer and reader. One aspect of the critical value of fictional narratives is the manner in which they represent cultural desires and the anxieties that spurred them. In this regard, I concur with new historicists who stress the contextual grounding of the novel's symbolic content. Scholarship of this sort broadens our awareness of the text's ability to signify and of the richness of social debates concerning issues within an historical period.

But novels aren't simply historical artifacts serving only to dramatize the consciousness of an era. They are active cognitive experiences that draw us into the conflict of authority that they delineate. This is yet another distinction between the novel and the romance. Although Michael Rogin's historical research in *Subversive Genealogies* contributes to a new understanding of *Moby-Dick*, just as Fisher and Tompkins show the value of historical research in recovering the significance of a text like *Uncle Tom's Cabin*, the radically different histories of reception of these texts illustrate the distinction between the romance and the novel.[7] Stowe's romance requires a knowledge of its contemporary context in order to rescue it from its twentieth-century lapse into obscurity. On the other hand, Melville's novel, despite being unread in its day, was rediscovered, one could argue, because it highlighted the problem of authority that throbs at the core of American ideology. What a novel like Melville's does, which a romance like Stowe's does not do, is to call into question the authority of language to represent experience and knowledge. Long before contemporary theory taught us its lesson about the dubiousness of unified discourse, the American novel was doing the same.

The definition of the novel that I've proposed attempts to keep that lesson before us. As a cultural performance that embodies the clash between the social limits in the actual world and the ideal of freedom in the utopian myth of America, the novel is a textually self-conscious, demythologizing critique of authority that could not be other than disunited. Its cross-hatching of modes alerts us not only to the heteroglossia of language in Bakhtin's theory but also to the dynamic structure of social relationships that language makes possible and that brought language forth. The American novel, specifically, functions to remind us that existence in a democratic society is a series of negotiations in which freedom and restraint are the terms of exchange. The ideological basis for forms like "romance" and "realism" was not the Manichean dichotomy to which Richard Chase attributed these twin components of the American novel's "tradition" but more closely related to the epistemological paradox that Horkheimer and Adorno describe as the Dialectic of Enlightenment.

The swindle and the burden that Twain discovered in the double-cross of novelistic discourse aroused in him a healthy skepticism about the viability of utopian schemes; it made him wary of the potential solipsism that the assumption of such total authority over an imaginary world can entail. Similarly, the novel's double-cross reminds us that the desire for individual freedom should not be confused with egocentrism. Personal freedom is always negotiated in a social relationship. We can see this even in Twain's late use of the Adamic myth. In his adaptation of this Genesis story, he focused not on a separate autonomous identity, as the American Adam generally portends, but on a domestically structured identity with responsibilities beyond the self.

Like Twain's diaries of Adam and Eve, the last effect of his discovery of the novel's double-cross is, as we might have expected, bittersweet: bitter because Twain's explorations within novelistic discourse finally made clear to him that the American promise of individual freedom does not deliver one from membership in "the damned human race," and sweet because the progress of Twain's dialectical career quietly points to the novel as a literary mechanism that springs from the desire to gain control over the discourses that give structure to society. By calling attention to those discourses and representing their inherent instability, the novelist reminds us of the ways in which language serves the interests of power. In a speech remarkable for its ironic foresight, twentieth-century America's most mythologized president, John Kennedy, warned about the distracting influence of mythology. "For the great enemy of the truth is very often not the lie – deliberate, contrived, and dishonest – but the myth – persistent, persuasive, and unrealistic."[8] The quality that sets the novel apart is its refusal merely to reiterate myth; instead, it interrogates myth and urges us to be critically aware of how the language we imagine we control may, in fact, control us.

NOTES

==========

Introduction

1. See Richard Sennett, *Authority* (New York: Knopf, 1980), pp. 134–7, who identifies the classic *Doppelgänger* relationship, of which Twain's double identity is an example, as a form of consciousness that allows one to disengage from authority in order to reconceive it.
2. See David M. Potter, *Freedom and Its Limitations in American Life* (Stanford: Stanford University Press, 1976), for an incisive analysis of the dynamic relation between freedom and control. See also Seymour Martin Lipset, *American Exceptionalism: A Double-Edged Sword* (New York: Norton, 1996). Lipset's analysis of the American paradox calls up a notion of doubleness related to the one I develop later in this introduction.
3. Emory Elliott, introduction to *The Columbia History of the American Novel*, ed. Elliott (New York: Columbia University Press, 1991), p. xi.
4. Frederick Jackson Turner's "frontier" thesis is premised on this ideological ground. But coming at the moment when the redemptive frontier has disappeared, Turner's thesis harbors its own skepticism about the durability of America's utopian possibilities.
5. See, for example, Sacvan Bercovitch and Myra Jehlen, eds., *Ideology and Classic American Literature* (Cambridge: Cambridge University Press, 1986).
6. See Michael Davitt Bell, *The Development of American Romance: The Sacrifice of Relation* (Chicago: University of Chicago Press, 1980), on the various distinctions propounded between the terms "romance" and "novel." But whereas these distinctions are largely stylistic, I want to emphasize the differences between modes on ideological grounds, along the lines of Frederic Jameson's views in *The Political Unconscious: Narrative as a Socially Symbolic Act* (Ithaca: Cornell University Press, 1981).
7. It seems hardly coincidental that Joseph Heller's phrase was not only the title of a novel in which the paradox of its discourse and American authority are explicit but also made a place for this kind of paradox in our popular lexicon.

231

8. Edward Said, *Beginnings: Intention and Method* (New York: Columbia University Press, 1975), pp. 82, 84.
9. D. A. Miller, *The Novel and the Police* (Berkeley and Los Angeles: University of California Press, 1988), p. xi.
10. Sigmund Freud, *Civilization and Its Discontents* (1930), ed. and trans. James A. Strachey (New York: Norton, 1962), p. 81.
11. Leslie A. Fiedler, *Love and Death in the American Novel* (1960; rpt. Cleveland: Meridian, 1962), pp. xxvii, xvii.
12. Nancy Armstrong and Leonard Tennenhouse, "The American Origins of the English Novel," *American Literary History*, 4 (1992): 386, 393, 391; Mitchell Robert Breitwieser, *American Puritanism and the Defense of Mourning: Religion, Grief, and Ethnology in Mary Rowlandson's Captivity Narrative* (Madison: University of Wisconsin Press, 1990).
13. Richard Poirier, *A World Elsewhere: The Place of Style in American Literature* (New York: Oxford University Press, 1966).
14. Louise K. Barnett, *Authority and Speech: Language, Society, and Self in the American Novel* (Athens: University of Georgia Press, 1993); Joyce A. Rowe, *Equivocal Endings in Classic American Novels* (Cambridge: Cambridge University Press, 1988), pp. 6–7.

Chapter 1. Mark Twain's Big Two-Hearted River Text

1. Ernest Hemingway, *The Green Hills of Africa* (New York: Scribners, 1935), p. 22.
2. By the term "representatively" I am denoting Twain's desire to embody personally the idea and the experience of America. This phenomenon is found throughout American literary history from the interpretive tradition of Puritan typology, to the tradition of secular autobiography established by Benjamin Franklin, to Emerson's "Representative Men." See Elizabeth Kaspar Aldrich, " 'The Children of These Fathers': The Origins of an Autobiographical Tradition in America," *First Person Singular: Studies in American Autobiography*, ed. A. Robert Lee (New York: St. Martin's, 1988); James M. Cox, "Autobiography and America," *Virginia Quarterly Review*, 47 (1971): 252–71; Robert F. Sayre, "Autobiography and the Making of America," *Autobiography: Essays Theoretical and Critical*, ed. James Olney (Princeton: Princeton University Press, 1980), and "The Proper Study – Autobiographies in American Studies," *American Quarterly*, 29 (1977): 241–62; Albert E. Stone, "Autobiography and American Culture," *American Studies: An International Newsletter*, 11 (1972): 22–36.
3. This idea of the representative use of biography appears in Twain criticism as early as the Brooks–DeVoto debate. See Guy Cardwell, *The Man Who Was Mark Twain: Images and Ideologies* (New Haven: Yale University Press, 1991), and Susan Gillman, *Dark Twins: Imposture and Identity in Mark Twain's America* (Chicago: University of Chicago Press, 1989), for recent examples of the representativity thesis.
4. Although Twain uses this expression to refer to his difficulty with *The Adven-

tures of Tom Sawyer, it's an apt description of his experience of composing virtually all of his major works.

5. Barriss Mills, " 'Old Times on the Mississippi' as an Initiation Story," *College English,* 25 (1964); 283–9. Mills's concern with the lack of formal unity in *Life on the Mississippi* exemplifies a New Critical bias that has endured well beyond the era of that critical methodology. Explanations of Twain's difficulty in fleshing out his book to the 600 to 700 pages required by the terms of subscription publishing include Hamlin Hill, "Mark Twain: Audience and Artistry," *American Quarterly,* 15 (1963): 25–40, and Walter Blair, *Mark Twain and Huck Finn* (Berkeley and Los Angeles: University of California Press, 1960), pp. 285–90. For an interesting speculation on the relationship between Twain's two professional roles dealing with the river, see Edgar J. Burde, "Mark Twain: The Writer as Pilot," *PMLA,* 93 (1978): 878–92. See also Dudley R. Hutcherson, "Mark Twain as Pilot," *American Literature,* 12 (1940): 19–35; Delancey Ferguson, *Mark Twain: Man and Legend* (Indianapolis: Bobbs-Merrill, 1943); Lucian R. Smith, "Sam Clemens: Pilot," *Mark Twain Journal,* 15 (1971): 1–5; and Thomas H. Pauly, "The 'Science of Piloting' in Twain's 'Old Times': The Cub's Lesson on Industrialization," *Arizona Quarterly,* 30 (1974): 229–38.

6. See Horst H. Kruse, *Mark Twain and "Life on the Mississippi"* (Amherst: University of Massachusetts Press, 1981), for a thorough study of the manuscript evidence supporting this conclusion.

7. See Georg Lukács, *Theory of the Novel,* trans. Anna Bostock (Cambridge: MIT Press, 1971). Lukács's description of the epic hero who embodies "the destiny of [the] community" (66) corresponds to one side of Twain's admiring portrait of Bixby as a representative of Mississippi authority. The antebellum world of "Old Times" lends itself both to Lukács's view that the epic represents "a totality of life that is rounded from within" (60) and to Mikhail Bakhtin's assessment of the epic's nostalgic view of the world within a period of irretrievable greatness that he calls the "absolute past" (*The Dialogic Imagination: Four Essays,* ed. Michael Holquist, trans. Caryl Emerson and Michael Holquist [Austin: University of Texas Press, 1981], 13).

The significance of the text's affinities with the bildungsroman are illuminated by Franco Moretti, *The Way of the World: The Bildungsroman in European Culture* (New York: Verso, 1987), who observes that the genre is a "symbolic form that more than any other has portrayed and promoted modern socialization" (10). This function of the genre seems to me emphasized in Twain's text by the symbolic correspondence between the protagonist's innocence and the national youthfulness. "Old Times," then, has both the structure of the epic behind it and the force of the novel, of the bildungsroman, within it.

8. William Dean Howells, "Mark Twain: An Inquiry" (1901), *My Mark Twain* (New York: Harper & Brothers, 1910), pp. 166–7.

9. See Roland Barthes, *S/Z,* trans. Richard Miller (New York: Hill & Wang, 1974), p. 5.

10. Blair, *Mark Twain and Huck Finn*, pp. 286–7. See *Mark Twain's Autobiography* (MTA), 2:959 for an expression of the same frustration with the humorist label when he feared that his seriousness about *Joan of Arc* would be misunderstood.

11. Mark Twain, *My Dear Bro: A Letter from Samuel Clemens to His Brother Orion*, ed. Frederick Anderson (Berkeley: Berkeley Albion, 1961), p. 6.

12. Everett Emerson, *The Authentic Mark Twain: A Literary Biography of Samuel L. Clemens* (Philadelphia: University of Pennsylvania Press, 1985), p. 16.

13. James M. Cox, *Mark Twain: The Fate of Humor* (Princeton: Princeton University Press, 1966), pp. 28–33.

14. Although Eric Partridge, *The "Shaggy Dog" Story: Its Origins, Development and Nature* (London: Faber & Faber, 1953), dates the origin of the term "shaggy-dog story" to the early 1940s and claims that the genre itself "was apparently invented in the 1930's," it should be clear that Twain's descriptions of Jim Blaine's tale and Mr. Brown's story about a dog are examples, perhaps inaugurations, of this narrative subgenre well before the dates that Partridge assigns.

15. See, for example, his letter to Orion in which he claims, "I wanted to be a pilot or a preacher, & I was about as well calculated for either as is poor Emperor Norton for Chief Justice of the United States" (*My Dear Bro*, p. 7). Burde, "Mark Twain: The Writer as Pilot," argues that "[b]y drawing for his analogy upon the California eccentric Joshua Norton, a financial failure and benign fraud who several years before had appointed himself Norton I, Emperor of the United States, Clemens emphasized the gulf that he felt between himself and figures of genuine authority and legitimate power" (p. 879).

16. See Burde, "Mark Twain: The Writer as Pilot," pp. 878–92.

17. Richard Bridgman, *Traveling in Mark Twain* (Berkeley and Los Angeles: University of California Press, 1987), p. 65.

18. On the connection between language and oedipality see Jacques Lacan, *Écrits: A Selection*, trans. Alan Sheridan (New York: Norton, 1977), especially "The Mirror Stage" (pp. 1–7) and "The Agency of the Letter in the Unconscious, or Reason since Freud" (pp. 146–78).

19. In a letter dated December 5, 1898, to a John Adams, Esq., of Glasgow, Scotland, Twain admits to never having read Locke ("An Unpublished Mark Twain Letter," ed. Laurence Clerk Powell, *American Literature*, 13 [1941–2]: 405–7). However, Jay Fliegelman, *Prodigals and Pilgrims: The American Revolution against Patriarchal Authority, 1750–1800* (Cambridge: Cambridge University Press, 1982), demonstrates that Lockean concepts were so prevalent in late-eighteenth-century American culture that we may infer Twain's access to these ideas despite his inability to attribute their origin.

20. This account shows the liberty Twain was willing to take with the facts of his autobiography. It was his curiosity about travel and his journalistic ambitions, not steamboating, that motivated his flight from the family hearth. After three years in journalism, he turned to the river, at the not so under-ripe age of twenty-one.

21. We should take care not to overestimate the degree of consciousness in Twain's desire to compensate for his lack of Civil War experience. In "The Private History of a Campaign That Failed," he hadn't yet worked up the courage to explain his absence from the Civil War, but his ability to repress the fact was not complete, even at this time. Similarly, in *Roughing It*, although Twain avoids mentioning the war until halfway through the book (when the war is all but over), he hints that the war may have influenced his decision to light out for the territory when he recalls that in traveling light he and his brother Orion "were reduced to a war-footing" (*Roughing It*, ed. Franklin R. Rogers and Paul Baender [Berkeley and Los Angeles: University of California Press, 1972], p. 45). On Twain's terming his lack of military service "disenlist[ment]" see Paul Fatout, ed., *Mark Twain in Virginia City* (Bloomington: Indiana University Press, 1964), p. 66.

22. The extent to which the Civil War was typologized as fratricide is suggested by the fact that the marquis of Lothian, in his book *The Confederate Secession* (Edinburgh and London, 1864), analogized strife-torn America in the biblical terms of Cain and Abel (cited in H. W. Wilberforce, "Causes and Objects of the War in America," *Dublin Review*, 56 [1865]: 331–5). In "The Private History of a Campaign That Failed," Twain similarly recalls the death of the "enemy" that he and his fellow Marion Rangers killed: "[H]e was sincerely mourned by the opposing force as if he had been their brother" (*CTSS&E*, 1:880).

23. Twain knew Frederick Douglass and interceded on his behalf with the Garfield administration. As early as 1869, in a letter to Olivia Langdon, he reports a conversation with Douglass (*MTP-L*, 3:426). In the *Autobiography*, when he describes the transfer of his contract from Bixby to Brown Twain even refers to Bixby as "my owner" (*AMT*, 98). In *Roughing It*, Twain's description of lighting out in 1861 for the Nevada territory as "emancipation from . . . slaving" (p. 47) similarly identifies his escape from war with the freedom of the slaves for whom the battle was fought. For a consideration of Twain's familiarity with slave stories, see also Shelley Fisher Fishkin, *Was Huck Finn Black?* (New York: Oxford University Press, 1993); William L. Andrews, "Mark Twain, William Wells Brown, and the Problem of Authority in New South Writing," *Southern Literature and Literary Theory*, ed. Jefferson Humphries (Athens: University of Georgia Press, 1990), pp. 1–21; and Sholom S. Kahn, "Mark Twain's 'Original Jacobs': A Probably Explanation," *Mark Twain Circular*, 8 (1994): 4–6.

24. Although Twain assumes the responsibility for Henry's death only implicitly in *Life on the Mississippi*, in the *Autobiography* he elaborates on his guilt and takes responsibility not only for their conversation but also for his own negligence in allowing inexperienced physicians to administer a "fatal" dose of morphine (*AMT*, 100–1).

25. Mitchell Robert Breitwieser, *Cotton Mather and Benjamin Franklin: The Price of Representative Personality* (Cambridge: Cambridge University Press, 1984), describes this conception of the self in Franklin, whose "public persona was a blank capacity in no way confined to special cause or faction

or passion. His self-presentation was primarily negational, a demonstration of the commitments to man to which he held" (p. 207). Whitman, however, was able to encompass such a wide scope in his affirmative verse that in "Song of Myself" he produces the unfamiliar juxtaposition of president and prostitute and acknowledges, even celebrates, the inevitability of self-contradiction ("Song of Myself," *Leaves of Grass: The First (1855) Edition*, ed. Malcolm Cowley [New York: Penguin, 1976], lines 302–5, 1314–15).

26. Howells, "My Mark Twain," p. 35.

27. *Faulkner in the University: Class Conferences at the University of Virginia, 1957–58*, ed. Frederick L. Gwynn and Joseph L. Blotner (Charlottesville: University Press, 1959), p. 281.

28. In *Roughing It*, there are two such figures. The old Admiral, looked upon by the Sandwich Islanders as a "father," creates history in order to silence anyone who dares oppose him. He receives his comeuppance when a quiet passenger, Williams, both flatters and turns the table on the Admiral by creating some history of his own. The second, an inveterate liar named Markiss, is not a father figure but an alter ego who haunts Twain, interfering with his ability to tell a story. Twain reports this as an eerie William Wilson–esque experience in which Markiss (Mark-ish?) repeatedly turns up to outdo him in conversation. (The reference to Poe in the chapter preceding the Markiss episode seems to reinforce the allusion.) In both of these cases, authority is at stake in a social competition.

29. Although Bixby wasn't a writer, it was he who first insisted that the cub learn the river by writing down his observations in a book. The analogy between filling up the blank pages and the inscription of experience on the *tabula rasa* of the cub's Lockean personality suggests analogies between the text and the self, between the self and the landscape, and between the individual and the nation.

30. In a culture that prides itself on change and innovation, the emphasis on tradition sets up a tension that is continually unsettling. Much of the authority that Twain appeals to or recoils from is authority based on priority. Captain Sellers's authority in *Life on the Mississippi*, for example, is based on his claim to having been around longer than any of the younger pilots – that is, he was there anterior to their arrival on the river. The same feature informs Twain's concern with plagiarism. Whoever writes or says something first has an authoritative claim based on priority.

Twain's remorse in the Seller's episode is similar to his despondency after the Whittier Birthday Speech. For an analysis of the Whittier Birthday Dinner speech, see Henry Nash Smith, *Mark Twain: The Development of a Writer* (Cambridge, MA: Harvard University Press, 1962). Even at a moment when Twain intended to honor figures of cultural authority, vernacular subversion complicated his performance.

31. On the Twain–Sellers connection, see Ernest E. Leisy, "Mark Twain and Isaiah Sellers," *American Literature*, 13 (1942): 398–405; George H. Brownell, "The Question as to the Origin of the Name 'Mark Twain,' " *Twain-*

ian, 1 (1942): 5; and Guy Cardwell, "Samuel Clemens' Magical Pseudonym," *New England Quarterly,* 48 (1975): 175–93.

32. See Edgar Marquess Branch and Robert Hirst, eds., "Editors' Note, 'River Intelligence,' " Mark Twain, *Early Tales & Sketches,* 2 vols. (Berkeley and Los Angeles: University of California Press, 1979), 1:126–30.

33. Bridgman, *Traveling in Mark Twain,* p. 115. Bakhtin, *The Dialogic Imagination,* p. 342.

34. Bakhtin, *The Dialogic Imagination,* p. 342.

35. Burde, "Mark Twain: The Writer as Pilot," p. 884.

36. Sigmund Freud, *Totem and Taboo* (1913), trans. A. A. Brill (New York: Vintage, 1918), p. 183.

37. Freud, *Totem and Taboo,* p. 184n. See George Forgie, *Patricide and the House Divided: A Psychological Interpretation of Lincoln and His Age* (New York: Norton, 1979), for a fuller explanation of this theory that the Oedipus complex underlay the Civil War. Likewise, on the Revolutionary period, see Fliegelman, *Prodigals and Pilgrims;* on the colonial period, see Perry Miller, *Errand into the Wilderness* (Cambridge, MA: Belknap/Harvard University Press, 1956); on the South during and after Reconstruction, see C. Vann Woodward, *The Burdens of Southern History* (New York: Vintage, 1960).

38. Mitchell Robert Breitwieser, "False Sympathy in Melville's *Typee,*" *American Quarterly,* 34 (1982): 396–417, identifies a parallel instance of this phenomenon.

39. In his autobiographical dictations, Twain claims, "I have studied the human race with diligence and strong interest all these years in my own person" (*MTE,* xxix), reinforcing the parallels between himself and Freud. But despite his attempts to become a citizen of the world, his representativity was always focused in American terms.

40. In a chapter edited out of the finished book, Twain noted with confidence that the "horror [of slavery] is gone, and permanently" (*LOM,* 332). Certainly, Twain could not have entirely overlooked the desperate condition of the South's former slaves, but his attention was more acutely focused on the monolithic character of the South's social and political identity.

41. Bakhtin, *The Dialogic Imagination,* pp. 376, 378.

42. Henry James, *Hawthorne* (Ithaca: Cornell University Press, 1966), p. 144.

43. See Steven Knapp, "Collective Memory and the Actual Past," *Representations,* 26 (1989). 123–49. See also James M. Cox, "Walt Whitman, Mark Twain, and the Civil War," *Sewanee Review,* 69 (1961): 185–204, and *Mark Twain: The Fate of Humor,* pp. 169–70.

44. The link between the two suggests a more direct and compelling version of the determinism that Twain would later elaborate in "The Turning Point of My Life." In that piece, commissioned by *Harper's Bazaar* in 1910, he argues humorously for the importance of intermediate steps, steps often overlooked for their seeming insignificance in the chain that leads to some watershed event, concluding, "I can say with truth that the reason I am in the literary profession is because I had the measles when I was twelve years old" (*CTSS&E,* 2:935). Despite his lack of seriousness in linking the destiny

of his career with his childhood illness, the relation between "Old Times" and *Life on the Mississippi* insists that the connection between the pilot and the writer is no such frivolous matter.

45. Richard Bridgman, *The Colloquial Style in America* (New York: Oxford University Press, 1966), p. 136, noted a "mixed style" as a distinctive feature of American writing; Bakhtin's theoretical explanation helps to amplify the ideological underpinnings of that constituent feature in the novel.

46. See Barbara Novak, *Nature and Culture: American Landscape and Painting, 1825–1875* (New York: Oxford University Press, 1980), pp. 18–33, 137–56.

47. Novak, *Nature and Culture*, p. 137.

48. See Ernst Robert Curtius, *European Literature in the Latin Middle Ages*, trans. Willard Trask (Princeton: Princeton University Press, 1967), pp. 28–9, for the background on the *translatio* concepts. American expressions of the notion include Philip Freneau and Hugh Henry Brackenridge, "The Rising Glory of America" (1772); Timothy Dwight, "Greenfield Hill" (1794); and Whitman, "A Passage to India" (1871) – all quoted in Henry Nash Smith, *Virgin Land: The American West as Symbol and Myth* (1950; rpt. New York: Vintage, 1962), pp. 9–11. J. Hector St. John de Crèvecoeur, *Letters from an American Farmer and Sketches from Eighteenth-Century American Life* (1782) (New York: Penguin, 1981), has his letter-writing farmer express the notion very directly: "Americans are the western pilgrims who are carrying along with them that great mass of the arts, sciences, vigour, and industry which began in the East; they will finish the great circle" (p. 70).

49. See Michael Riffaterre, *Fictional Truth* (Baltimore: Johns Hopkins University Press, 1990), and Jacques Lacan, "Seminar on 'The Purloined Letter,' " trans. Jeffrey Mehlman, *Yale French Studies*, 48 (1972): 38–72, for similar distinctions between two registers of truth.

50. Bridgman, *Traveling in Mark Twain*, p. 305, notes that, like Samuel Clemens, Huck assumes a pseudonym, "Charles William Allbright," suggested by the haunted-barrel story he has just overheard. Another of the more surprising connections Bridgman discovers is the anticipation in Huck's pseudonym of "The Burning Brand," the story of the convicted burglar–confidence man, Charles Williams, in chapter 52. Bridgman astutely conjectures that just as Williams is discovered as a fraudulent letter writer and "not a Christian man, but a dissolute, cunning prodigal," we should also perceive society's views of Huck and Mark Twain in this revelation. Further, like Williams, Huck and Twain employed pseudonyms and fictional narrative – the latter, even more like Williams, authored a fictional narrator to endear himself to members of the provincial New England establishment, who held his disregard of conventional authority in contempt.

51. Bridgman, *Traveling in Mark Twain*, p. 113.

52. Bakhtin, *The Dialogic Imagination*, p. 342.

53. See Frank Kermode, *The Sense of an Ending: Studies in the Theory of Fiction* (New York: Oxford University Press, 1967), on the two Greek concepts of "chronological" and "kairological" time as fundamental to the narrative process.

54. Daniel Aaron, *The Unwritten War: American Writers and the Civil War* (New York: Knopf, 1973), p. 343.
55. See Forrest G. Robinson, "Why I Killed My Brother: An Essay on Mark Twain," *Literature and Psychology*, 30 (1980): 168–81, for an analysis of Twain's egocentrism in a letter describing Henry's death to his sister-in-law. In this account, Twain assumes the role of "sacrificial cross-bearer" and, ironically, displaces Henry as the victim.

Chapter 2. Catching Mark Twain's Drift

1. Twain alludes to the epic slant of these school texts in the scene where Huck proves his literacy by reading just such a passage, "something about General Washington and the Wars" (*HF*, 24), to his disapproving father early in the story.
2. Roy Harvey Pearce, " 'The End. Yours Truly, Huck Finn': Postscript," *Modern Language Quarterly*, 24 (1963): 253–6, has claimed more modestly that "even in the Territory, [Huck] will be only one step ahead of the rest: boomers, dukes and dauphins, Aunt Sallies, Colonel Sherburns, and Wilkses – civilizers all" (256). I contend that were Huck to get to the territory, civilization would have arrived when he set down his foot, shod or unshod.
3. For the details of *Tom Sawyer*'s compositional history, see Hamlin Hill, "The Composition and Structure of *Tom Sawyer*," *American Literature*, 32 (1961–2): 379–92, and Charles A. Norton, *Writing Tom Sawyer: The Adventures of a Classic* (Jefferson, NC: McFarland, 1983).
4. Neil Schmitz, *Of Huck and Alice: Humorous Writing in American Literature* (Minneapolis: University of Minnesota Press, 1983), p. 82. Schmitz's interpretation parallels Leo Marx's reading of this scene as an emblem of the contest between the pastoral and the technological (*The Machine in the Garden: Technology and the Pastoral Ideal in America* [New York: Oxford University Press, 1964], pp. 327–30).
5. David Noble, *The Paradox of Progressive Thought* (Minneapolis: University of Minnesota Press, 1957), p. vi.
6. James M. Cox, *Mark Twain: The Fate of Humor* (Princeton: Princeton University Press, 1966), p. 162.
7. See Forrest G. Robinson, *In Bad Faith: The Dynamics of Deception in Mark Twain's America* (Cambridge, MA: Harvard University Press, 1986), who claims that a form of bad faith inherent in Twain's narratives is a reflection of the reader's desire, a desire borne out by the persistent identification of Huck with nature. See Bruce Michelson, "Huck and Games of the World," *American Literary Realism*, 13 (1980): 108–21, who observes that the novel's civilized characters perceive Huck as some kind of fortunate savage. See also Sigmund Freud, *Civilization and Its Discontents* (1930), ed. and trans. James Strachey (New York: Norton, 1962), who argues that "civilization is built upon the renunciation of instinct, . . . [I]t presupposes precisely the non-satisfaction (by suppression, repression or some other means?) of powerful instincts" (44).

8. Marx, *The Machine in the Garden*, pp. 331–4.
9. Henry David Thoreau, *Walden* (1854); reprinted in *A Week on the Concord and Merrimack Rivers; Walden: or, Life on the Woods; The Maine Woods; and Cape Cod* (New York: Library of America, 1985), p. 461. In May of 1876, around the time he was beginning *Huckleberry Finn*, Twain wrote to Howells praising Dean Sage as "the best & happiest narrative-talent that has tackled pen since Thoreau" (*MTHL*, 1:138). James L. Colwell, "Huckleberries and Humans: On the Naming of Huckleberry Finn," *PMLA*, 86 (1971): 70–6, cites this connection but without the ironic reading of the romanticism of nature.
10. D. A. Miller, *Narrative and Its Discontents: Problems of Closure in the Traditional Novel* (Princeton: Princeton University Press, 1981).
11. Laurence B. Holland, "A 'Raft of Trouble': Word and Deed in *Huckleberry Finn*," *American Realism: New Essays*, ed. Eric J. Sundquist (Baltimore: Johns Hopkins University Press, 1982), views Tom's tardy revelation similarly. See also Frederick Woodard and Donnarae MacCann, "Minstrel Shackles and Nineteenth-Century 'Liberality' in *Huckleberry Finn*," *Satire or Evasion? Black Perspectives on Huckleberry Finn*, ed. James S. Leonard, Thomas A. Tenney, and Thadious M. Davis (Durham: Duke University Press, 1992), pp. 141–53, who see Jim's concealment of the identity of Pap's corpse as the full development of Jim above the plantation stereotype.
12. On his 1882 river voyage, Clemens renewed his acquaintance with George Washington Cable, perhaps the most outspoken Southerner on the issue of racial injustice; the two subsequently toured together on the lecture circuit. It's hard to imagine that Cable's committed critique of racism in the South did not influence Twain's burlesque of freeing a free Negro in *Huckleberry Finn*. See Charles H. Nilon, "The Ending of *Huckleberry Finn*: 'Freeing the Free Negro,' " *Satire or Evasion?*, ed. Leonard, Tenney, and Davis, pp. 62–76, for an astute development of this idea. For further considerations of how Twain's text reflects contemporary racial injustice in the South, see Louis J. Budd, "The Southward Currents under Huck Finn's Raft," *Mississippi Valley Historical Review*, 46 (1959): 222–37; James M. Cox, "Walt Whitman, Mark Twain, and the Civil War," *Sewanee Review*, 69 (1961): 185–204; Neil Schmitz, "Twain, *Huckleberry Finn*, and the Reconstruction," *American Studies*, 12 (1987): 59–67; and Victor A. Doyno, *Writing Huck Finn: Mark Twain's Creative Process* (Philadelphia: University of Pennsylvania Press, 1991).
13. René Girard, *Deceit, Desire, and the Novel: Self and Other in Literary Structure*, trans. Yvonne Freccero (Baltimore: Johns Hopkins University Press, 1965), pp. 9, 16.
14. Girard, *Deceit, Desire, and the Novel*, pp. 16, 143.
15. Girard, *Deceit, Desire, and the Novel*, pp. 140–1, 143.
16. Cox, *Mark Twain: The Fate of Humor*, blazed a very productive trail on this aspect of Twain's writing, and Michelson, "Huck and Games of the World," extended our understanding of the role of games in *Huckleberry Finn*. See also Bernard Mergen, "The Discovery of Children's Play," *American Quar-*

terly, 27 (1975): 399–420, on the pioneering anthropological interest in children's play that was launched in the same era in which Twain was writing.

17. Only the board game has survived, housed in the Mark Twain Papers at the Bancroft Library, University of California, Berkeley. The board lists a patent dated 1885 and a copyright dated 1891.

18. See Samuel Charles Webster, *Mark Twain, Business Man* (Boston: Little, Brown, 1946); Jeanie M. Wagner, "*Huckleberry Finn* and the History Game," *Mark Twain Journal*, 20 (1979–80): 5–10.

19. To my knowledge, Dale B. Billingsley, " 'Standard Authors' in *Huckleberry Finn*," *Journal of Narrative Technique*, 9 (1979): 126–31, is the first to make this interpretation based on the names of the feuding families. See Allison Ensor, *Mark Twain and the Bible* (Lexington: University of Kentucky Press, 1969), for a more complete account of biblical allusions in Twain's work.

20. Walter Blair, *Mark Twain and Huck Finn* (Berkeley and Los Angeles: University of California Press, 1960), links the Judith Loftus episode to a similar scene in a popular novel, *The Cloister and the Hearth*, by British author Charles Reade, whom Twain knew. Regarding Twain's use of Carlyle, see Henry Nash Smith, *Mark Twain: The Development of a Writer* (Cambridge, MA: Harvard University Press, 1962), pp. 135–6.

21. Lawrence Levine, *Highbrow/lowbrow: The Emergence of Cultural Hierarchy in America* (Cambridge, MA: Harvard University Press, 1988). See Doyno, *Writing Huck Finn*, who uses these two Shakespearean scenes as an illustration of how "Twain treats a topic first in a serious and then in a comic or parodic fashion" (p. 31), which I elaborate upon later in this chapter.

22. See Gregg Camfield, *Sentimental Twain: Samuel Clemens in the Maze of Moral Philosophy* (Philadelphia: University of Pennsylvania Press, 1994).

23. See Billingsley, " 'Standard Authors' in *Huckleberry Finn*"; Billy G. Collins, "Huckleberry Finn: A Mississippi Moses," *Journal of Narrative Technique*, 5 (1975): 86–104; and Kevin Murphy, "Illiterate's Progress: The Descent into Literacy in *Huckleberry Finn*," *Texas Studies in Language and Literature*, 26 (1984): 363–87.

24. T. J. Jackson Lears, *No Place of Grace: Antimodernism and the Transformation of American Culture, 1880–1920* (New York: Pantheon, 1981), p. 147.

25. Stephen Greenblatt, "What Is the History of Literature?", Keynote address at a conference by the same title, University of California, Berkeley, March 2–3, 1991.

26. All references to the History Game are from the board in the collection of the Mark Twain Papers.

27. James M. Cox ("*A Connecticut Yankee in King Arthur's Court*: The Machinery of Self-Preservation," *Yale Review*, 50 [1960]; reprinted in Mark Twain, *A Connecticut Yankee*, Norton Critical Edition, ed. Allison R. Ensor [New York: Norton, 1982]) attributes Twain's success as a writer of travel books to "his pervasive concern with attitudes toward history" (p. 395).

28. See Susan Derwin, "Impossible Commands: Reading *Adventures of Huckleberry Finn*," *Nineteenth-Century Literature*, 47 (1993): 437–54, who sees the

notice as a command that must be violated in order for the narrative's critique of morality to emerge (454).

29. Clemens's often cited patronage of two African Americans, a sculptor in Paris and a Yale law student, were explicit acts of retribution that he felt the whites owed blacks. See Doyno, *Writing Huck Finn*, who notes in his introduction that "Twain's creative imagination is extraordinarily repetitive, creating a book which resembles an intra-textual echo-chamber. An idea, topic, problem, or situation will be brought up and developed, often to re-appear in a matching but contrary form" (30). Doyno's last chapter, "Repetition, Cycles, and Structure," expands on this notion and elaborates on the resonance between the text's racial elements and contemporary anxiety about a second slavery imposed in the South after the Civil War.

30. Henry Louis Gates, Jr., "The Blackness of Blackness: A Critique of the Sign and the Signifying Monkey," *Black Literature and Literary Theory*, ed. Gates (New York: Methuen, 1984), p. 172; Frederick Douglass, *The Narrative of the Life of Frederick Douglass an American Slave Written by Himself* (1845; New York: Penguin, 1982), p. 107; Thomas Mermall, "The Chiasmus: Unamuno's Favorite Trope," *PMLA*, 105 (1990): 376.

31. The first half of the manuscript, rediscovered subsequent to my initial observation of the structure that I've elaborated here, shows that the narrative division corresponds to the textual division resulting from Twain's interrupted composition. It seems likely that Twain's deployment of the chiasmus in *Huckleberry Finn* was derived from his having devised the structure of *Life on the Mississippi* similarly.

32. Walter Blair's review of Twain's own copy of W. E. H. Lecky's two-volume work, *The History of European Morals* (1869), illuminates the influence of the moral historian on "The Facts Concerning the Recent Carnival of Crime in Connecticut" and on Huck's crisis of conscience. But Twain's annotations of his copy of Lecky's text highlight his significant opposition to what Lecky defines as "intuitive morality." And Huck's ambivalent subordination to Tom's authoritative management of Jim's escape underscores Twain's disagreements with Lecky.

Chapter 3. Reinventing and Circumventing History

1. David E. E. Sloane, *"Adventures of Huckleberry Finn:" American Comic Vision* (Boston: Twayne, 1988), p. 33.

2. Clarence Stedman, *Life and Letters of Clarence Stedman*, 2 vols. (New York: Moffatt, Yard, 1910), 1:370–2. The letter, dated July 7, 1889, is included in the Norton Critical Edition of *A Connecticut Yankee*, ed. Allison R. Ensor (New York: Norton, 1982). The passage quoted appears on page 298 of the Norton edition.

3. See Walter Blair, *Mark Twain and Huck Finn* (Berkeley and Los Angeles: University of California, 1960); Roger B. Salomon, *Twain and the Image of History* (New Haven: Yale University Press, 1961); Henry Nash Smith, *Mark Twain's Fable of Progress: Political and Economic Ideas in "A Connecticut Yankee"*

(New Brunswick, NJ: Rutgers University Press, 1964); Harry B. Henderson III, "Twain: The Varieties of History and *A Connecticut Yankee*," *Versions of the Past: The Historical Imagination in American Fiction* (New York: Oxford University Press, 1974); Rodney O. Rogers, "Twain, Taine, and Lecky: The Genesis of a Passage in *A Connecticut Yankee*," *Modern Language Quarterly*, 34 (1973): 436–47; and Sherwood Cummings, *Mark Twain and Science: Adventures of a Mind* (Baton Rouge: Louisiana State University Press, 1988). See also Bernard Bailyn, *The Ideological Origins of the American Revolution* (Cambridge, MA: Belknap/Harvard University Press, 1967), on the influence of Whig historiography on early American culture generally, and Sacvan Bercovitch, *The American Jeremiad* (Madison: University of Wisconsin Press, 1978), on the tradition of eschatological interpretations of progress, beginning with the Puritan "errand" and running through George Bancroft's epic of America's revolutionary destiny.

4. T. J. Jackson Lears, *No Place of Grace: Antimodernism and the Transformation of American Culture, 1880–1920* (New York: Pantheon, 1981), offers a compelling historical analysis of this cultural phenomenon. However, such a crisis runs throughout American culture even before industrialization, as shown in work on earlier periods, such as Bercovitch, *The American Jeremiad*; Emory Elliott, *Revolutionary Writers: Literature and Authority in the New Republic: 1725–1810* (New York: Oxford University Press, 1982); and Jay Fliegelman, *Prodigals and Pilgrims: The American Revolution against Patriarchal Authority, 1750–1800* (Cambridge: Cambridge University Press, 1982).

5. Michel de Certeau, *Heterologies: Discourse on the Other*, trans. Brian Massumi (Minneapolis: University of Minnesota Press, 1986), pp. 200–1.

6. Joe Goodman to Samuel Langhorne Clemens, October 24, 1881: Mark Twain Papers, Bancroft Library, University of California, Berkeley, CA. Justin Kaplan, *Mr. Clemens and Mark Twain: A Biography* (New York: Simon & Schuster, 1966), p. 238. In a letter to Mrs. Fairbanks, in February 1878, Clemens conveys his sense of authorial social climbing with *The Prince and the Pauper* by indicating why he intended to publish it anonymously – "such a grave & stately work being considered by the world to be above my proper level" (*Mark Twain to Mrs. Fairbanks*, ed. Dixon Wecter [San Marino, CA: Huntington Library, 1949], p. 218). He underwrites his seriousness about this move into a new class of writing by declaring, "I have been studying for it, off & on, for a year & a half." Although Albert Bigelow Paine attributes *The Prince and the Pauper* to the influence of Yonge's *The Prince and the Page*, Howard G. Baetzhold, "Mark Twain's *The Prince and the Pauper*" *Notes and Queries*, 1 (1954):401–3, argues that Twain's story shares virtually nothing beyond a similarity of title. *The Little Duke*, on the other hand, could have called Twain's attention to Edward Tudor. But if Yonge's tales had influenced him at all, it seems not unlikely that both *The Prince and the Page* and *The Little Duke* may have worked together to suggest the idea of importing the mistaken-identity theme into the biography of the Prince of Wales. See also Everett Emerson, *The Authentic Mark Twain: A Literary Biography of Samuel L. Clemens* (Philadelphia: University of Pennsylvania Press, 1985), pp.

107–9; Kaplan, *Mr. Clemens and Mark Twain*, p. 239; and David E. E. Sloane, *Mark Twain: Literary Comedian* (Baton Rouge: Louisiana State University Press, 1979), p. 118. Kenneth R. Andrews, *Nook Farm: Mark Twain's Hartford Circle* (Cambridge, MA: Belknap/Harvard University Press, 1950), emphasizes the genteel influence of Twain's family and neighbors in the case of *The Prince and the Pauper*, suggesting that the book was "the product of community collaboration" (p. 192).

7. Beecher's letter is quoted in Andrews, *Nook Farm*, pp. 132–3. With regard to *The Jukes*, we should note that Dugdale's tendency toward concluding that these phenomena were hereditary is distinctly different from Twain's portrayal of Tom Canty. Cindy Weinstein, *The Literature of Labor and the Labors of Literature* (Cambridge: Cambridge University Press, 1994) turns up interesting ambiguity in the meanings of the term "tramp" in that era, which is precisely the focus of the "Contributors' Club" item titled "Tramps," *Atlantic Monthly*, 45 (May 1880):717–19. On the reform sentiments of Twain's Hartford circle see Andrews, *Nook Farm*, pp. 128–34. See also Laura Skandera-Trombley, *Mark Twain in the Company of Women* (Philadelphia: University of Pennsylvania Press, 1994), for a thorough investigation of Twain's association with progressive reform.

8. Henry George, *Progress and Poverty: An Inquiry into the Cause of Industrial Depressions and of Increase of Want with Increase of Wealth: The Remedy* (1880; rpt. New York: Doubleday, 1905), pp. 283–4, 288. Influenced by Henry Fawcett's account of English political economy in *Pauperism: Its Causes and Remedies* (1871), George argued that the divided American economy was an outgrowth of English developments in England, striking a parallel to Twain's portrait of Renaissance England as the root of American liberalism. Coincidentally, George and Clemens appear to have crossed paths throughout the years. Both were contributors to the *Californian* in the spring of 1865. George is reported to have served as a ticket taker during Twain's lecture in Sacramento the following year. In 1869, they corresponded to arrange a complimentary exchange of copies of Clemens's *Buffalo Express* and George's *Oakland Daily Transcript* (*MTP-L*, 3:401–2). We don't know, however, if Clemens read the San Francisco socialist's economic treatise when it appeared in 1880; his library shows only the volumes of George's work that were issued by Clemens's own Charles L. Webster Publishing Company in the early 1890s. But George's best seller was widely noted, including a two-part review of *Progress and Poverty* in the *Atlantic Monthly*, a magazine that Clemens read devotedly.

9. See Lears, *No Place of Grace*, especially chapter 4, "The Morning of Belief: Medieval Mentalities in a Modern World," pp. 141–81.

10. George, *Progress and Poverty*, p. 479.

11. Edith Colgate Salsbury, *Susy and Mark Twain* (New York: Harper & Row, 1965), p. 318; Emerson, *The Authentic Mark Twain*, p. 110; Sloane, *Mark Twain: Literary Comedian*, p. 120.

12. For an example of genteel pressure, see Kaplan, *Mr. Clemens and Mark Twain*, who quotes a letter from the Reverend Edwin Pond Parker exhort-

ing Clemens to rise to "first-class serious or sober work" (p. 238). Cummings, *Mark Twain and Science*, suggests that Twain's mortification about the Whittier Birthday Dinner Speech brought his progress on *The Prince and the Pauper* to "a screeching halt" (p. 86).

13. Blair, *Mark Twain and Huck Finn*, pp. 190, 192. Sloane, *Mark Twain: Literary Comedian*, has extended Blair's observations, noting that many of the topoi Twain deploys in *The Prince and the Pauper* were the stock-in-trade of the vernacular literary comedians from whom Twain first learned his craft.

14. See Bernard Wishy, *The Child and the Republic: The Dawn of Modern American Child Nurture* (Philadelphia: University of Pennsylvania Press, 1968), pp. 81–93.

15. Quoted in Lears, *No Place of Grace*, p. 163.

16. Howells is quoted in Philip S. Foner, *Mark Twain, Social Critic* (New York: International, 1958), p. 113. John Macy, *The Spirit of American Literature* (New York: Boni & Liveright, 1913), p. 262; James M. Cox, *Mark Twain: The Fate of Humor* (Princeton: Princeton University Press, 1966), p. 154.

17. Louis J. Budd, *Mark Twain: Social Philosopher* (Bloomington: Indiana University Press, 1962), p. 76.

18. Kaplan, *Mr. Clemens and Mark Twain*, p. 136.

19. See Cathy N. Davidson, *Revolution and the Word: The Rise of the Novel in America* (New York: Oxford University Press, 1986), especially chapters 3 and 4, "Ideology and Genre" and "Literacy, Education, and the Reader," pp. 38–79.

20. See Frederic Jameson, *The Political Unconscious: Narrative as a Socially Symbolic Act* (Ithaca: Cornell University Press, 1981), who emphasizes the fact of history as a referent to the text of historiography. Following Louis Althusser, Jameson characterizes history as an "absent cause . . . inaccessible to us except in textual form" (p. 35). The textual transformation of events from history into historiography is an interpretive act in which referential reliability is a suspect matter of ideological subjectivity, either of an individual, a community, or a national culture.

21. See Hayden White, *Topics of Discourse: Essays in Cultural Criticism* (Baltimore: Johns Hopkins University Press, 1978), pp. 31–5.

22. Friedrich Nietzsche, "The Use and Abuse of History," *Thoughts out of Season*, pt. 2, *Complete Works of Friedrich Nietzsche*, vol. 2, ed. Oscar Levy, trans. Albert Collins (Edinburgh: Tn. Foulis, 1910), pp. 19, 11, 16. As in my comparisons between Twain and Freud and between Twain and George, I am not suggesting that Nietzsche was a direct influence on Twain. Twain's library shows acquisition of Nietzsche's books much later than the era of *The Prince and the Pauper*. However, they share much in their philosophical outlooks, as Twain's secretary, Isabel Lyons, had observed. In her journal she notes that she quoted Nietzsche to Twain – "some telling passages – for Nietzsche is too much like himself" (quoted in Alan Gribben, *Mark Twain's Library: A Reconstruction*, 2 vols. [Boston: Hall, 1980], 2:508).

23. Nietzsche, "The Use and Abuse of History," p. 29.

24. Lears, *No Place of Grace*, pp. 21–2.

25. This is not to overlook the fact that Twain originally thought about focusing his tale on Queen Victoria's heir Edward Albert. Rather, it seems even more suggestive that the Victorian setting didn't work out. We don't know why Edward was the character to settle upon when Twain "followed back through history, looking along for the proper time and prince" (Albert Bigelow Paine, quoted in Lin Salamo, introduction to *The Prince and the Pauper*, vol. 6 of *The Works of Mark Twain* [vol. ed. Victor Fisher; project ed. Robert Hirst] [Berkeley and Los Angeles: University of California Press, 1979], p. 3). But any attempt to answer the question must account for the choice of a reign anterior to the English colonization of America.

26. The Puritan jeremiad's model of history as the fulfillment of biblical typology makes no appearance in *The Prince and the Pauper*, but religious enthusiasm of a related kind enters the tale in the figure of the deranged hermit. Ironically, this madman is the only one to take seriously Edward's claim that he is the king. Unfortunately for Edward, the hermit has lofty delusions about his own status: he believes that he is a favorite of God and the patriarchs "Abraham and Isaac and Jacob," and that he had been divinely chosen to become pope until Henry VIII's Reformation discredited his religion. He views Edward's arrival as a divinely inspired opportunity for retribution against Henry. Because the hermit's aspirations lie with Roman Catholicism, he does not directly represent the Protestant tradition of the Puritans, but his delusion that he was to have been elected a latter-day patriarch equal to the Old Testament ones resonates with Puritan typology.

27. Georg Lukács, *The Historical Novel*, trans. Hannah Mitchell and Stanley Mitchell (Lincoln: University of Nebraska Press, 1962), pp. 53, 20, 27, and 32.

28. See Ernest Lee Tuveson, "A Connecticut Yankee in the Mystical Babylon," *Redeemer Nation: The Idea of America's Millennial Role* (Chicago: University of Chicago Press, 1968), on *A Connecticut Yankee*'s place in Twain's changing view of America as the vanguard of civilization.

29. Nietzsche, "The Use and Abuse of History," p. 24. A notebook entry by Twain that mentions the palimpsest at the same time he is considering ending the novel with Morgan's suicide, among a number of other plot details left out of the published text, indicates that the idea for the palimpsest was part of Twain's plan from early on. See Adam Seligman, *The Idea of a Civil Society* (New York: Free Press, 1992), on the transformation of Locke's idea of a civil society from its roots in Christian individualism to a secularized religion of human perfectibility in America. See James M. Cox, "*A Connecticut Yankee in King Arthur's Court*": The Machinery of Self-Preservation," *Yale Review*, 50 (1960); reprinted in the Norton Critical Edition, pp. 390–401, for a comparison of the Yankee and the writer: "The Yankee was not simply a businessman, but an *inventor*, and his power, which was as benign inside the creative imagination as it was malign outside it, was indissolubly linked with Twain's artistic life" (399).

30. Michel Foucault, *The Archeology of Knowledge and the Discourse on Language*, trans. A. M. Sheridan Smith (New York: Pantheon), p. 141. See George

Dekker, *The American Historical Romance* (Cambridge: Cambridge University Press, 1987), especially the chapter titled "Historical Romance and the Stadialist Model of Progress," pp. 73–98.

31. This was a common complaint when the book first appeared. See, for example, the anonymous review in the Boston *Literary World*, 21 (February 15, 1890), 52–3, reprinted in the Norton Critical Edition, pp. 334–6. See James D. Williams, "The Use of History in Mark Twain's *A Connecticut Yankee*," *PMLA*, 80 (1965): 102–10, for a modern echo of this criticism.

32. Cable mentioned this in his remarks at a memorial service for Clemens on November 30, 1910, in New York. Quoted in Arlin Turner, *Mark Twain and George W. Cable* (Lansing: Michigan State University Press, 1960), pp. 135–6.

33. See Michel Foucault, *Language, Counter-Memory, Practice* (Ithaca: Cornell University Press, 1977), who distinguishes between history and what he terms "genealogy," a kind of counterhistory modeled on the "wirkliche historie" that Nietzsche hoped would prevent the "monumental" approach that occluded creativity with veneration.

34. Cox, "*A Connecticut Yankee*: The Machinery of Self-Preservation," emphasizes the sense of the text's desperation by comparing it to the place of *Pierre* in Melville's career: "Before both books stand single masterpieces; after them come books of genuine merit, books even greater than they themselves are, but books more quietly desperate, as if the creative force behind them had suffered a crippling blow and had trimmed itself to the storm of time" (p. 390).

35. Granted, as Cox has noted, "[M]ost of [the Yankee's] attitudes were the same ones Mark Twain swore by at one time or another during his public life" ("*A Connecticut Yankee*, The Machinery of Self-Preservation," p. 393). But one view that Twain never held was Morgan's approbation of Scott. Even Cox's seemingly innocent phrase "at one time or another" is loaded with more weight than his assertion suggests. Morgan has no doubt about the perfection of modern civilization; Twain, on the other hand, though often a cheerleader of the era of progress, was nearly as often pessimistic about that moment in American history that he dubbed the "Gilded Age." His concern about the avaricious spirit of the day was matched by his vexation with the resiliency of class and caste distinctions in a presumably egalitarian society – and in neither of these attitudes was Twain entirely free of hypocrisy.

36. Smith, *Mark Twain's Fable of Progress*, p. 104.

37. Mark Twain, *Mark Twain's Letters to His Publishers*, ed. Hamlin Hill (Berkeley and Los Angeles, University Press, 1967), pp. 221–2.

38. Kenneth S. Lynn, *Mark Twain and Southwestern Humor* (Boston: Little, Brown, 1960), was the first to note the connection and to suggest that Twain's fascination with the typesetter was the inspiration for the techno-utopian novel. Cox, "*A Connecticut Yankee in King Arthur's Court*: The Machinery of Self-Preservation," goes farther by detailing Twain's perception of a twinned identity between machine and text, expressed in his wish to

complete the novel on the very day on which Paige was to complete his technological marvel. Cox argues that the novel's publication "break[s] the vicious identification between it and the machine" and "signifies a victory for the writer . . . In bringing Morgan to death Twain was symbolically killing the machine madness which possessed him" (p. 398). Frederick Crews, "A Yankee in the Court of Criticism," *The Critics Bear It Away: American Fiction and the Academy* (New York: Random House, 1992), applauds Cox's shrewd analysis of the correspondence between Morgan's technologically inspired dreams of social reform and Twain's own grandiose expectations of the typesetter's beneficial social influence. But Crews goes still farther to speculate that Twain's aspirations for the Paige typesetter are in conflict with the text's exaggerated democratic yearnings: "Twain flew into his unappeasable rage against aristocracy because he *needed* to make a show of solidarity with the workers – the workers, that is, whose jobs would be imperiled by the very automation that would supposedly propel Twain himself into the top rank of America's plutocracy" (p. 87). Weinstein, *The Literature of Labor and the Labors of Literature,* offers a cultural interpretation of the Paige typesetter's influence in A *Connecticut Yankee* and beyond in "No. 44, The Mysterious Stranger," arguing that Twain's financial and emotional investment in labor-saving machinery is a symptom of a cultural crisis in which literary and economic anxiety in nineteenth-century America intersect.

39. Like Bliss and Osgood, Twain's nephew Charles Webster came under severe attack. Twain insists that he himself did everything right, except for allowing Webster to remain in his titular position. But Webster, according to Twain, did everything wrong, finally running the author into bankruptcy (*MTE,* 186–95). Notably, Twain makes no mention of the Paige typesetter, preferring instead to heap the responsibility for his losses on Webster.

40. Steven Spielberg's film *Back to the Future* turns on this same dilemma of its hero's time travel. David Butler's film version of *A Connecticut Yankee* (1931), starring Will Rogers in the title role, drew out the same implication in Twain's time-travel story by having Hank encounter his own ancestors in Clarence and Sandy, who initiate the genealogical chain culminating in Hank's birth. Revising the narrative for the screen in this way takes obvious liberties with Twain's text, but they are liberties which underscore the effects that Hank's technological project imposes on subsequent eras.

41. Lynn, *Mark Twain and Southwestern Humor,* p. 258; Crews, "A Yankee in the Court of the Critics," p. 87. Chadwick Hansen, "The Once and Future Boss: Mark Twain's Yankee," *Nineteenth-Century Fiction,* 28 (1978): 62–73, most bluntly observes Morgan's totalitarianism. But despite mentioning that "dozens of commentators, from Tocqueville to the present, have reminded us that the possibility of dictatorship is always latent in the American democratic character" (p. 68), Hansen doesn't work out the implications of Twain's having represented Morgan in this manner.

42. Indeed, we might measure Morgan in light of Max Horkheimer and Theodor W. Adorno's aphorism, "[T]he burgher, in the successive forms of

slaveowner, free entrepreneur, and administrator, is the logical subject of the Enlightenment" (*Dialectic of Enlightenment*, trans. John Cumming [New York: Herder & Herder, 1972], p. 83).

43. Martha Banta, "The Boys and the Bosses: Twain's Double Take on Work, Play, and the Democratic Ideal," *American Literary History*, 3 (1991): 487–520, makes a comparable point about the evolution of industrial management under Fredrick Winslow Taylor's principles of efficiency.

44. Claude Lefort, *Democracy and Political Theory*, trans. David Macey (Cambridge: Polity, 1988), pp. 169, 176, 167, 176, 166; Lefort cites the revised Henry Reeve translation of Tocqueville as his source. Twain's library contained a copy of Tocqueville's *Democracy in America*; in an excised section of the manuscript of *Life on the Mississippi*, he included the political philosopher among the many Europeans who had come to observe the young nation.

45. See David Hume, "Of National Characters," *Essays: Moral, Political, Literary*, ed. Eugene F. Miller (Indianapolis: Liberty Classics, 1985), p. 208, n. 10; George, *Progress and Poverty*, pp. 487–502. See David R. Sewell, "Hank Morgan and the Colonization of Utopia," *American Transcendental Quarterly*, 3 (1989): 27–44, for an analysis of Morgan's colonial impulses.

46. The striking resonances between Twain's text and Horkheimer and Adorno's critique in *Dialectic of Enlightenment* can be gauged in a quotation they give from the marquis de Sade's *Histoire de Justine*, which the Frankfurt philosophers cite as a literary critique of the bourgeois sensibility of the Enlightenment. In Sade's text, Verneuil scoffs at the notion of human equality: "But what impudence I ask you, could allow the pygmy of four feet two inches to compare himself with the stature that nature had endowed with the strength and form of a Hercules? The fly might as well rank itself with the elephant" (quoted in Horkheimer and Adorno, *Dialectic of Enlightenment*, p. 98). This brief passage brings together nearly all of the analogies that Morgan makes to differentiate himself from the inhabitants of Camelot. He is a "giant among pigmies" (p. 67), who has awakened in Camelot after receiving a blow from a laborer named "Hercules" with whom he had fought in nineteenth-century Hartford; he notes that the English view people without titles as "bugs, insects," and that they regard him much as "the keeper and the public regard the elephant in the menagerie, . . . full of admiration for his vast bulk and strength" (p. 65), but with no respect. There is no record of Twain having owned any book by the notorious marquis de Sade; there's little likelihood that his wife would have admitted such a book into her home. But the uncanny resemblances between the terms of Verneuil's aristocratic sentiments and Morgan's self-assessment suggest a common economy of scale in Enlightenment perspective.

47. Critics have often noted that Clemens expressed a similar ambivalence toward the Paige typesetter, at times viewing it as a perfect achievement that surpassed human ability and at other times cursing it as a cunning devil. (See Cox, "*A Connecticut Yankee*: The Machinery of Self-Preservation.")

48. See Budd, *Mark Twain: Social Philosopher*, pp. 111–44; Cox, *Mark Twain: The Fate of Humor*, pp. 216–18; Henry Nash Smith, "Mark Twain's Images of Hannibal; From St. Petersburg to Eseldorf," *Texas Studies in Literature*, 37 (1958): 3–23.

49. See Nadia Khouri, "From Eden to the Dark Ages: Images of History in the World of Mark Twain," *Canadian Review of American Studies*, 11 (1980): 151–74, who describes the Dark Ages as "frozen history" into which Twain's protagonist "is able to infuse some energy . . . only to cause this character to be himself eliminated by the system's own entropy" (p. 165). Sewell, "Hank Morgan and the Colonization of Utopia," offers a systematic reading of the different narrative modes associated with the various explorers typed here and emphasizes their desire to dominate through language. Twain's library shows a copy of Emerson's famous "Concord Hymn"; in "To the Person Sitting in Darkness," he quotes Emerson's famous line to describe McKinley's announcement of his Cuban policy as "another 'shot heard round the world' " (*CTSS&E*, 2:466). Cox, *Mark Twain: The Fate of Humor*, p. 218, also observes how the text restages the Civil War.

50. Lears, *No Place of Grace*, p. 21. I am indebted to Frederick Crews for pointing out the appropriateness of Yogi Berra's malapropism.

51. Horkheimer and Adorno, *Dialectic of Enlightenment*, p. 90.

52. Horkheimer and Adorno, *Dialectic of Enlightenment*, p. 90.

53. Horkheimer and Adorno, *Dialectic of Enlightenment*, p. 19. At the Battle of the Sand Belt, Morgan and Clarence mark off such a sacred space – none other than Merlin's cave, suggesting that they have identified their technological power with magic. See Lynn, *Mark Twain and Southwestern Humor*, p. 258, who points out that the cave topos of Morgan's last stand resonates with the use of the cave locale in *Tom Sawyer*.

54. Sewell, "Hank Morgan and the Colonization of Utopia," reads this failed erasure as a symbol of how Twain's own text dialogizes "Malory's monologic language . . . as it is variously framed, mocked, parodied, and questioned" (p. 35). But this interpretation doesn't account for the full trajectory of the narrative. Morgan's language may attempt to ignore the authority of traditional institutions, but to do so doesn't eradicate them. To the contrary, the narrative resolution shows that such dialogism creates the illusion of subversive power. The habits of training are far more resistant to attack than Morgan has calculated.

55. Herbert Marcuse, "The Affirmative Character of Culture," *Negations: Essays in Critical Theory*, trans. Jeremy J. Shapiro (Boston: Beacon, 1968), pp. 88–133.

Chapter 4. Twaining Is Everything

1. See the headnote to Notebook 30 (*MTNJ*, 3:573).

2. This change of plans appears in Notebook 23 from September of 1884 (*MTNJ*, 3:79).

3. Toni Morrison, *Playing in the Dark: Whiteness and the Literary Imagination* (Cambridge, MA: Harvard University Press, 1992), p. 45.

4. Hawthorne's "American Claimant" manuscripts were published in 1882 and 1883, when "The Ancestral Footstep" was serialized in the *Atlantic Monthly* and the composite text *Doctor Grimshawe's Secret* that Julian Hawthorne had edited from two separate manuscript stories appeared in book form.

5. Twain's aversion to Austen is documented in a letter to Howells in which he admits to finding her prose so "entirely impossible" that he would be unable to read it "on salary" (*MTHL*, 2:841). In *Following the Equator*, he wryly approved of the absence of Austen's books from the ship's library: "Just that one omission alone would make a fairly good library out of a library that hadn't a book in it" (*FE*, 2:289).

6. Susan Gillman, " 'Sure Identifiers': Race, Science, and the Law in *Pudd'nhead Wilson*," *Pudd'nhead Wilson: Race, Conflict, and Culture*, ed. Susan Gillman and Forrest G. Robinson (Durham, NC: Duke University Press, 1990), p. 87.

7. Hershel Parker, *Flawed Texts and Verbal Icons: Literary Authority in American Fiction* (Evanston, IL: Northwestern University Press, 1984).

8. George M. Frederickson, *The Inner Civil War: Northern Intellectuals and the Crisis of the Union* (New York: Harper & Row, 1965), pp. 53–64.

9. Mark Twain, *The Tragedy of Pudd'nhead Wilson and the Comedy Those Extraordinary Twins* (Hartford: American Publishing, 1897), p. 425.

10. Philip S. Foner, *Mark Twain, Social Critic* (New York: International, 1958), p. 99; Alfred H. Holt, *Phrase and Word Origins: A Study of Familiar Expressions* (New York: Dover, 1961), p. 183; Twain, *Pudd'nhead Wilson* (1897 edition), p. 158. I am grateful to Kerry Walk, who located Holt's reported source of the mugwump fence-straddling joke. Holt credits it to Harold Willis Dodds, president of Princeton from 1933 to 1957 (p. 183). Although *Pudd'nhead Wilson* predates Dodds's utterance of this joke by as much as a half century, Twain seems to anticipate it, much as his description of Mr. Brown's shaggy-dog story in "Old Times on the Mississippi" provides the label long before the subgenre is recognized.

    This electoral figure forecasts in "Those Extraordinary Twins" the racial electoral politics that Eric J. Sundquist argues, in "Mark Twain and Homer Plessy," *To Wake the Nations* (Cambridge, MA: Harvard University Press, 1993), pp. 225–70, are at the center of *Pudd'nhead Wilson*.

11. On the cultural anxiety about the miscegenation the mulatto represented see Joel Williamson, *New People. Miscegenation and Mulattoes in the United States* (New York: Free Press, 1980).

12. Alexis de Tocqueville, *Democracy in America*, 2 vols., ed. J. P. Mayer and Max Lerner, trans. George Lawrence (New York: Harper & Row, 1966), 1:370–2. By suggesting that Twain *discovers* that Tom is a mulatto, I intentionally break with the convention in which writers are thought to create their characters. Twain is, of course, the creator of this tale and the characters that inhabit it, but his uncertain authority makes him more like the townspeople

than Roxana with respect to Tom's racial heritage. Twain didn't *transform* Tom from a white to a mulatto as much as he *discovered* his character's racial identity as a consequence of Roxana's presence in the story.

13. See George Templeton Strong, *The Diaries of George Templeton Strong*, 4 vols., ed. Allen Nevins and Milton Halsey Thomas (New York: Octagon, 1974), who – while hardly an abolitionist – referred to the "wild men of the South" (2:275) and to "civilization at the South" as "retrograde" (2:274) and came to believe that "slavery demoralizes and degrades the slave owners" (2:480). For the pervasiveness of the criminal image of the Negro in America, see Gary B. Nash and Richard Weiss, eds., *The Great Fear: Race in the Mind of America* (New York: Holt, Rinehart, & Winston, 1970).

14. Georg Lukács, *Studies in European Realism*, trans. Edith Bone (London: Hillway, 1950), p. 11.

15. See Carolyn Porter, "Roxana's Plot," *Mark Twain's "Pudd'nhead Wilson": Race, Conflict, and Culture*, ed. Gillman and Robinson, pp. 121–36.

16. Cox, *Mark Twain: The Fate of Humor* (Princeton: Princeton University Press, 1966), pp. 241–4; Kenneth Lynn, *Mark Twain and Southwestern Humor* (Boston: Little, Brown, 1960), pp. 265–6; Frederick Anderson, "Mark Twain and the Writing of *Pudd'nhead Wilson*," introduction to the first American facsimile edition of *Pudd'nhead Wilson/Those Extraordinary Twins* (San Francisco: Chandler, 1968), pp. vii–xxii; reprinted in the Norton Critical Edition of *Pudd'nhead Wilson* and *Those Extraordinary Twins*, ed. Sidney E. Berger (New York: Norton, 1980), p. 285.

17. Twain had to have known about Harriet Jacobs's text, since the question of its authorship was a topic of some controversy at the time. Recently, Sholom S. Kahn, "Mark Twain's 'Original Jacobs': A Probable Exlanation," *Mark Twain Circular*, 8 (1994): 4–6, has speculated that the title of chapter 50, "The Original Jacobs," in *Life on the Mississippi* is a direct reference to the controversy about Jacobs's use of the pseudonym "Linda Brent," which allusively comments on Clemens's adoption of the name "Mark Twain." Hazel V. Carby, *Reconstructing Womanhood: The Emergence of the Afro-American Woman Novelist* (New York: Oxford University Press, 1987), p. 47. See also Julia Cherry Spruill, *Women's Life and Work in the Southern Colonies* (1938; New York: Russell & Russell, 1969); Barbara Welter, "The Cult of True Womanhood, 1820–1860," *Dimity Convictions: The American Woman in the Nineteenth Century* (Athens: Ohio State University Press, 1976), pp. 21–41; Ann Douglas, *The Feminization of American Culture* (New York: Knopf, 1977); and Nancy F. Cott, *The Bonds of Womanhood: "Woman's Sphere" in New England, 1780–1835* (New Haven: Yale University Press, 1977).

18. Quoted in Douglas, *The Feminization of American Culture*, pp. 74–5.

19. Alan Gribben, *Mark Twain's Library: A Reconstruction*, 2 vols. (Boston: Hall, 1980), notes Twain's ownership of a volume of Sigourney's *Sketches* (1844). Perhaps even more important, though, was Sigourney's influence among the Hartford literati over whom she presided until her death in 1865; see Kenneth R. Andrews, *Nook Farm: Mark Twain's Hartford Circle* (Cambridge, MA: Belknap/Harvard University Press, 1950), pp. 146–7. Certainly this

wasn't limited to Hartford. Cott's study of private diaries and letters of nineteenth-century women, *The Bonds of Womanhood,* reveals the extensive influence of ideas like Sigourney's.

20. Mark Twain, "The Art of Authorship," *The Art of Authorship,* ed. George Bainton (New York: Appleton, 1890), pp. 87.

21. Evan Carton, "*Pudd'nhead Wilson* and the Fiction of Law and Custom," in *American Realism: New Essays,* ed. Eric Sundquist (Baltimore: Johns Hopkins University Press, 1982), pp. 82–94.

22. Cox, *Mark Twain: The Fate of Humor,* p. 227. Attempting to rationalize away the peculiarity that Cox finds in this passage, Hershel Parker suggests, "Maybe the image can be explained as Mark Twain's remembering having pulled the farce pages out of the big typescript and leaving on the table the pages he was going to use for *Pudd'nhead Wilson*" (*Flawed Texts and Verbal Icons,* p. 131, n. 10). Although the thoroughness of Parker's textual detective work is generally admirable, his conclusions are hamstrung by a much too simple concept of intentionality, as this speculation exemplifies. Twain may have literally pulled out pages of the suppressed farce, but the question of why he would choose to describe that as obstetric surgery remains to be answered. By adhering too doggedly to the literal, Parker closes off the opportunity to consider the significance of the metaphor.

23. Cox, *Mark Twain: The Fate of Humor,* p. 238. Aside from the hostility that Twain vented on Franklin, it seems worth noting that Twain's interest in twins shows up in "The Late Benjamin Franklin" (1870), where he writes of the founding father, "He was *twins,* being born simultaneously in two different houses in the city of Boston" (*CTSS&E,* 1:425).

24. Hayden White, *The Content of the Form: Narrative Discourse and Historical Representation* (Baltimore: Johns Hopkins University Press, 1987), p. 16. White's characterization of chronicle versus historical narrative proper helps also to explain the insufficient closure of *Pudd'nhead Wilson.* The chronicle, Hayden points out, has greater narrative coherency than the annal, because it is organized around a topic, but failing to achieve the closure of historical narrative, the chronicle "does not so much 'conclude' as simply terminate; typically it lacks closure, that summing up of the 'meaning' of the chain of events with which it deals that we normally expect from the well-made story" (16).

25. D. A. Miller, *Narrative and Its Discontents: Problems of Closure in the Traditional Novel* (Princeton: Princeton University Press, 1981), p. ix.

26. We might also note the similarity between the community's puzzlement over Wilson's joke and Jim's interpretation of the King Solomon story. Both the Dawson's Landing townsfolk and Jim are dismayed at the idea that an organic body could be divided, but whereas the former chalk this up to Wilson's ignorance, Jim reads Solomon's solution to the dispute from the perspective of a slave who has seen this sort of authoritarian callousness all too frequently.

27. See Jay. B. Hubbell, *The South in American Literature* (Durham: Duke University Press, 1954), p. 835.

28. Quoted in Justin Kaplan, *Mr. Clemens and Mark Twain: A Biography* (New York: Simon & Schuster, 1966), p. 21.
29. See Michael Rogin, "Francis Galton and Mark Twain: The Natal Autograph in *Pudd'nhead Wilson*," *Mark Twain's Pudd'nhead Wilson: Race, Conflict, and Culture*, ed. Gillman and Robinson, pp. 73–85, for an examination of the alteration in Wilson's legal career between "Those Extraordinary Twins" and *Pudd'nhead Wilson* with regard to the late-nineteenth-century fascination with ethnological arguments for racial difference. Around the time that Twain was writing *The Prince and the Pauper*, he published "Edward Mills and George Benton: A Tale," which surprisingly anticipates the nature–nurture element of *Pudd'nhead Wilson*, though without the racial angle. In both, the narrative rhetoric moves from emphasizing the different moral temperaments of the pair of characters to critiquing society's backward response to their fates.
30. Notebook 38, typescript p. 32, Mark Twain Papers, University of California, Berkeley.
31. For examples of the view of Wilson as a hero, see Leslie A. Fiedler, "As Free as Any Cretur . . . ," *New Republic*, 133 (August 15 and 22, 1955): 130–9, and Robert Regan, *Unpromising Heroes: Mark Twain and His Characters* (Berkeley and Los Angeles: University of California Press, 1966), pp. 207–19. Henry Nash Smith, *Mark Twain: The Development of a Writer* (Cambridge, MA: Harvard University Press, 1962), pp. 173–83, represents a slightly different view, one that questions the success of Twain's characterization of Wilson but nonetheless sees Wilson as the hero. Cox, *Mark Twain: The Fate of Humor*, pp. 222–46, focuses on Wilson as a repressive agent and has influenced to a degree the critical reading that I suggest here. More recently, a lot of attention has been focused on cultural constructions of race in Twain's novel; see, for examples, Sundquist, "Mark Twain and Homer Plessy"; Susan Gillman, *Dark Twins: Imposture and Identity in Mark Twain's America* (Chicago: University of Chicago Press, 1989), pp. 53–95; and Myra Jehlen, "The Ties That Bind: Race and Sex in *Pudd'nhead Wilson*," *Mark Twain's "Pudd'nhead Wilson": Race, Conflict, and Culture*, ed. Gillman and Robinson, pp. 105–20. My argument pursues the question of race and the genre of detective fiction as exhibited in Twain's novel, in a direction compatible with these more recent interpretations and with particular attention to James M. Cox, "*Pudd'nhead Wilson* Revisited," *Mark Twain's "Pudd'nhead Wilson": Race, Conflict, and Culture*, ed. Gillman and Robinson, pp. 1–21, who suggestively points to the Poe–Twain connection in this tale.
32. Arthur G. Pettit, *Mark Twain & the South* (Lexington: University Press of Kentucky, 1974), traces the influence of Clemens's southern background on his lifelong struggle with racial prejudice.
33. George M. Fredrickson, *The Black Image in the White Mind: Debate on Afro-American Character and Destiny, 1817–1914* (New York: Harper & Row, 1971), p. 4, quotes northern abolitionists at the turn of the eighteenth century either lamenting "that many free blacks were 'given to Idleness, Frolicking, Drunkenness, and in some few cases Dishonesty' " or even de-

crying Negroes as "degraded and vicious." The knife-wielding black was so pervasive an image that a British journalist, D. J. Bannatyne, focused especially on it in his depiction of America's violent tendencies: "Even where it is unlawful to carry weapons, it is customary for citizens to go about armed . . . Negroes are partial to large razors (the blade being stuck in a wooden handle) carried in a sheath" ("Despotism, Anarchy, and Corruption in the United States of America," *Blackwood's*, 149 [1891]: 735). The implication here is that the "citizens" must arm themselves for protection from the Nat Turners among them. For analyses of the polarized images of the Negro as docile or threatening see John W. Blassingame, *The Slave Community: Plantation Life in the Antebellum South* (New York: Oxford University Press, 1972), and Ronald Takaki, "The Black Child-Savage in Antebellum America," *The Great Fear: Race in the Mind of America*, ed. Nash and Weiss, pp. 27–44.

34. Metta Victor, *Maum Guinea and Her Plantation Children Or, Holiday-Week on a Louisiana Plantation* (1861; Fredonia, NY: Books for Libraries, 1972), p. 160. George S. Sawyer, *Southern Institutes; or an Inquiry into the Origin and Early Prevalence of Slavery and the Slave Trade* (Philadelphia, 1858), pp. 197, 222.

35. Pettit, *Mark Twain & the South*, p. 24.

36. Sundquist, "Mark Twain and Homer Plessy," points out that "Twain leaves unsettled the question of whether it is the 'nigger' in Tom that leads to the killing, though as allegory it can be read no other way" (p. 266).

37. D. A. Miller, "Language of Detective Fiction: Fiction of Detective Language," *The State of the Language*, ed. Leonard Michaels and Christopher Ricks (Berkeley and Los Angeles: University of California Press, 1980), p. 481.

38. Miller, "Language of Detective Fiction: Fiction of Detective Language," pp. 480–1.

39. Jacques Lacan, "Seminar on 'The Purloined Letter,' " trans. Jeffrey Mehlman, *Yale French Studies*, 48 (1972): 38–72.

40. With regard to Poe's influence on *Pudd'nhead Wilson*, Cox, "*Pudd'nhead Wilson* Revisited," observes, "Certainly Poe is deeply inscribed in this book, not only in the name of the titular hero, but also in his role as amateur detective" (p. 10). And, after detailing the ways in which he reads this inscription, he explains, "I dwell on Poe, who fell from birth in Boston into the South, because he is a true forerunner of Mark Twain, with his recognition that the reader is the double of the author, that the text is thus like a mechanically designed invention relating them, and that the issue for the modern world will be original crime, not original sin." A number of other critics have also cited parallels between Twain and Poe. For example, see Lynn, *Mark Twain and Southwestern Humor*, pp. 274–6, who notes similarities between Poe's *Narrative of Arthur Gordon Pym* and Twain's plans for "The Great Dark"; Minnie M. Brashear, *Mark Twain: Son of Missouri* (Chapel Hill: University of North Carolina Press, 1934), p. 213, n. 39, who suggests the influence of "William Wilson" on Twain's "Concerning the Recent Carnival of Crime in Connecticut"; Margaret Augur, "Mark Twain's Reading"

(1939), p. 65, who observes the resemblance between "A Descent into the Maelstrom" and Twain's sublime descriptions of Hawaii in *Roughing It* (cited in Gribben, *Mark Twain's Library*, 2:551; see Gribben, 2:551–3, for a list of the various volumes of Poe's works in Twain's library). See also Stuart Levine, *Edgar Poe: Seer and Craftsman* (Deland, FL: Everett/Edwards, 1972), p. 57, who notes a number of striking correspondences between Poe's "Thou Art the Man" and *Pudd'nhead Wilson*. Jack Scherting, "Poe's 'The Cask of Amontillado': A Source for Twain's 'The Man That Corrupted Hadleyburg,' " *Mark Twain Journal*, 16 (1972), p. 18n, suggests that "William Wilson" was perhaps an analogue for *Pudd'nhead Wilson*. And Steven E. Kemper, "Poe, Twain, and Limburger Cheese," *Mark Twain Journal*, 21 (1981–2), pp. 13–14, finds "an elaborate spoof of Poe in Twain's 'The Invalid Story.' " My analysis of Twain's anxiety of influence is of course informed by my reading of Harold Bloom, *The Anxiety of Influence: A Theory of Poetry* (New York: Oxford University Press, 1973).

41. Edgar Allan Poe, *Collected Works*, 3 vols., ed. Thomas Ollive Mabbot (Cambridge, MA: Belknap/Harvard University Press, 1978), 3:796, 858.

42. Poe, *Collected Works*, 2:533.

43. I do not dispute the evidence of Twain's interest in Galton. Michael Rogin's interpretation of the importance of Galton for Twain, especially with regard to racial issues, is particularly compelling. Nonetheless, fingerprinting was a fascination for Twain long before he read Galton: chapter 23 of *Life on the Mississippi*, "A Thumb-Print and What Came of It" (written originally in 1879 for *A Tramp Abroad*), uses fingerprinting as a means of criminal detection in a tale as gothic as any by Poe. Although Dupin's facsimile of the orangutan's fingerprints has no explicit bearing on the "Thumb-Print" case in *Life on the Mississippi*, the latter complicates the question of influence on Twain and opens up the possibility that Dupin's methods may have played as much of a role as Galton's book in the conclusion of *Pudd'nhead Wilson*.

44. Rufus Wilmot Griswold, "A Memoir of the Author," *Works of the Late Edgar Allan Poe* (New York: Redfield, 1857), vol. 1, p. xxiii. We should note, however, that although Alan Gribben does find evidence in Twain's notebooks to suggest that he was familiar with Griswold's biographical account of Poe (*Mark Twain's Library*, 2:552), Gribben did not locate a copy of the notorious memoir of Poe in his research on Twain's personal library.

45. Griswold, "A Memoir of the Author," p. xxvi.

46. Metta Victor (pseud. Seeley Regester), *The Dead Letter* (New York: Beadle, 1867; rpt. Boston: Gregg, 1978), p. 115.

47. See my essay "Poe and the Critical Pun; or The Revenge of the Detective Tales," *LIT: Literature Interpretation Theory*, 3 (1992): 189–203, in which I argue that Poe inaugurated the genre as a satiric weapon.

48. Joel Williamson, *A Rage for Order: Black/White Relations in the American South since Emancipation* (New York: Oxford University Press, 1986), p. 86.

49. See Williamson, *New People*, pp. 100–9, on the extent of cultural anxiety about "passing" in this era.

50. See Poe's review of James Kirke Paulding's *Slavery in the United States* and of

NOTES TO PP. 220–7

the anonymous volume *The South Vindicated from the Treason and Fanaticism of the Northern Abolitionists (The Complete Works of Edgar Allan Poe*, Virginia Edition, 17 vols., ed. James A. Harrison [New York: de Fau, 1902], 8:265–75) as an indication of his sympathy with the southern cause.

51. Following Levine, *Edgar Poe: Seer and Craftsman*, we might also consider the influence of Poe's "Thou Art the Man," which explicitly acknowledges Oedipus as a detective in the tale's opening line.

52. Henry Louis Gates, Jr., "The Blackness of Blackness: A Critique of the Sign and the Signifying Monkey," *Black Literature and Literary Theory*, ed. Henry Louis Gates, Jr. (New York: Methuen, 1984), quotes Roger D. Abrahams's description of the very slippery word "signifying" as

> a Negro term, in use if not in origin. It can mean any of a number of things; . . . it certainly refers to the trickster's ability to talk with great innuendo, to carp, to cajole, to needle, and lie. It can mean in other instances the propensity to talk around a subject, never quite coming to a point. It can mean making fun of a person or situation . . . Thus it is signifying to stir up a fight between neighbors by telling stories. (288)

Much of this applies to the general attitude inhering in Twain's writing and the effect in *Pudd'nhead Wilson* specifically. In addition, some of "the black rhetorical tropes" that Gates categorizes under signifying – "marking," "loud-talking," "calling out" (of one's name), and "sounding" – we might recognize as a large measure of the vernacular talk in much of Twain's work. Thus, insofar as "signifying" characterizes black discourse, it is not exclusive to it. See also Shelley Fisher Fishkin, *Was Huck Black? Mark Twain and African American Voices* (New York: Oxford University Press, 1993), especially chapter 3, for an informative discussion of Twain's exposure to this category of discursive practice.

53. See Daniel Harris's review, "Interracial Etiquette and All That Jive: *The Terrible Threes*, by Ishmael Reed," *New York Post*, April 9, 1989, p. 7, which disparages Reed's book as a "mongrel" that fails as a novel because of its diffuse parodic textuality. Oddly, the criterion by which this reviewer judges Reed's novel a failure is both what black narrative discourse, in Gates's estimation, is about, and what I argue makes Twain's novels so representative of the American strain of the genre.

Epilogue

1. Kenneth S. Lynn, *Mark Twain and Southwestern Humor* (Boston: Little, Brown, 1960), p. 273.

2. Edward Said, *Beginnings: Intention and Method* (1975; rpt. Columbia University Press, 1985), p. 83.

3. Richard Sennett, *Authority* (New York: Knopf, 1980), p. 155.

4. Charles W. Chesnutt, *The Marrow of Tradition* (1901; rpt. Ann Arbor: University of Michigan Press, 1969), p. 304.

5. On this point, I concur with Barbara Bardes and Suzanne Gossett, who, in

the course of highlighting the political intentions encoded within nine-teenth-century American women's fiction, acknowledge that "[u]ltimately the impact of fiction on the political culture is circumscribed" (*Declarations of Independence* [New Brunswick, NJ: Rutgers University Press, 1990], p. 16). But in doing so, they call attention to a problem within the title of their book; to call these fictive critiques of the political and economic plights of American women "declarations of independence" is a misnomer, because, as Bardes and Gossett concede, these texts don't function as performative speech acts in the way that the American Declaration did.

6. Philip Fisher, *Hard Facts: Setting and Form in the American Novel* (New York: Oxford University Press, 1985); Jane Tompkins, *Sensational Designs: The Cultural Work of American Fiction* (New York: Oxford University Press, 1985). See Dominick LaCapra, *History, Politics, and the Novel* (Ithaca: Cornell University Press, 1987), who sees novels as being "worked over" by ideologies but suggests that they also "work through" ideologies "in potentially transformative fashion" (p. 4). But no sooner does he make this claim than he qualifies the issue by acknowledging that a novel "may have transformative effects more through its style or mode of narration than in the concrete image or representation of any desirable alternative society or polity." In fact, I argue that the novel's influence is not *through* its style, but *in* its style or mode of narration; that is, the transformation it is likely to achieve is almost entirely literary and not political in any active sense. Citing Derrida's claim that there is nothing outside the text doesn't wash. As Twain knew only too well, Huck and Tom's charade of setting Jim free did not achieve their captive's freedom, any more than Twain's own fiction of freeing a boy's conscience from his culture changed American racial attitudes.

7. Michael P. Rogin, *Subversive Genealogies: The Politics and Art of Herman Melville* (New York: Knopf, 1983).

8. Quoted in the untitled introductory film for visitors at the John F. Kennedy Library, dir. Robert Stone (Boston: John F. Kennedy Library Foundation, 1993).

INDEX